DISCIPLINED
EXUBERANCE

Linda Elaine Neagley

DISCIPLINED EXUBERANCE

The Parish Church of
Saint-Maclou
and
Late Gothic Architecture
in Rouen

The Pennsylvania State University Press
University Park, Pennsylvania

Library of Congress Cataloging-in-Publication Data

Neagley, Linda Elaine.
   Disciplined exuberance : the Parish Church of Saint-Maclou and late Gothic architecture in Rouen / Linda Elaine
Neagley.
      p.   cm.
   Includes bibliographical references and index.
   ISBN 0−271−01716−3 (alk. paper)
   1. Saint Maclou (Church : Rouen, France)   2. Robin, Pierre, Master mason—Criticism and interpretation.
3. Architecture, Gothic—France—Rouen.   4. Church architecture—France—Rouen.   5. Rouen (France)—
Buildings, structures, etc.   I. Title.
   NA5551.R616N43   1998
   726.5′0944′25—dc21   96−38117
                                                                                                               CIP

Published by The Pennsylvania State University Press,
University Park, PA 16802−1003

It is the policy of The Pennsylvania State University Press to use acid-free paper for the first printing of all clothbound
books. Publications on uncoated stock satisfy the minimum requirements of American National Standards for Information Sciences—Permanence of Paper for Printed Library Materials, ANSI Z39.48−1992.

To My Parents
William and Vivian Neagley

Contents

List of Illustrations

A note on nomenclature: Throughout the text and illustrations I use a nomenclature or numbering system that is generated from the transept crossing in north, south, east, and west, directions. Upper-case letters and numerals indicate spaces, while lower-case letters and numerals indicate supports. All spaces and supports are identified on my plan in Figure 76.

List of Tables

Acknowledgments

My interest in the architecture of Saint-Maclou began twenty years ago when I arrived in Rouen in search of a dissertation topic. At that time the church was in a disastrous state of repair, having suffered extensive damage in the 1944 bombing of the city. Although under restoration, the exterior was shrouded in scaffolding; the chapel of Sainte-Clothilde was missing; the lantern tower, blocked of its clerestory windows, was listing to the south; and the choir, the portion of the church most seriously damaged, was still separated from the transept and nave by a provisional wall. As the restorers sought to recover the medieval appearance of the monument, I endeavored to reclaim its architectural history; while we have both made progress, much work is still to be done.

I extend my deepest appreciation to the people of Rouen, especially Jean-Marc Lanfry, president of the Entreprise Georges Lanfry restoration company, Jean-Louis Durand, titular organist of Saint-Maclou, and M. L'Abbé Raymond Prévost, curate of Saint-Maclou. They have provided me with documents, access to the monuments, and assistance from the very beginning. I am particularly indebted to Michael T. Davis for his insights and comments on various versions of the manuscript and to Stephen Murray who is responsible for my initial interest in late gothic architecture and whose shadow can often be detected in my ideas.

I particularly thank my students for their tolerance of my musings on late gothic architecture, especially Melanie Holcomb, Jane Chung, and Abby McGehee Proust and for the unflagging assistance of Leslie Cavell, Mayra Rodriguez, and Rebecca Price-Wilkin during the long weeks of the summer plan survey of Saint-Maclou in 1988. I have relied on the computer-drafting abilities of several architecture students, especially Heman Shih and Ari Seligmann, who introduced me to the potential of AutoCAD and Adobe Illustrator to mask my lack of drafting skills.

Along the way I have received a number of grants from the University of Michigan, Rice University, and ACLS that permitted my frequent travel to Rouen. I am especially indebted to Dean Allen Matusow of Rice University for granting a faculty leave to write the final chapter of the book. In the end, it was the friendship of Terryl, Donna, and Karin that gave me the patience, perseverance, and pugnaciousness to bring the work to completion.

Introduction

In 1432, the same year that Jan van Eyck recorded his authorship on the frame of the Ghent Altarpiece in Bruges, plans were put in motion for the construction of a new parish church in Rouen that, like the Ghent Altarpiece, would both summarize and surpass medieval traditions and standards of craftsmanship. Financed by the newly acquired wealth of the merchant class and designed by the Parisian master Pierre Robin, the architecture of Saint-Maclou was no less a masterpiece than the altarpiece, elevating the art of geometry and the craft of masonry to an astonishing level of sophistication and providing an articulate and public expression of complex fifteenth-century sociopolitical, artisanal, and religious values. As contemporaries, Pierre Robin and Jan van Eyck were kindred spirits. Both had risen to the highest levels of their respective crafts, receiving recognition through employment in the royal and ducal houses of northern Europe. Jan van Eyck entered the service of Philip the Good as a *valet de chambre* in 1425 while Pierre Robin was employed by both English and French kings in Paris sometime between 1422 and 1437 and held the prestigious position of master mason of the cathedral of Paris. Both artisans worked in thriving cities, Ghent and Rouen, whose expanding economies were driven by growth in the cloth industry, and both found greater freedom of expression and outlet for their talents in commissions of the new merchant class made wealthy by trade and commerce.

Perhaps the strongest bond between these two masters, is the new level of art they brought to their craft: a mastery of materials, design, technique that expanded the expressive potential of their respective media. The trompe l'oeil of Jan van Eyck's painted sculpture and metalwork collapsed the viewer's distinctions between earthly and celestial realities. Pierre Robin's sophisticated manipulation of space and proportion monumentalized small-scale architecture while his technical dexterity transformed stone into lithic lace providing equally ambiguous and emotive spatial realms. At the same time both van Eyck and Robin had a profound respect for the "classic" elements of late medieval art. The symmetry and frontality, hieratic compositions, and focus on Marian subjects of van Eyck's painting indicates indebtedness to a well-established tradition of devotional images. Likewise, Pierre Robin's guiding design principles were rooted in gothic building traditions that had originated two hundred and fifty years earlier in the workshops of northern France. Bartolomeo Facio writing in 1454 stated that Jan could be considered the greatest painter of his time "cultivated as well in letters but chiefly in geometry."[1] Likewise, geometry was the foundation of Robin's designs as he skillfully wielded complex matrices that gave shape and proportion to his architecture.

Yet our perception of the role and impact of these two masters within the artistic milieu of the fifteenth century is dramatically different. While library shelves bend under the weight of twentieth-century Eyckian scholarship, the designer of Saint-Maclou, Pierre Robin, remains relatively unknown, even to scholars of medieval architecture. Robin's design of Saint-Maclou transformed late gothic style by its reinterpretation of the gothic canon and by its dazzling technical proficiency, profoundly influencing architecture in the second half of the fifteenth century. The absence of twentieth-century appreciation of Saint-Maclou has more to do with the modern historiography of late gothic architecture than the lack of ingenuity by Pierre Robin and the patrons of Saint-Maclou.

Although the documents are silent concerning the theoretical and practical basis for Robin's creative methods, contemporary appreciation for the monument of Saint-Maclou was unmistakable. Greater institutional status of the church among other parishes in the fifteenth and early sixteenth centuries is indicated by the high reputation of its clergy. The curate of Saint-Maclou, Arthur Fillon, who contributed significant sums to the church and presided over its dedication in June 1521, had served as canon to the cathedrals of Rouen and Evreux, bishop of Senlis, and vicar general to the archbishop Georges d'Amboise.[2] Greater prestige was afforded the parish church owing to its close physical proximity to the archbishop's palace. It was from the porch of Saint-Maclou that the results of the election of new archbishops were announced. The church was also granted the privilege of keeping and distributing holy oil to other parishes in 1517.[3] More important, however, the flamboyant architecture of Saint-Maclou was considered a visible and public symbol of urban identity in late medieval Rouen. The finely crafted and richly decorated architecture was a progressive vision that reflected Rouen's modernity, urban prosperity, and civic pride. Royal and episcopal entries into the city, marked by elaborate processions and spectacles meant to symbolize institutional affiliations and loyalties, were also carefully calculated to showcase the material assets of the city. Entries, whether they took place through the Porte Martainville in the parish of Saint-Maclou, the Porte Beauvoisine, or across the Pont

Mathilde from the Left Bank of the Seine, passed by the cathedral, the abbey of Saint-Ouen and Saint-Maclou and paused at the Pont du Robec in front of the church (Figs. 1 and 2).[4]

In the years following the dedication of the church in 1521, numerous strategic "portraits" of the church also appeared suggesting urban pride and Rouennais identity with their chief parish church. Saint-Maclou is depicted twice in the famous *Livre des fontaines* map of Rouen executed in 1525 commemorating the construction of city fountains (Figs. 3 and 93); twice in the *Grand cartulaire* of 1531 (a record of gifts by the Dufour to the parish) (Figs. 88 and 92); and is depicted alongside the cathedral of Rouen in the stained glass of Saint-Vincent in Rouen executed in the first third of the sixteenth century (Fig. 4). The controversial model of Saint-Maclou, possibly dating to the sixteenth century, celebrates its reliquary-like preciousness; François Farin's early history of the city of Rouen in 1668 describes prints of Saint-Maclou being sold as souvenirs in the city of Rome, attesting to both local and international fame of the parish church (Figs. 5a and 5b).[5] Perhaps more than any other monument in late gothic Rouen, Saint-Maclou symbolized the material prosperity of the city and the professional and social status of its builders and patrons.

The parameters of this study are somewhat dictated by the present state of research on French flamboyant monuments. Because of the basic foundation provided by early twentieth-century art historians such as Friedländer, Baldass, Weale, and Panofsky, current Eyckian scholarship is free to explore a variety of interpretive and contextual discourses surrounding the production and meaning of Jan's work.[6] However, the historical contours of the construction of Saint-Maclou based on documentation and a descriptive language characterizing flamboyant architecture in terms other than an identification of decorative motifs have yet to be established.

The literature on Saint-Maclou mirrors the overall historiographic scholarship of the late gothic period. The first useful records of the church history were included in Farin's *Histoire de Rouen*, published in 1668. Although only a few pages are devoted to Saint-Maclou, he includes transcriptions of lost tomb inscriptions useful in establishing chronology of construction and identification of patrons. A preliminary review of archival documentation and the first attribution of Saint-Maclou to the master mason Pierre Robin was made by Charles Ouin-Lacroix, curate of Saint-Maclou and author of the first monograph, published in 1846. Major contributions in the area of local documentation were made by the nineteenth-century archivist, Charles de Robillard de Beaurepaire, who published numerous texts related to Rouennais architects and construction in the fifteenth century. Two subsequent monographs followed, one published by Julien Loth in 1913 and another by René Herval in 1933, providing the first compendium of pre–World War II photographs, and sheding new light on chronology, patronage, and the style. The brief articles by Jouen in the 1926 *Congrès archéologique*, and Chirol in 1970 summarized the work of earlier authors, while Taralon in 1958 documented the devasting damage and subsequent repair to the church following the bombing of Rouen in 1944. A general history of the curates and parish by Canon Prevost (1970) and a gathering of documents pertinent to foundations and rent in Catherine Bodin-Cerné's 1962 thesis provide important contributions; neither, however, addresses the architectural history.[7]

With a self-conscious eye on method, I attempt here to redefine the traditional medieval architectural monograph by bringing to bear an array of analytical and interpretive strategies to the examination of a single monument and historic moment. The two-part structure of this study straddles methodologies, examining both intrinsic evidence of documents and architectural style on the one hand, and providing a format for interpretive essays that explore the sociopolitical, artisanal, and cultural context of the monument. This book reinterprets flamboyant architecture in these terms and portrays flamboyant as an embodiment of the discipline provided by the high gothic canon (inherited from the workshop practices of the thirteenth century) but made exuberant by the technological display of the late gothic craft (necessitated by new professional and social demands on architecture). In the wake of the Hundred Years' War, Normandy and Northern Europe saw a reordering of major financial, political, and social institutions, and the forward/backward-looking stylistic character of Saint-Maclou reflects a society in transition, turning to the past to maintain social order while defining new roles for individuals. The justification of an individual's place in society was no longer fully restricted by birthright and class. Public displays of wealth, talent, material, and skill—whether by the specialized master/mason emerging as the architect/draftsman/theorist or the merchant/tradesman emerging as the city councilor/landowner and title-holder—used architecture as a form of social self-definition and a visible assertion of new social and professional status.

Using a variety of written sources, including the church fabric accounts and cartularies, Chapter 1 establishes the temporal time line for the construction of the church between the beginning of construction in the 1430s and its dedication in 1521. A variety of evidence—including the identification of funding sources, patrons, and master masons and craftsmen, as well as size of workshops, the nature of the work, and evidence for the reconstruction of the earlier thirteenth-century chapel on the site—provides a background against which the archaeological and design evidence of Chapters 2 and 3 can be tested and anchors the interpretive analysis of Chapters 4, 5 and 6.

Chapter 2 undertakes the articulation of the formal elements of Saint-Maclou, not just as a descriptive exercise to establish chronology but as an outline of the design principles and models that underlay Pierre Robin's theory of design. Robin's work indicates a major reassessment of gothic architecture and design that defined the direction of much flamboyant architecture in remaining decades of the century. A discernible pattern emerges in the choices made by Robin and in his method of transforming gothic vocabulary. He clearly rejects the fashionable trends in Rouen or Paris since the 1380s but reclaims certain design rules more evident in architecture of the thirteenth century and transforms these principles by the application of sophisticated geometry and technical skill characteristic of the late gothic craft (the motives for the retrospection and transformation of the high gothic canon will be explored in Part II).

No element of architecture is more revealing of late gothic design theory than geometry, the focus of Chapter 3. What had been the primary tool of the master mason and chief vehicle for design in the thirteenth century became the subject of design in the fifteenth century. The geometric underpinnings of late gothic design provided the spatial scaffolding for plan, elevation, and structure and were revealed to express a new prismatic clarity in space and form. This chapter focuses on plan design and outlines a relationship between the use of constructive geometry and the pragmatic task of setting out a building at the site. It also demonstrates that the idiosyncratic features of Saint-Maclou are directly linked to the priority given to geometric precision over conventional composition of mass and space. In addition, the orderly unfolding of construction from the transept, first to the choir and then to the west facade, is due to the use of a transept module as the key design unit for all major dimensions of the plan.

Chapter 4 considers the social group most directly involved in assigning meaning to the architectural forms: the patrons. The funding for the construction arises almost exclusively from within the parish and written evidence suggests full participation of all residents of the parish. However, the leading merchant-class families, most of whom were related through marriage, played a primary role in soliciting funds, providing major contributions, and overseeing the construction. The fabric accounts illustrate a steady but small amount of money available over a long period of time, enough to maintain a small workshop. With the conception of the design of Saint-Maclou anchored in the politics and economics of the 1430s in Rouen, an examination of the historic events surrounding the English occupation of the city reveals a decisive change in economic (and hence political) allegiances of this new class of patrons. This analysis supplies motives for the retrospective character of Saint-Maclou that depend heavily on the pre-1380 portions of the cathedral of Rouen for inspiration. The reference to the rayonnant Rouennais architecture, updated by the fashionable and highly crafted Parisian vocabulary of Pierre Robin, provides a very visible and public vehicle for the new social and professional identity of the Dufour and related families in a period of increasing upward mobility.

Chapter 5 reconsiders the architectural language of Pierre Robin against the immediate architectural context of Paris, the Vexin, Rouen, and Normandy. Scant documentation permits only a brief outline of his career and projects; the evidence suggests that Robin worked primarily as a draftsman/designer. Seen against the backdrop of contemporary work in Paris and Rouen, the innovative character of Robin's work is emphasized. In addition, the immediate impact of Saint-Maclou is registered in the most significant projects in Rouen following Robin's departure from the city.

In order to explain the artisanal display and the value placed on craftsmanship in fifteenth-century architecture, Chapter 6 broadens the basis of discussion by examining the construction of professional status and the cultural values of the craftsmen who constitute a large portion of the parish of Saint-Maclou. Both the artisans associated with the cloth industry and the building industry are uniquely clustered in the parish and exhibit similar social ranking and shared taste and values. Two cultural phenomenon are explored that underlie the value placed on properties of materials, extravagant display of technical dexterity, and sophisticated design. By examining both physical and written evidence, we find that the professional identity of the master mason in the fifteenth century is more closely associated with the architectural drawing than with the actual monument. Because of the increasing importance of the drawing as the primary communicator of idea, the initial vision becomes farther removed from execution and the drawing becomes an arena receptive to capricious flourishes of design as well as highly intellectual and sophisticated relationships. Also, the architectural competition based on public and patronal approval of drawings places new demands on the drawing to be impressive and visually seductive.

Finally, greater regulation of time—illustrated by the introduction of the mechanical clock into masons' lodges in Rouen—is played out in the control of productivity of labor and is crucial to the transformation of artistic expression. Patrons consciously manipulate perceptions of new regulations involving time by melding religious virtue with regulatory control, thereby convincing artisans to value the investment of time as much as patrons worried about the cost of time. This results in perhaps the most significant dilemma of the late gothic period, one that contributed to the disappearance of flamboyant architecture in the early sixteenth century: conflict between economy of production (mercantile values rooted in commercial mentality of trade and profit) and efflorescence of style (that is, costly and extravagant expressions of professional status and investment of time).

PART I

THE MONUMENT
Intrinsic Evidence

1

The History of Construction Through Written Sources

It is not a coincidence that the earliest extant fabric account of Saint-Maclou should begin in 1436, the same year that construction of the new church got under way.[1] This lavish and expensive monument was paid for with revenues secured and judiciously distributed by the church treasurers, members of the prominent bourgeois families of the parish. To ensure continual construction revenues, they applied the same astute business acumen honed in the fifteenth-century financial markets of international trade and the cloth industry to the business of ecclesiastical building. The written accounts of weekly expenses and receipts provided careful regulation of building costs just as the architectural drawings of Pierre Robin provided precise control over the design and execution of construction. Thus, paper documentation, functioning as a regulatory agent facilitated the carefully calculated visual effects, the assiduous homogeneity, and exquisite precision characteristic of Saint-Maclou. In addition, these records furnish intimate details about gothic building practice. Although the building accounts of Saint-Maclou were diligently kept, only four sets have survived dating to the period of construction, and none are so detailed or complete as other well-known late gothic French examples such as those of Troyes Cathedral or the château of Gaillon.[2]

To augment the records of ordinary expenses and receipts documented in the fabric accounts, the treasurers also commissioned two cartularies, identifying extraordinary sources of revenues as well as commemorating their participation as patrons of the church. The *petit cartulaire*, composed between 1430 and 1450, contains a collection of royal letters of amortizement, indulgences, titles of rents and properties, donations, and foundations.[3]

Similar documents dating from the fourteenth to the early sixteenth century were assembled in the *Grand Chartrier* sometime between 1531 and 1533 on the order of Nicolas Dufour.[4] Thus, the building accounts of 1436–37, 1443–46, 1477–79, and 1514–17, the cartularies, as well as chapel inscriptions and a variety of city documents including notary records and cathedral deliberations, provide sufficient temporal anchors to outline a clear sequence of construction that would have been impossible from the archaeological evidence alone.[5] The building history of Saint-Maclou appropriately begins with the written records.

The 1430s and the Beginning of Construction

The construction of the new church began sometime after 1432. On 16 September of that year, Hugues d'Orgues, archbishop of Rouen, granted an indulgence for the rebuilding and repair of the thirteenth-century parish church of Saint-Maclou (Fig. 6).[6] The letter describes this structure as old, neglected, and recently collapsed in the transept area:

> indeed a petition recently delivered to us [Hugues d'Orgues] on the part of our beloved sacristans and parish church of Saint-Maclou of Rouen, related that same church of Saint-Maclou of Rouen, among all the rest of the parish churches subject to us the more distinguished in reputation by a chance occurrence and because of its great age, was turned to great ruin and within a few days was cast down to the earth in its middle part, so much that for sustaining a fourth part of the parish clergy and to others thronging into the same place, it was not sufficient nor does the remaining part suffice, it stands in need of rebuilding and considerable and costly repairs which indeed without the alms and charitable gifts of the devoted Christian faithful cannot be done.[7]

The degree to which the parish treasurers undertook the rebuilding and repair following the incentive provided by the indulgence is not clear, but the urgency of the project is confirmed by a second request in June 1433 from Pope Eugene IV.[8] The papal bull, once again, solicited "alms and charitable gifts" from the parishioners.

By 1436 and perhaps earlier, a decision was finally made to rebuild, not just repair, the high gothic chapel. The fabric account of 1436–37 indicates that the treasurers paid the considerable sum of 43 livres 10 sous to the master mason Pierre Robin for a complete drawing of the church.

> the 12th of May 1437 to Master Pierre Robin for the account made of his wages from the day of the year until the 19th day of May and for the parchment where the church is drawn completely and for the said time paid to him as it appears by his receipt.[9]

[le dit jour a maistre Pierres Robin par compte fait a luy de ses gaignes depuys le jour de lan jusques au xixe jour de may et pour le parchemin or leglise est gestee toute complecte et pour le dit temps luy fu paie si comme il appert par sa quittanche, 43 livres 10 sous]

Although only one drawing is mentioned at this date, a careful examination of the fabric of the church indicates that dozens of drawings were needed to account for the rigorous uniformity of the whole and precise interrelationship of details.[10] The amount of payment is substantially more than Robin received for other single drawings. Thus, *le parchemin* described in the account may refer to more than one drawing or the payment of 42 livres 10 sous may have covered the cost of drawings received earlier by the treasurers.[11] Nevertheless, it is reasonable to assume that these drawings constituted the blueprints for the new church and that the design of Saint-Maclou must be attributed to Pierre Robin.

Two additional documents suggest that some work on the new church had been executed shortly after 1432, prior to the payment for Robin's last drawing in 1437. A contract dated 19 October 1434 between the treasurers of Saint-Maclou and Tassin Amyot and his wife Guillotte records the foundation of a low mass in the chapel of Notre-Dame "nouvellement encommencée à faire" (recently begun).[12] The location of the chapel of Notre-Dame to the east of the transept is alluded to in a later entry. In addition, an unusual poem written on the verso of the cover of the *petit cartulaire* and dated 23 May 1436 states that "it is the church proper of Saint-Maclou which is begun a while ago."[13] Both of these documents suggest that new construction was undertaken in addition to the repair work. Certainly work on the new church could not have been done by 1434 without Pierre Robin's drawings; therefore he may have been present in Rouen at least two years before he is identified in the building accounts of 1436–37.[14]

Other clues concerning the form of the earlier thirteenth-century church and the nature of the new work in the choir are suggested by the 1436–37 account. Nothing remains of the church of Saint-Maclou constructed after the city fire of 1211. The first mention of the high gothic chapel is in the letter of indulgence of 1432, which describes the church in ruin. Even after the 1944 bombing of the church and during the major restorations of the twentieth century, no vestiges of the earlier chapel were found and excavations have never been carried out on the site.[15]

The account identifies major restoration of the carpentry of the nave roof and portal of the old church under the direction of master carpenters Jehan de Soissons (Soyson) and Martin Le Douen as well as various kinds of decorative work executed by the *huchiers* or wood workers.[16] Jehan de Soissons is paid by contract for the carpentry of the "nef de moustier" or nave. *Souschevrons, soliveau, chevrons,* and *fillière,* in addition to tiles, lead, gutters, and laths, are purchased for reroofing the nave.[17] *Trefs* or tie beams for a new chapel are placed against a tower for support. Jehan de Soissons is also paid 4 livres tournois for "la façon du portail devant leglise" (making the portal in front of the church) and a plasterer was paid for repairs to "le pignon de leglise de devant le pignon du portail" (the gable of the church in front of the portal gable). Other entries mention a "chambre Saint Leu au grant porche" (room of Saint Leu near the large porch) and "pour avoir fait et rapplique les fers locquetes et les vergues de verrieres du pignon du portail de lestage de dessoubz ou est listoire de la nativite" (window lancets above the portal near the gable with stained glass depicting the story of the nativity). With such random references it is difficult to reconstruct the appearance of the chapel, but one is tempted to visualize a parish church with a transept crossing tower, a western porch with a gable and a gabled facade—a description containing the essential components of the present flamboyant church. Some temporary repairs on this structure may have been carried out before 1432. On 28 March 1428 Jehanne Capperon established a mass for her husband, Jehan, with funds given to the "treasurers and fabric of the said church of Saint-Maclou and for augmentation of the work."[18]

In addition to the extensive repairs by the carpenters on the old church, the fabric account indicates the presence of a mason's workshop with three master masons. Master Pierre Robin is paid for his year and for his drawings of the church (Table 1).[19] He is never again mentioned in the Rouen documents and disappears from the workshop in 1437. A second mason, Oudin de Mantes, while never qualifying under the title of master, is paid the equivalent of a master's wages of 5 sous per day (the ordinary masons at Saint-Maclou were paid 3 sous 9 denier per day).[20] As his name indicates, he comes from the Vexin and along with his son, he is given a house on the rue de Sac (Bac?) in the parish of Saint-Maclou for the duration of his work. The account indicates a considerable yearly pension of 67(?) livres.[21] In another entry, Oudin is advanced 100 sous tournois. A third mason who does bear the title of master is Simon Le Noir. He arrives in Rouen from Paris with Robin and by the 1440s is one of the most successful and active masters in the city. During his first year at Saint-Maclou he earns a daily wage of 4 sous 2 denier and within a few months is appointed master of the works of masonry of the king's bailiff in Rouen, which position he holds until 1448.[22]

Seven masons work sporadically throughout the year of 1436–37. Friset Le Mestre, Pierre Cossart, Alain Le Boulenguier, and Jehan Le Large are paid by the day (4 sous 2 denier, 3 sous 9 denier, 3 sous 9 denier and 3 sous 7 denier, respectively) while three other

Table 1   Daily wages of masons

Fabric Account for 1436–1437		
Master Pierre Robin	unspecified	master mason, architect/designer
Oudin de Mantes	5 sous	master mason
Master Symon Le Noir	4 s 2 d	master mason/appareilleur
Friset Le Mestre	4 s 2 d	appareilleur
Perrin Cossart	3 s 9 d	mason
Alain Le Boulenguier	3 s 9 d	mason
Jehan Le Large	3 s 7 d	mason
Tassin de Porqueroult	12d per buistes	quarryman/mason
Jehan Moreau	"	quarryman/mason
Jehan Duval	"	quarryman/mason

masons including Tassin de Porqueroult, Jehan Moreau, and Jehan Duval, are paid for cutting *buistes* (also *buites* and *buytes*) at a rate of 12 denier per buiste. The translation of *buistes* is problematic. Godefroy cites it as a variation of the spelling for *boîtes* or box; it may, however, be related to the modern masonry term *boutisse*, meaning a header or bondstone which could refer to a large block used for foundations.[23] The accounts reveal that these three masons cut several hundred *buistes*. To earn the equivalent of an ordinary mason's wage in one day, they needed to cut fewer than four *buistes* per day, suggesting that *buistes* may be large rough-cut stones. The discrepancy in method of payment may also indicate that the three masons are not working on the site but at the quarry. One of the suppliers of stone is the quarryman Jehan de Porqueroult, perhaps associated with Tassin de Porqueroult who is cutting *buistes*. Because of the high cost of shipping stone up the Seine to the construction site, and the standardization in size and shape of footer stones, it would seem logical to rough-cut the foundation stone at the quarry in order to eliminate excess weight.

The same account shows significant purchases of stone, lime, and sand costing a total of 68 livres 10 sous. Between May and February, only 31 tonneaux of stone were purchased from Jehan de Porqueroult and son at 12 sous 6 denier per tonneau, while between February and May 1437, some 171 tonneaux of stone were purchased at the same price from the quarrymen Raoul Tretart, Robin Lasseur, and Bertran Le Bonnelier.

There is no indication of the location of the quarry in the 1436–37 account, but a document of 1408 identifies Jehan de Porqueroult as a quarryman from Val-des-Leux.[24] The superstructure of Saint-Maclou is built out of a fine grain and expensive stone from the quarries of Vernon costing twice the amount of Val-des-Leux stone. The letters of amortizement from Henry VI of 1446 to the treasurers of Saint-Maclou describe the church as begun without deniers or good quality stone. It is unlikely that such a large quantity of stone was used for temporary repair work on the old nave. On the other hand, stone of inferior quality from Val-des-Leux may have been used for the foundations in the new choir.[25]

The laborforce carrying out unspecified work and designated under the heading of *mennouvriers* or *ouvriers des bras* in the account consisted of six men who were paid 18 denier per day between November and May. Additional laborers were hired to assist in putting tile on the roof of the old nave.

Despite lengthy references to materials, masons, and laborers, almost nothing is mentioned in the account of the nature of the new work being executed. Numerous expenses for *bors dilland* used for making templates indicate that construction had advanced beyond the foundations, and that patterns were needed for more complex stone carving of piers, shafts, or moldings of some type.[26] The location is suggested by a payment on 23 December to Jehan Le Fort, Jehan Le Puost, and Jehan Gibes "pour maistre des estroix contre la tour et pour soustenier les quatres trefs de la chapelle notre dame" (for putting the beams against the tower and for supporting the four beams of the chapel of Notre-Dame). This is probably the same chapel of Notre-Dame mentioned two years earlier in the foundation contract and described as "recently begun." The only location where roof or scaffolding beams of a new chapel could be supported against an old tower is at the transept. Because the old nave was being reroofed, it is likely that the new work began in the first straight bays and chapels of the choir adjacent to the transept, an assumption that is confirmed by the archaeological and design evidence discussed in Chapters 2 and 3.

Thus, the building accounts indicate that by 1437, the nave of the old church was being repaired and reroofed, foundations were being laid to the east of the old transept, and at least one chapel, Notre-Dame, was above ground.

The Completion of the Choir, 1437–1452

Seven years later, the next extant fabric account dating from 26 September 1443 and running until All Saints' Day 1446, indicates an active workshop under the direction of Simon Le Noir.[27] In this three-year period, two additional masons, Friset Le Mestre (mentioned in the earlier account) and Guillaume Le Prevost, are paid the same daily wage of 5 sous as Simon Le Noir but do not bear the title of master. Nor do they receive the yearly pension of 4 livres 10 sous granted to the master, yet these *appareilleurs* provide continuity in the workshop by their daily presence, whereas Simon, occupied with other projects throughout the city, works only one or two days per week.

During this period, the treasurers purchased 218 *tonneaux* of stone from the quarries at Vernon, 43 *toise*, 28 *quartier*, and 69 *parpain* of stone from the quarries at Val-des-Leux. Once again little can be gleaned about the actual state of construction. In November 1443, a *couvreur de rosel* was paid to cover the chapels around the choir and the masons' lodge with reeds to protect the exposed stone over the winter months.[28] Thus, after ten years of construction only some of the choir chapels were completed to their upper parts. Three entries describe the placement of *piscine* stones. These were large carved stones passing through the entire thickness of the wall and located in every chapel. The full height of at least three of the chapels must have been reached, as suggested by an entry recording the fall of Jehan Le Prevost from the chapel of Notre-Dame.[29] Second, a payment was made to a carpenter for the placement of an altar in the chapel of Saint-Louis (although this may refer as well to the chapel in the old nave).[30] Finally, four carpenters place the "engin grenouville" in the chapel of Saint Catherine.[31] This undoubtedly was a lifting machine used to raise stone to the upper parts of the building. A payment for a cord that would lift ten pounds perhaps indicates that chapel vault severies were being placed.

While the construction at Saint-Maclou seems to be progressing at a steady but slow pace, the economic situation in Rouen during the fourth decade of the century was dismal. A series of letters from Henry VI, expressing his desire to see the completion of the church, suggests only his nominal interest in the project. A letter of 15 March 1444 to the English king from the Rouen notary requests an amortizement of twenty pounds sterling on the occasion of the reconstruction of Saint-Maclou. This may have been in response to similar letters of amortizement granted by Henry VI to the cathedral of Rouen. In one such letter of 15 January 1444, Le Moyne, the notary, mentions the decrease in cathedral revenues "à l'occasion des guerres et mesmement de la destruction du pays de Caux" (due to wars and the destruction of the Pays de Caux).[32] In a similar fashion, the king granted sums for the reconstruction of the parish church of Saint-Laurent in Rouen.[33]

Two letters in the Rouen archive from Henry VI relate to Saint-Maclou. The state of construction and the needs of the parish are described in the first letter given by Henry from Windsor on 22 April 1446.

> We, having found that this church because of its age formerly has been a great part demolished such that the divine service cannot be honorably celebrated as before as was accustomed to be celebrated in one day forty masses or more, which church the said suppliants having undertaken and began to build without *deniers* and materials of good stone they can neither complete nor accomplish without our grace and the help of our loyal subjects because this church does not have the sufficient treasury to make that which is proper but hope to collect and have gifts and alms for the accomplishment of the said work of who love the church. Making known to all by these presents that we the king of France and England wish the prosperity and continuation of the same duly support and seek, we regard favorably the good, holy, and laudable proposal of the said suppliants and their ruling and we sanction all as with God. In order that we by the grace of the holy spirit are made participant on the masses, sermons and other approbations which are celebrated in the said church, by royal authority full and powerful in special thanks to those suppliant treasurers have given gifts and concessions by our pity that they may and deserve in our land or in the land of our vassals, property, rents, works, or alms made to the said fabric by gifts or purchase in whatever place that they can find them. We grant further the sum of 40 pounds perpetually fixed and we wish in future time then as now and we order that these treasurers and parishioners can be compelled in such a manner to abandon the said properties and rents.[34]

The document describes a church that is partially demolished and in such a disruptive state that the forty masses per day formerly said at various altars cannot be carried out. The work on the new church was begun without the assurance of money to buy good building stone and the description confirms the state suggested in the 1443–46 account. The choir is under construction but not vaulted and the nave of the thirteenth-century church is being used for services. The letter further acknowledges the treasurers for their major support, initiation, and direction of the work. Henry's gift of forty pounds annually (which would last only two more years until the recapitulation of Rouen), and the suggestion of the return of properties to the church "either by gift or purchase" allows for the expansion of the nave into the *petit aître*. The royal participation in funding is relatively modest and once again underscores that the support of construction came directly and indirectly through internal parish resources.[35]

A second letter, given by Henry on 6 February 1447, and notarized by Robin Le Vigneron on 29 July 1448, provides additional information concerning the location of the land acquired.

> With the help of other devoted persons who stretched out helping hands toward this church which from old age for a long time stood, fallen and in ruins they will raze it and have it be rebuilt altogether anew at their own expense larger and more beautiful than it was before and already for many years this work has been begun, for the completion of which work and also for the enlargement of the cemetery of the same church the suitors themselves have acquired one piece of land for this use bordering on the same church or thereabouts upon which stands one house with the token called in the vulgar tongue Les Flagons and on the other part it is attached to lord (archbishop) of the church of Rouen and on another part to the public house in front of the church.[36]

By this letter Henry again encourages the donation or the sale of properties to the church that are situated in the area needed for the expansion of the nave to the west (toward the archbishop's palace) and to the south (into the cemetery) and the expansion of the cemetery. Therefore, preparations for setting out foundations in the nave may have been under way soon after 1448. The document also confirms that the parishioners were responsible for funding construction and that the old church had been under reconstruction for some time.

The Construction of the Nave, 1452–1489

In May 1452, shortly after the recapitulation of Rouen to Charles VII, the archbishop of Rouen and abbot of Saint-Ouen, Cardinal Guillaume d'Estouteville, granted an indulgence to the parishioners to fund construction.

> desiring therefore, that the parish church of Saint-Maclou of Rouen be completed, repaired, and enlarged so that it may be filled with a multitude with appropriate dignity, and that the Christian faithful may more willingly gather together in the same church for the sake of devotion and more readily extend helping hands for the completion, repair, and increase of buildings and structures, books, and other adornments of the same because they will perceive themselves filled more copiously with the gift of heavenly grace. Through the love of Almighty God and of Blessed Peter and Paul his Apostles and by the trusted authority which we exercise in these parts, to each and every one, truly penitent and shriven, who on the feasts of the Conception and Assumption of the Blessed Virgin Mary and on the feasts days of

Saints Maclou, Gilles, Leu, and Clair and also on the Sundays on which "Letare Jerusalem" and "In Ramis Palmarum" are sung and on the holy day of ———— will devoutly have visited the said church annually and also will have extended helping hands for the completion, repair, and enlargement of these buildings, structures, chalices, books, and adornments of the same namely, we mercifully remit in the Lord, on the feasts Saint Maclou and Saint Gilles and Leu for whichever, one year, and for each of the aforesaid feasts and days 100 days indulgence from the penance enjoyed on them.[37]

Further acceleration of the work was made possible by a parish subscription undertaken to raise money for construction. The archive contains a list of nearly four hundred parish families (almost the entire number of property owners) who contributed money for the work.[38] Although the document is not dated, the handwriting is midcentury and it must have been written in 1448, before the death of Etienne Dufour, who is listed as a donor and a *centenier*.[39]

By the mid-1450s, the choir vaults were completed. On a stylistic basis, François Perrot suggests that the stained glass of the choir clerestory representing the Apostles' Creed was contemporary with the transept roses of the nearby Abbey of Saint-Ouen. These roses are generally attributed to Alexandre and Colin de Berneval and therefore must date before 1450.[40] On 8 August 1453, Master Jean Pajot, curate of Notre-Dame-de-la-Ronde, and his brother Pierre Pajot, curate of Saint-Laurent-en-Caux, donated their house on the rue des Crottes to the work at Saint-Maclou: "in consideration of the excellent, notable, and sumptuous building by the grace of God marvelously begun and detailed in chapels made, foundations and other parts, in honor of God and the said glorious patron well advanced."[41]

The completion of the choir is further confirmed by a dated tomb inscription found in the first radiating chapel on the south side: "Here lies Master André Pajot for the salvation of the soul of which Master Jean Pajot, canon of the Cathedral of Rouen and Pierre Pajot, his brother, patron of the said church, child of the said André, died in the year 1460 has founded."[42]

Another inscription found in the choir chapel of the Virgin (NEIAII), and still visible today in the chapel of the same dedication, provides additional information concerning the patronage of the work (Fig. 7).

> Here lies Jean de Grenouville
> Prudent man, merchant, born in Etteville
> . . . in this parish
> Came to live at the time of his youth
> By his *deniers* and by his great largess
> Has made built most of this church
> Who died in the year 1466 in August
> On the 14th day

His wife, the daughter of Etienne Dufour
and his children be all under this earth
where his wife died the year 1464
In the month of March, she died
On the twenty-fifth day
We pray to God to complete the poem
That their souls after judgment
thereupon in glory safely lead.[43]

By 1454 Simon Le Noir had been replaced by Jehan Chauvin as master mason at Saint-Maclou. An account dated 14 January 1454 of Jean de Montcaudon, chaplain of Sainte-Catherine du Mont, identifies "Jol Chauvin" as "maistre macho de S. Maclo."[44] Nothing is documented of his work at Saint-Maclou but one can assume he was supervising the completion of the choir, the beginning of the transepts and possibly, the setting out of the nave foundations. Four years later, Chauvin is mentioned in a letter to the treasurers of Saint-Maclou from Guillaume Gombaut, viscount of Rouen, concerning the construction of a stone wall around the *petit aître*. The letter, dated 17 May 1458, describes the wall

around and enclosing the space of the church and in the place where the old wall is on the street making closed and separation between the cemetery adjoining the church and the street made by master Richard des Bustz, Estienne Le Marie, Martin Le Bourgois, Colin Duval, Jehan Le Prevost, Robin Riviere, Jehan Pontis, Jehan Chauvin, jurers of the craft of masonry and carpentry in Rouen from and around the Hôtel des Flagons, to the old wall of the cemetery to the place of the chapel Sainte Katherine.[45]

Due to the enlargement of the new nave, which extended into the old cemetery, the treasurers sought permission from the city to expand the new wall into the city street. The Hôtel des Flagons, already mentioned in the 1448 letter of Henry VI, was situated southwest of the church. On the advice of a lawyer and procurer to the king, Gombaut turned down their request and in the same letter declared that the city is "to be responsible for, to keep, and maintain the street of the king in its former course and state without which no one from any state or condition no matter who can undertake, begin or innovate buildings on the street."[46]

The conflict must have been resolved in favor of the treasurers; construction had progressed steadily so that at least some of the nave chapels on the south side were completed by 1465. An inscription in the chapel of the Annunciation, currently under the dedication of Saint Anthony of Padua (SIIWII) is dated 23 October 1465 (Fig. 8).

Here lies the honorable and prudent man
Jean de la Cayne, in his life,

Curate of Saint-Antoine-de-la-Foret
Who has been vicar of this church and
Who died 23 October 1465.[47]

Two sources of funding facilitated the rapid pace of construction. Although building accounts do not exist for this period, the archive possesses a summary of expenses recorded by the treasurer Jehan Le Roy for the years 1465–70 that shows 4,598 livres 18 sous 2 denier from parish funds were paid out for construction.[48] Nominal support from the French king Louis XI is indicated in letter from the counsel of the Exchequer of Normandy to the bailiff of Rouen dating November 1469, declaring that the cathedral chapter was exempt from a property tax on street frontage of 2 sous 6 denier "affectée à l'achèvement de l'église Saint-Maclou" (destined for the completion of the church of Saint-Maclou).[49] In the same year, the king levied a parish tax for a period of three years at a rate of 2 sous 6 denier on each foot of property built and placed on the streets in the parish, with revenue going to the work at Saint-Maclou.[50]

The next extant account of 1476–79 provides a more precise picture of the construction.[51] Large sums of money are expended on the purchase of roofing timbers including *trefs*, *chevrons*, and *soliveaux*, and a lifting machine is installed to raise the beams for roofing the nave prior to placing the vaults. Large quantities of stone are purchased from the quarries of Vernon and Val-des-Leux. The workshop is under the direction of a new master, Ambroise Harel, who is supervising eight masons including Jehan Le Prevost, Friset Le Mestre, Jehan Le Canne, Olliver Le Rebours, Guillaume Ouye, Gillet Luce, and Jehan Guillet. Harel was directing work at Saint-Maclou from as early as 1467 when he is mentioned as "Ambroise de Saint-Maclou" in a expertise called by the cathedral chapter concerning work on the tour Saint Romain.[52] At the same time Harel was supervising work on the parish church of Saint-Vincent in Rouen, where he was referred to as "maitre machon de l'oeuvre Saint-Maclou."[53] The similarity of the polygonal porch at Saint-Vincent with the western porch of Saint-Maclou has led scholars to suggest that Harel was responsible for the design of the innovative porch of the latter monument. This porch no doubt was constructed during Harel's tenure as master of Saint-Maclou, but it is unquestionably a design of Pierre Robin.[54]

The donation of the tracery for the western rose in 1487 provides the terminus ante quem for work on the nave and lower porch. On 19 August of this year, Colette Masselin, wife of Pierre Dufour, bequeathed to the treasury "all the *denier* that it is advisable for the completion of tracery necessary for the rose of the central portal and six small tracery lancets which are below the said rose and to pay the expense of the pavement and passage in the place of the chapel of Saint Symon Saint Jude."[55]

It is unlikely that the fragile tracery and glass of the rose and gallery would have been inserted before the construction of the adjacent nave vaults. Nine years later in 1496, Colette Masselin also paid for the erection of the vault before the chapel of the Three Nativities of Christ, the Virgin, and John the Baptist. On this occasion she gave to the fabric an ecu d'or du roi and une surplus et un doublier d'oeuvre de Vienne.[56] The western porch needed to support the western wall and nave vaults, must also have been in an advanced stage of construction.

The Lantern Tower, *Clôture*, *Jubé*, and Spire, 1487–1521

There is a substantial lacuna in the building accounts until 1514.[57] In this interim, Jacques Le Roux and Jehan Le Boucher are mentioned in unrelated documents as master of the works at Saint-Maclou. Nothing is known of their actual work at Saint-Maclou but Jacques Le Roux, master mason of the cathedral of Rouen between 1496 and 1510, is listed in the accounts of the tabellionage of Rouen on 6 September 1492 as "maitre des oeuvres de l'eglise Saint-Maclou."[58] In the cathedral accounts of 3 January 1508, Jehan Le Boucher, architect for the king, is designated as master mason of Saint-Maclou on the occasion of an expertise to the central portal of the cathedral.[59]

Building revenues for the work during the last decades of the fifteenth century were secured through generous gifts from parish families recorded in the *Grand Chartrier*. Cardinal Olivier de Sabine granted an indulgence in April 1500, and in 1511, Louis XII granted to the treasurers the same privilege of taxation on property bordering the street of the king.[60] A tax of 12 deniers for each foot of property was levied to assist the work on the lantern tower.[61]

Detailed descriptions of the completion of the lantern tower, *jubé*, and spire are provided by the accounts of 1514–17 and 1517–28.[62] By August 1514, Pierre Grégoire was master mason of the works; along with Roulland Le Roux, the master mason of the cathedral, he visited a house that blocked the portal of Saint-Maclou and requested that it be demolished.[63] In the same year, again with Roulland Le Roux and two other masons, he visited the tower at Saint-Maclou. Other entries record him making templates and drawings and executing work on two piers between the turrets of the tower, "Paid to Master Pierre Grégoire for two piers between the turrets by contract made with him . . . 44 livres" (Paie a Maistre Pierre Grégoire pour deux pilliers dentre lesquel tourelles par marche fait a luy ainsi quil appert par sa quittance, 44 livres). "This includes 4 livres tournois given to him for his work for having drawn the stones of the accompanying two turrets" (A ce comprins quatre livres tournoi quy luy ont este donnees pour sa paine davoir trace les pierres aux compaignons de deux tourelles).[64]

Between 1518 and 1519 he is paid a total of 205 livres for work on the organ staircase of the *jubé*.[65] At the same time, a payment of 200 livres was made to Nicolas Castille, *menuisier* (woodworker), for work on the organ buffet.[66] Grégoire is still master mason in 1530 but all major work seems to have been executed by the time of the dedication of the church in 1521.

During the three-year period of 1514–17 a workshop consisting of nine masons is involved in cutting and placing the stone of the staircase turrets around the lantern tower. A mason named Etienne Cauchée is paid 102 livres 2 sous for "making a stone staircase of the tower of the said church" (Item paie a Estienne Cauchee macon pour avoir fait en parfait une vis de pierre cy la tour de la dite eglise pour paine de macons faicte et maconniers la somme), and 7 livres 19 sous are paid for the week "for the last tower staircase to Etienne Cauchée and his companions" (Item paie le dernier jour de may 1516 pour la dernier tourelle vis laure a Estienne Cauchee et a ses compaignons pour leur sepmaine). Cauchée was an *appareilleur* in the tradition of Friset Le Mestre and Jehan Le Prevost.[67]

The last major construction of the flamboyant church involved the completion of a wooden spire to be placed over the lantern tower. Designed and executed by master carpenter Martin Desperrois, it was a masterwork of carpentry.[68] Shortly after Desperrois completed the spire for Saint-Maclou, he was commissioned by the cathedral who would not be outdone by the diminutive parish church, to execute a similar one.[69] In 1517 the treasurers of Saint-Maclou paid him 50 livres for unspecified work and a payment of 30 sous "for a piece of walnut on which is cut the said prophet". Other entries describe the spire decoration. An ironworker (serrurier), Martin Le Bourc, was paid 73 livres for an iron cross weighing 756 livres to surmount the spire, and the painter, Noel Barante, received 8 livres for the leading of the cross and the gilding of dolphins around the cross and for painting black fleur-de-lis on the tower.[70]

The fabric accounts also list numerous entries concerning the decoration of the church interior in preparation for its dedication. Pierre Huillard is paid for gilding the eight piers around the choir and cleaning the chandeliers of both the choir and nave. On 25 June 1521, the completion of the church was celebrated at its dedication by the cardinal and archbishop of Rouen, Georges II d'Amboise. To commemorate this event, Arthur Fillon, canon of the cathedral and curate of Saint-Maclou, gave four red damask copes to the church.[71]

Summary of Construction Chronology Based on Written Sources

Thus, from the written sources a clear sequence of construction emerges. Work appears to be slow in starting, owing to a lack of funds and the unavailability of good building materials, but progressed steadily through the third quarter of the fifteenth century. It continues uninterrupted into the last years of the century and first two decades of the sixteenth century when the pace slows and the expenses increase due to the elaborate detailed work on the lantern tower, upper parts of the west facade and transepts, and the stone liturgical furniture including the *jubé* and choir screen. The documents identify at least eight men as master mason of Saint-Maclou over the ninety-year period of construction between 1432 and 1521, yet there are no distinct breaks in construction activity. Neither are there indications in the fabric of the church of a pause or interruption of work.

Therefore, based upon the written sources alone, the following sequence of construction emerges against which the archaeological and design evidence will be tested:

I. 1432–1437 (Fig. 9). Work began soon after the request for funds in 1432. A foundation of 1434 mentions the initial stages of construction of a chapel of Notre Dame and a poem of 1436 describes the church which was "begun a while ago." Three masters appear in the 1436–37 account including Pierre Robin, Oudin de Mantes, and Simon Le Noir. Timber is purchased for reroofing the old nave and large quantities of stone are purchased. "*Buistes*," probably foundation stones, are being cut and templates are being made suggesting that work is above ground. Beams for the chapel of Notre Dame are placed against the tower of the old church indicating that work had begun in the choir.

II. 1437–1450 (Fig. 10). Work is under the direction of Simon Le Noir in 1443–46. The chapels are completed to their upper parts but not all of them are vaulted. Land is purchased to the south of the church in preparation for expansion of the nave and transepts.

III. 1450–1460 (Fig. 11). Construction accelerates after the recapitulation of the city to Charles VII. An indulgence of Cardinal Estoutville in 1452 suggests that the choir is completed and Jehan Chauvin, master mason, is supervising work on the transepts and the beginning of the nave.

IV. 1460–1490 (Fig. 12). The next three decades saw the construction of the nave. By 1465 some of the nave chapels were completed and the fabric account of 1476–79 shows that the nave is being roofed. Ambroise Harel directs the workshop from 1467 until 1480. With the donation of the western rose window in 1487, the nave vaults and western porch were in an advanced stage of completion.

V. 1490–1521 (Fig. 13). Work on the lantern tower was begun by the next master Jacques Le Roux and continued by Jehan Le Boucher. Pierre Grégoire saw the project to completion after 1514. He also worked on the *jubé* staircase, and the *appareilleur*, Etienne Cauchée, finished the lantern-tower staircases. The accounts show that the tower was vaulted by 1514 and the wooden spire was erected by master carpenter, Martin Desperrois in 1517. Expenses for decoration, cleaning, gilding, and so forth, prepared the church for its dedication in 1521.

2

The High Gothic Canon and the Late Gothic Craft

The Formal Language of Pierre Robin

The complexity of form and meaning in gothic architecture stems in part from the corporate nature of the design process and lengthy duration of construction. Because the conditions and rules that governed the design and execution of a gothic church were constantly shifting over the course of construction, the architectural fabric of any single monument embodies a succession of discrete and often unconnected visions. Artistic intent is more difficult to decipher because of the absence of written architectural treatises that would articulate the theoretical and conceptual basis for gothic design. However, with varying degrees of success, scholars have skillfully unraveled building histories by relating the changing fabric of the gothic monument to external events such as changes in master mason, patronal vision, construction revenue, site conditions, and function, or to less precise internal forces such as "stylistic evolution" or artistic development. Despite a long history of unbroken building activity of masons' workshops in northern France between 1140 and 1500, only occasionally was a master mason assigned the task of designing an entire structure from foundation to spire; even less frequently was his vision executed in its entirety. Even seemingly uniform structures such as Jean d'Orbais's Reims Cathedral or Robert de Luzarches's Amiens Cathedral, bear the distinct hand of subsequent masters who deviated from the vision of the original master. Although the monumental cathedrals of the high gothic period create challenging chronological puzzles for the scholar, their frequent adjustments to historical conditions over their long periods of construction have provided few opportunities to recover a coherent set of academic precepts that underlie the initial conceptualization of the overall design and to investigate the interrelationships between the design and conception of details with those of plan, elevation, and massing.

The parish church of Saint-Maclou is a rare example in the history of gothic architecture where a clear and coherent vision is manifested in the totality of its execution (Figs. 14–21).[1] Although there are occasional marginal elaborations in the surface decoration of Saint-Maclou during the later campaigns of construction (especially the upper west facade and crossing tower), these embellishments did not alter the underlying integrity or coherency of the initial design. Thus, not only does Saint-Maclou articulate late gothic style; it also provides an opportunity to extract a general set of design principles that guided the master mason at the moment he began to trace his ideas on parchment and plaster.

The continuity between concept and execution at Saint-Maclou can be attributed to a fortuitous convergence of circumstances: the presence of an exceptional master mason; the use of architectural drawings to provide consistency over the long period of construction; the guidance of a corporate patron who, over successive generations, insisted on adherence to the original drawings; the availability of steady funding that prevented abrupt starts and stops in construction; and the small scale of the monument, which permitted greater control over design, execution, and coordination of parts to the whole. Pierre Robin, the experienced and gifted master mason from the cathedral of Notre-Dame in Paris, was called to Rouen sometime before 1437 to provide the drawings for the new parish church. These drawings, mentioned in the building accounts were no doubt the blueprints for the construction, which lasted until 1521, although the vaults of the church were in place by 1490. Even though Pierre Robin left Rouen in 1437, the church treasurers, chosen from the dominant merchant parish families, played a significant role in overseeing the work, and insisting that these drawings be followed, despite pressures to concede to more fashionable trends of rouennais architecture after 1480.[2]

Thus it is possible to extract a clear set of rules that guided the conceptualization of the plan, elevation, and details of design from a visual analysis of the artistic language of Pierre Robin. In addition, an investigation of the underlying geometric framework that guided design will illuminate the practical and oral traditions that must have existed in the late gothic workshops of northern France. From this analysis, two primary observations emerge, the implications of which are developed in later chapters. First, the primary point of departure for Pierre Robin was the high gothic cathedral. When Pierre Robin was assigned the task of designing a complete church, there were few models of contemporary architecture in either Rouen or Paris to inspire him. Owing to the political turmoil following the death of Charles V, the subsequent decentralization of power under his successor Charles VI, the civil war brought on by the Burgundian/Armagnac conflict, and the economic devastation following the renewed efforts of the English to claim the French throne, very little large-scale ecclesiastic building was undertaken after 1380.

On the other hand, masons' workshops were augmenting or altering older structures by adding chapels or completing towers and facades or were involved in the construction of civic buildings, secular residences, and fortifications. Although there are numerous references connecting Pierre Robin with work in Paris, none suggest that he ever designed an entire church. Robin turned to the cathedral of Rouen for inspiration, but no single model proved to be his source. Rather, he was attracted to the coherency, clarity, and visual logic provided by high gothic architectural design in contrast to the excessive refinement, foreign influence, and additive nature that characterized the work of his contemporaries in Paris and Rouen.[3] It is not clear if Pierre Robin and the patrons of Saint-Maclou would have distinguished the architecture constructed under Louis IX from that of Philip the Fair or Charles V; thus the term *high gothic* is used here in its broadest sense encompassing rayonnant monuments constructed between the second quarter of the thirteenth century to the mid-fourteenth century. The success of Saint-Maclou in rejuvenating gothic architecture and contributing to the longevity of this style is due to Robin's insistence in recovering the order and clarity of design inherent in older monuments and by transforming design with the sophisticated academic logic and craftsmanship characteristic of late gothic workshop practice.

Second, because of the absence of architectural treatises and because of the rich diversity of architectural styles within this period of 1230–1350, it is difficult to identify a single set of principles that governed the design of high gothic monuments. Yet the most influential monuments of Paris and Rouen express certain common stylistic conventions. The most useful articulation of design rules is provided by Erwin Panofsky and Michel Bouttier, who borrowed a descriptive language from contemporary Scholasticism.[4] The purpose here is not to debate the nature and validity of the connection between Scholastic thought and gothic articulation but merely to adopt the descriptive language used by Panofsky and Bouttier. Thus, Panofsky's explanation of visual logic and the abstract concept of *manifestatio* with its constituent principles of sufficient enumeration, progressive divisibility, and distinctive and deductive cogency, along with Bouttier's use of the concepts of "hierarchization" and "crystallization," will form the basis for my characterization of the high gothic canon. Various parts of the cathedral of Rouen were the primary expressions of this canon for Pierre Robin. Consequently, the use and transformation of these principles by Pierre Robin provides a new criterion for understanding late gothic architecture.

The Formal Language of Pierre Robin

The plan

The design of the ground plan of Saint-Maclou was the most crucial stage in the conceptualization of the church: from it, mass, space, and structure were generated (Fig. 20). Pierre Robin had first to accommodate the requirements of his patrons, who would have stressed the functional needs of the parish church including chapels, a preference for a lantern tower and ambulatory and perhaps a porch, as well as their desire to associate their monument through imitation with the most prestigious monument in their city, the cathedral.[5] Second, he examined the size, shape, and impediments of the site that might pose limitations on his design scheme. With these considerations in mind, Robin then composed the plan according to a geometric framework that would assure structural and aesthetic integrity. The unorthodox and radical departures from traditional parish church plans as well as the rigorous uniformity in dimensions are owed to the uncompromising geometry underlying the plan design. The investigation of the precise geometric design schemes and the relationship between the abstract geometric design concepts and the pragmatic procedures of constructive geometry used to lay out the plan at the site will be examined in Chapter 3.

The compact and uniform ground plan of Saint-Maclou includes a nonprojecting transept with enlarged crossing piers that support a lantern tower centrally placed between the short, three-bay nave and two-bay choir. The nave consists of a central vessel, aisles with deep chapels; the relatively large choir is composed of two straight bays, aisles and chapels, and four polygonal radiating chapels off the ambulatory. Although almost identical to the collegiate church of Saint-Urbain, Troyes, in overall dimensions, the central placement of the transept, and the presence of idiosyncratic porches, the plan of Saint-Maclou includes a number of unique features that did not evolve from any single model.[6] The presence of an axial pier and the absence of an axial chapel are radical departures from conventional east-end designs and yet this feature complements the equally anomalous polygonal porch at the west end. Although the plan is uniform, the bays are of different dimensions and emphasis falls on the transept because of its placement midway between the nave and choir.

The structurally and liturgically complex features of the ambulatory and radiating chapels were most likely inspired by large-scale buildings. Because Pierre Robin has chosen an unorthodox solution for his east end (employing an axial pier and rejecting an axial chapel), he was able to resolve design irregularities that occur in gothic plans at the point where the turning bays join the straight bays of the choir. Saint-Maclou is the first gothic monument with identical turning bays and radiating chapels creating a perfectly symmetrical, precise, and uniform east end. The private chapels of the nave and choir straight bays were features normally added to existing plans in high gothic and a majority of late gothic churches, but at Saint-Maclou they were designed from the outset as an integral part of the ground plan, providing the historian with the opportunity to examine an all-embracing design scheme not easily recognized in other monuments. Finally, by placing the transept crossing midway between the nave and choir, by calling attention to the crossing through the dominating presence of the lantern tower, and by the complementary polygonality that directed movement from both the east and west to this area, Pierre Robin made both the spatial focus and the design center explicit. In his discussion of "visual logic," Panofsky wrote that the "membrification of the edifice permitted (the viewer) to reexperience the very processes of architectural composition."[7] Although Panofsky is referring only to the articulation of an elevation, at Saint-Maclou it might be applied in a more profound sense to the entire composition of space, mass, and structure.

Elevation

It is significant that the elevation of Saint-Maclou is most comparable to large-scale monuments of the high gothic period. Saint-Maclou continued the three-story elevation characteristic of monumental architecture, although unlike the more recent and fashionable Norman choirs of Saint-Ouen, Sées, and Evreux with their stunning glazed triforia and dense decoration, he returned to the more conservative and older blind triforium. This formula is characteristic of a significant group of early fifteenth-century parish and collegiate churches in Normandy and the Vexin of similar scale to Saint-Maclou, including the nave of Saint-Germain at Argentan, nave and choir of Notre-Dame at Les Andely, nave of Notre-Dame at Vernon, nave of Notre-Dame at Alençon, and the nave and choir of Notre-Dame at Caudebec-en-Caux. The unmitigated verticality that imparts an impression of a supercharged monumentality to Saint-Maclou, however, is owed to Robin's distinct vocabulary of forms and an illusionistic manipulation of proportional relationships.

The choir and nave both have a "classic" three-story elevation of an arcade, blind triforium, and clerestory.[8] Each narrow straight bay of the choir and nave is outlined by linear, continuous fillet moldings rising from the arcade piers and inscribing a bay composed of a four-lancet clerestory with cusped double-curved tracery above a four-lancet triforium screen subdivided into four pairs of smaller lancets. A triforium balustrade of truncated lancets provides a strong horizontal element to balance the insistent verticality of the framing moldings that rise uninterrupted from the floor level (Figs. 22 and 23). The elevation design reveals the same visual logic established in the high gothic architecture and expressed through the "principle of progressive divisibility." All moldings of the articulation scheme are fully integrated into the whole by both inscribing a unit and by being inscribed by a larger identical unit. The problem of linkage and continuity among levels, arcade, triforium, and clerestory—which often presented problems for the high gothic masters in terms of placement of capitals—has been fully resolved by the use of continuous moldings, yet the integrity of each unit is preserved by the presence of individual bases for each mullion, molding, and shaft. Pierre Robin never inserts sculptural flourishes such as bouquets of foliage or uncanonic forms such as the lozenge-shaped balustrade employed in the contemporary churches of Saint-Germain at Argentan or Notre-Dame at Caudebec-en-Caux. Neither does he indulge in marginal elaboration of the scheme, which might detract from a clear and systematic progressive division of parts within the whole. Pierre Robin reclaims the inherent clarity and systematic organization provided by the triforium and clerestory of the cathedral of Rouen and transforms it by the substitution of double-curved tracery for geometric tracery and continuous fillet moldings and for round shafts and capitals (Fig. 106). By choosing an older model, he was able to recover the academic explicitness of linkage and progressive divisibility that was absent in construction after 1380.

Yet the interior of Saint-Maclou could never be confused with the cathedrals of Rouen or Amiens, the abbey of Saint-Ouen, or the collegiate church of Saint-Urbain in Troyes.

Robin knew how to transform the precious scale of Saint-Maclou through a manipulation of proportions and articulation in order to create the illusion of monumentality as well as to energize the space defined by architectural elements. The sharp continuous moldings, narrow central vessel, and proportional scheme of the elevation create an unmitigated sense of verticality. A comparison of overall proportions between Saint-Maclou and a number of large-scale and small-scale monuments illustrates Robin's manipulation of scale and illusion. Although the high vaults of Saint-Maclou are approximately half the height of the vaults of Amiens or Saint-Ouen, Robin uses the same ratio between the height of the arcade to the height of the triforium/clerestory (A:A). Likewise, the proportion of the height of the vault to the width of the central vessel has a similar ratio of 1:3 among the three monuments. This provides the impression of a miniature monumental building. His only deviation from the elevation of large-scale monuments is in the relationship between the clerestory and triforium. In order to compensate for the proportionally smaller clerestory window and to permit more light into the church, Robin reduces the triforium in relationship to the clerestory. Thus, while the triforium/clerestory proportion at Saint-Ouen is 1:1.5, at Amiens it is 1:2, and at Saint-Maclou it is 1:3 (Table 2).

Table 2 Comparative proportions in elevations

	Height of arcade / triforium and clerestory		Width of central vessel / height of central vessel		Height of triforium / clerestory
Saint-Maclou (Vincent)*		A:A	7.6 m / 22.8 m	1/3.3	1/3
Saint-Ouen (Pugin)*	52″ / 51″	A:A	31″ / 103′ 2″	1/3.4	1/1.5
Amiens Cathedral (Prak and Durand)*	22 m / 22 m	A:A	14 m 60 / 42 m 30	1/3	1/2

*Indicates source of measurement.

Vocabulary of Forms

The academic precepts that governed Pierre Robin's design are perhaps most evident in his highly individualized vocabulary of forms including moldings, piers, window tracery, and keystone sculpture.

The fillet base, plinth, and molding. No single element of architecture more perfectly summarized the aesthetic aims of Pierre Robin than the fillet base and molding. It is the hallmark of his style and the building block of all the articulation systems at Saint-Maclou. The fillet base provided the means for achieving rigid geometric control and order following rules laid out in the high gothic period, thus displaying his technical mastery of masonry. Through various combinations and highly sophisticated designs, Pierre Robin was able to achieve maximum visual explicitness, unrestrained verticality, an organic arboreal frame or enclosure for space, and a vehicle by which line and geometry—the primary expressive in-struments of the architectural draftsman—were supremely manifested.

Although there is evidence that the fillet base, plinth, and molding developed a decade or so earlier, Pierre Robin introduced a new sleek and elegant version at Saint-Maclou (Figs. 24–30).[9] Except for variations in scale that indicate responses to different functions, these three components are used throughout, from the basic compositional unit of the pier base, the articulating systems of the triforium and clerestory, the chapel mullions and for-merets and wall shafts, and the jambs and embrasures of the western and transept facades and the lantern tower. A consistent and coherent use of the fillet base, plinth, and continuous moldings account for the stunning uniformity of the interior space. No single element was more influential or became more ubiquitous in northern late gothic design of the late fifteenth century. The celebrated early sixteenth-century masters, Roulland Le Roux and Martin Chambiges, are both indebted to Pierre Robin for this building block in their own designs.[10]

The nave arcade piers, chapel opening piers, transept crossing piers, and choir hemicycle piers are all composed of combinations of five sizes of individual plinths, bases, and mold-ings that rise from complex socles designed around polygons defined by concave scoops and flat faces (Fig. 25).[11] All the piers, attached and freestanding on the north side of the church, are complemented by an identical pier on the opposite south side. However, no two piers on the same side of the church are identical. In addition, with the exception of the axial pier (a) and the radiating chapel piers (n1a1, a1, and s1a1), no two piers are perfectly sym-metrical. Pierre Robin designed each pier to accommodate its unique function in the church and adjusted its geometry to reflect individual bay sizes. Despite the apparent vari-ety in outward appearance, pier design follows a rigid set of coherent rules.

1. All interior pier bases are composed of five sizes of fillet plinths, bases and moldings (Fig. 25). The nave arcade piers consist of 20 individual bases (Figs. 26 and 27), the chapel opening piers consist of 19 individual bases (Fig. 28), and the transept crossing piers in-clude 32 individual bases (Fig. 29). The size of the individual bases reflects the impor-tance of its function so that the intrados of the chapel-opening molding is supported by a massive fillet base and plinth cut from the same template as the base that supports the in-trados moldings of the lantern tower found on the transept crossing piers. Pierre Robin introduced a triplet of fillet bases for the intrados of the arcade piers that both signifies the importance of this molding in the hierarchy and softens the profile providing an ele-gant tone to the arcade central vessel articulation. This systematic and assiduous applica-tion of scaled bases may be construed as a logical conclusion to the introduction of graded components in the rayonnant period.[12]

2. All bases rise from polygonal socles composed of combinations of short flat faces and broad concave scoops.

3. In addition to combinations of five graded individual fillet plinths, bases, and moldings, every pier also has three moldings wrapping the core of the entire pier (Fig. 24a.E). The

profiles of these moldings vary depending on the depth of the recession but they have a similar profile to the fillet bases. These moldings of the chapel-opening piers and other attached piers extend beyond the pier and form the wall moldings of the chapels and inner transept and west walls, creating a continuous horizontal band approximately one meter above ground level around the entire inner wall of the church (Fig. 30). The walls of the church become visual extensions of the pier bases.

4. Each molding that rises from the pier has its own individual plinth and base. These individual plinths and bases rise above the core moldings of the piers. Every molding is continuous, springing uninterrupted from a base until it meets the apex of the arch of the ribbed vault, the formeret, or the arcade. Once a molding springs from a base, its profile never changes. Consequently, the rib profile can be read by examining the pier molding.

5. Dying or disappearing moldings are rare and usually interpenetrate first. This occurs most frequently when complex moldings have to be adjusted to smaller dimensions of bays or chapels (Fig. 31).

6. Groups of moldings are always connected by concave scoops, sometimes with a sharp angle between each molding.

7. The piers appear to be composed of the sum total of the moldings they support without having a mass of their own.

8. The individual plinth, bases, and moldings are clustered in each pier to indicate differences in the sizes of the bays. For example, in the nave arcade pier, the individual plinths and bases that support the molding of the diagonal ribs of the central vessel are spaced further apart than the individual plinths and bases that support the diagonal ribs of the side aisles. This difference reflects the fact that the angle is greater than 45 degrees for the rectangular bay of the central vessel whereas the ribs of the aisles are close to 45 degrees.

This description, although tedious, underscores the pervasive control that Pierre Robin exercised through every detail of design. Every pier, very directly, reflects not only the idea of a ribbed vault or a formeret, but also the very shape and size of the profile of the ribs. The hierarchy assigned to the individual molding establishes its level of importance; the subtle adjustments to the geometry of the pier indicates the proportions of the bay that are inscribed by the moldings. In other words, each pier base contains within it the exact form and geometry of the surrounding spaces and is a virtual synecdoche for the entire structure. No gothic building more perfectly expresses the high gothic canon of "visual logic" in pier design. Panofsky identified the compound piers of Saint-Denis as the perfect expressions of this ideal. He writes "the classic style demands that we be able to infer, not only the interior from the exterior, or the shape of the side aisles form that of the nave but say, the organization of the whole system from the cross section of one pier."[13] This claim may be an exaggeration for Saint-Denis but accurately suits Saint-Maclou. This degree of explicitness would not have been possible unless Pierre Robin understood the inherent design rules of the thirteenth-century architect, and set out to express the full implications of these principles. At Saint-Maclou, the level of visual logic has become so utterly sophisticated that the precise geometric relationship of the individual shafts to the pier is not readily comprehensible and can only be completely understood through the studied contemplation of sections provided by drawings. Although the fillet plinth, base, and continuous molding became the sign of contemporeneity in Norman architecture of the second half of the fifteenth century, no master mason was able to reproduce the exact form of the Saint-Maclou piers. Without access to drawings, regional architects employed idiosyncratic and sometimes comical variations of the fillet pier base in a large number of churches in Normandy, including Saint-Germain at Argentan, Saint-Michel at Pont L'Evêque, and Saint-Ouen at Pont Audemer.[14] Perhaps the best illustration of the importance of drawings for construction of a Saint-Maclou pier is demonstrated by the modern blueprints drawn to replace the axial pier damaged in 1944 (Figs. 33–35). Similar drawings must have existed to instruct the fifteenth-century carpenters on the forms for templates and the *appareilleurs* on carving and assembly. In addition to the complex set of vertical profiles, for the axial pier alone, drawings were needed for at least seven horizontal courses. Besides containing all the forms for elevation and vault articulation and bay geometry, this pier (like all the choir arcade piers) also contains the design instructions for the minuscule bases and lintel forms of the choir *clôture*—perhaps the only gothic piers to do so. Thus, it was the late gothic dependency on drawings that contributed to an almost incomprehensible complexity in design that consciously flaunted the sophisticated knowledge possessed by the gothic mason.

The elimination of the capital was fundamental to Robin's ability to create a sense of monumentality through the illusion of verticality. From the very beginning of gothic architecture the capital had been a problem for the gothic builder. Although perfectly suited for the round column, the capital had a limited ability to express structural forces and to link the vault and wall articulation visually with the supporting member. Panofsky points out the problems of accommodating the capital to the more explicit supports of the *pilier cantonné* and the compound pier. But in a very real sense, the capital was an archaic Romanesque vestige that had no appropriate role in the "modern" architecture of the gothic period.[15] For Pierre Robin, the capital was an anomaly and it inhibited his desire for an integrated and fully explicit system of articulation. The capital was an intrusion or interruption in the linear and geometric design process. It would not submit to line, the straight edge, the compass, or a rule of measure. Nor could it be conveyed by the economic use of templates and the prefabrication process of cutting stone. The capital impeded the upward flow of articulating and supporting members that framed space and permitted the full integration of mass and space. The same moldings that clustered together forming the piers rose uninterrupted to inscribe the space of the bays, aisles, and chapels. Supporting mass flowed to frame space. Although continuous moldings were occasionally employed in thirteenth-century monuments, they were key to the vision of Pierre Robin and applied at Saint-Maclou with absolute consistency.[16] It must have appeared to his contemporaries a radical and daring solution, but because of the new priority given to craftsmanship, by eliminating the capital he was able to resolve an inherent contradiction between absolute visual logic of the gothic pier and the interruptive effect of the Romanesque capital.

Wall shafts and portal jambs. Two small but significant variations in the design of the fillet base indicate Robin's interest in illusionism and his awareness of manipulating the perceptions of the viewer. A distinctly different profile belongs to the fillet bases found on the exterior of the church and on all the bases above the arcade level (Figs. 24b and 32). Although the bases, plinths, and moldings are identical in section, the base profile consists of strong rolls on both the upper and lower tori that are absent in the interior pier bases. These more durable bases may have been considered by Robin to be more appropriate for the harsher conditions of the exterior and for the bolder visual profile they created at the upper levels of the elevation. Thus, the change in base form has more to do with practical considerations of location than the morphology of forms or individual style.[17] Second, optical illusionism was a conscious design consideration of fifteenth-century architects, just as it was for contemporary painters and sculptors.[18]

Window tracery. Tracery patterns, the focus of most discussions on flamboyant architecture, provide the earliest and most visible signs of change in gothic style after the 1380s; to earlier scholars, "double-curved" tracery was considered the hallmark (and sometimes the only mark) of late gothic style. Although the characteristic ogees, mouchettes, and soufflets were present in early flamboyant monuments such as the La Grange chapels at Amiens, Jean de Berry's fireplace in the Palace at Poitiers, the Sainte-Chapelle at Riom, and the new facade screens of the Rouen Cathedral, important distinctions must be made between these works and Saint-Maclou. Prior to the construction of Saint-Maclou, all appearances of double-curved tracery were in combination with geometric tracery. A good map of the changes that took place between the fourteenth and fifteenth century can be demonstrated by the three great lancet windows of the west facade of the parish church of Saint-Vivien in Rouen (Fig. 124).[19] Built directly behind the abbey of Saint-Ouen, the three vessels of this hall church are terminated in the west by large mullioned windows. The northern facade window was completed in the early fourteenth century and must be contemporary with the construction of the choir of Saint-Ouen (1319–38). The disposition of two pairs of lancets with small quatrefoils surmounted by a larger sexfoil is typical of the tracery found in the rayonnant choir chapels at Saint-Ouen.

The central vessel, completed sometime in the late fourteenth century, is terminated by ogees above the major and minor lancets as well as mouchettes and soufflets filling the irregular spaces. These are combined with the more regular geometric tracery including sexfoils above the lancet pairs and an idiosyncratic rose of four cinquefoils and four soufflets. This mannerist and eccentric combination of forms was probably inspired by the equally unusual inner north transept blind tracery of Saint-Ouen or the panels of Jean de Bayeux on the Porch of the Marmosets and the facade of the cathedral executed sometime between 1380 and 1399. In all cases, the mullions are composed of refined almond-shaped shafts rising from tiny trumpet bases on octagonal plinths with fragile foliate bands as capitals. "Hierarchy" and "crystallization," which provided discipline to the articulation of tracery in high gothic windows, is absent in the diverse and inconsistent designs of Saint-Vivien. Patterns recall the seemingly endless variety of geometric shapes that appear in the dado spandrels of the Virgin Chapel at Lisieux Cathedral of around 1432. These lithic doodles seem to be taken from a page of the mason's sketchbook. It is easy to see how this academic playfulness and experimentation could have been inspired by similar motifs first appearing in small-scale ivories, metalwork, and manuscripts, or imported from English decorated sources.

These works stand in stark contrast to the tracery of Saint-Maclou and to the third lancet window of Saint-Vivien that reflects the influence of the new work at Saint-Maclou. Pierre Robin introduced to French architecture for the first time a coherent and consistent use of flamboyant or double-curved tracery. He completely eliminated the use of geometric patterns in tracery design and discarded the overrefined capital, fragile almond shaft, and trumpet base. Strong, fluid contours of tracery patterns restored power to design and created a more appropriate form for architecture distinct from the more fastidious and precious decoration of small-scale objects. His choice of patterns is much closer in formula to tracery of high gothic architecture and distinguished primarily by the transformation of geometric to double-curved forms, which allowed him to express the innate fluid linearity of draftsmanship. In addition, although there is diversity expressed in the patterns, these stylistic differences can be linked not to traditional explanations of changes in campaigns or stylistic evolution, but to the new ideology of individualism, which permitted variety within a carefully coordinated whole in order to display the technical and design skill of the individual craftsman.[20]

An examination of two windows, one from the radiating chapel and one from the nave chapels, will demonstrate Pierre Robin's tracery design and "system." The most typical Saint-Maclou window is represented by a nave chapel window (the same pattern is repeated in the entire clerestory). It is a flamboyant version of a thirteenth-century window of the cathedral of Rouen (Figs. 36 and 106), and follows the same rules of "hierarchization" (a hierarchy of planes: primary, secondary, and tertiary) and "crystallization" (the repetition of forms concerning the two-dimensional design, tracery subdivided according to geometric figures common to the whole) found in the cathedral clerestory.[21] At Saint-Maclou, the four lancets are arranged in two pairs, each surmounted by a soufflet containing two mouchettes and two soufflets. Between the pairs is another soufflet composed of similar two mouchettes and two soufflets. A hierarchy of mullions governs the articulation. The heaviest mullion of the primary plane frames the entire window (separated from it by a deep concave scoop) and rises from the largest fillet plinths and bases.

On the secondary level, all lancet mullions are equally weighed and of identical size; they rise from the second-level fillet plinths and bases. On the exterior, these plinths are located on the sloping *glacis* of the window but on the interior, at the chapel level, the mullions penetrate the *glacis* and extend to the stone wall molding above the floor level (Figs. 39 and 146). This creates a dado of recessed panels directly below the window in each chapel. Aside from being a more efficient and economic method of designing an elegant dado arcade, the linked panels repeat the more complex pattern of the triforium/clerestory of the central vessel, creating overall visual uniformity in the interior design. The third level or tertiary plane in the tracery hierarchy is the cusping itself. Carved in lower relief than the lancet mullions and tracery, it adds to the flickering quality of the stone patterns.

The greatest discrepancy of the Saint-Maclou windows with those of the cathedral is that hierarchy does not extend to differentiate the size of the mullions between the individual lancets and the pairs of lancets. Pierre Robin chose overall uniformity and texture. This choice was necessary because the choir chapel windows and the transept windows consist of triple lancets, where hierarchy of pairs within the whole is not possible. Neither is it possible in other variations found in the nave chapels. For instance, the center nave chapel of both the north and south also has four lancets but the patterns above create three soufflets composed of two smaller soufflets and two mouchettes (Fig. 37). These three are then surmounted by another pair of soufflets consisting of the same patterns. In every window design by Robin, however, the same divisions between primary (formeret), secondary (tracery and lancet mullion) and tertiary (cusping) apply. All his tracery is composed of variations of ogee lancets with soufflets and mouchettes and an occasional ogee trefoil to fill in corners; all these variations, however, are essentially double-curved versions of the same geometric patterns found at the cathedral. He never uses geometric forms, spherical triangles or rectangles, spinning panels, stars, or other motifs frequently found in the work of his contemporaries or immediate predecessors. Compare, for example, the unregulated patterning of the early flamboyant cathedral facade panels in Rouen or the Porch of the Marmosets of Saint-Ouen.

How then can the tremendous variation in tracery patterns be explained at Saint-Maclou if we suppose that Pierre Robin was interested in uniformity—particularly as the architectural style in other ways is utterly homogeneous? Although there are at least ten variations in tracery patterns, they are not randomly placed. Every window on the north side of the church has an identical counterpart opposite to it on the south side of the church.[22] In addition, other patterns of placement emerge. Every radiating chapel window consists of two types of triple lancets forming "tulips" (Figs. 19 and 39).[23] In each choir chapel, two tulip-patterned windows frame a slightly more complex tulip tracery window. Because each chapel has three windows, the pattern of placement of all the four radiating chapels from north to south is 1–2–1, 1–2–1, 1–2–1, and 1–2–1. The same tulip windows appear in the arms of the transept clerestory but are adjusted to accommodate the various widths of the bays. The nave chapels use a similar pairing. The center chapel on both the north and south displays the flickering four-lancet solution while the chapels on each side display the cathedral version. The chapels adjacent to the transepts are adjusted to three lancets to accommodate the intrusion of the staircase turrets; the underlying pattern, however, is the same as the western most chapels of the nave. Thus, on the north side, the chapel patterns are 3–4–3-transept-3, and on the south the same 3–4–3-transept-3 patterns are found. All the clerestory windows of the central vessel employ identical four-lancet windows (repeating the patterns found in the outer nave chapels and first choir chapel-3), and turning bays of the hemicycle display a simplified two-lancet version.

Planned and patterned diversity within a uniform whole confirms that drawings were the agent of control; they provided continuity and order to the work. This patterning could not have been maintained had the eight masters who directed the workshop in the fifteenth century been allowed the freedom to design as well as to oversee construction. Changes in patterns at Saint-Maclou in no way suggest changes in campaigns, masters, or stylistic evolution; instead they suggest new freedom and a rather self-conscious and academic display of the virtuosity of draftsmanship as well as the importance of drawings in maintaining control despite the diversity. Planned and patterned diversity adds a decorative effect that draws attention to itself, to display the cunning skill and inventiveness of the master. In the late gothic period, variation within a building takes on an additional meaning. It would be difficult to argue that the variety of pier forms in the ambulatory of Saint-Severin in Paris or in the nave of Saint-Gervais and Protais in Gisors were constructed in a separate campaigns (Fig. 133). Rather, the master mason seems to be demonstrating his skill as a draftsman, delighting in the variety of forms for their own sake, and drawing attention to himself as an accomplished craftsman, one who asserts his individuality very publicly and visibly—at modest expense to overall uniformity. Richness and diversity of surface articulation within the boundaries of careful overall control distinguish Saint-Maclou. Individuality of form granted within the whole is also linked to the double function of the parish church that needed to incorporate private devotional spaces, often bearing the distinct emblems or marks of its donor (coats-of-arms or sculpture portraits), within the public corporate space of the central vessel.

Late gothic keystones. With great priority placed on architectural draftsmanship and the communication of design through line that could be transferred to templates, there was little room left for architectural sculpture. Bands of neatly paired leaves articulate the horizontal stringcourse in assembly-line fashion, at three levels of the triforium (Fig. 40). In addition, the western porch and facades provide a few opportunities for exquisite vignettes of dense naturalistic vines of grape leaves and strawberries inhabited by birds, snails, and fantastic creatures (Figs. 41 and 42).

On the other hand, Pierre Robin redesigned the artistic format of the keystone to accommodate his aesthetic aims and to maintain his control over the uniformity of production (Fig. 43). Traditionally a location for foliate or figurative carving, the keystones of Saint-Maclou have become displays of geometric elegance. Geometry, formerly in service of design, became the subject of design.[24] With two exceptions—the scene of the Baptism of Christ on the vault for nave aisle bay NIIWI (Fig. 44), and the coat-of-arms of the Amyot family on the vault of nave aisle bay NIIWIII (Fig. 45)—the keystones are designed around variations of exquisite geometric discs of openwork double-curved tracery articulated with small bouquets of foliage and occasionally a center rose (Figs. 46–49). The true keystone boss was unarticulated and placed at the joining of the ribs with the decorative geometric keystone disc suspended from it by an iron rod and hook. Viollet-Le-Duc describes these as characteristic of fifteenth-century architecture and closer in form to metalwork, but the Saint-Maclou geometric keystones are among the earliest and indeed, may have been an invention of Pierre Robin.[25]

In addition to providing a new format for the display of both design and carving skill, the keystone became a vehicle by which Pierre Robin could, once again, explore illusionism in architecture. The keystones of the central vessel vaults are slightly larger and more elaborate versions of aisle, chapel, and porch-vault keystones. The increased size makes them more visible from below (Fig. 50). However, to enliven their presence in the transept vault, Robin projected the geometric discs into three dimensions. Their pendant form is not visible from the ground level but the flat keystone discs used in the nave have been transformed into animated stars in the transept (Fig. 51). Thus, as with his design of the base profiles used above the arcade level (where he gives greater visual power to the form by increasing its plasticity), Robin seems aware of the position of the viewer and the optical distortion that takes place through space by adjusting his design accordingly.

Transept Facades and the West Facade Porch

Pierre Robin's dependency on the high gothic cathedral of Rouen as a point of departure is most apparent in the design of the transept facades, while his ability to transcend his models with a highly creative and novel solution boasting the sophistication of his craft is evident in the design of the west facade and porch. The north transept of Saint-Maclou faced the rue Martainville, the major east/west axis of the city. Entry through the Porte Martainville would lead dignitaries, processions, and grand entrances, past the north transept of the parish church, across the Pont du Robec to the rue St. Romain, an extension of the rue Martainville, past the archbishop's palace, and finally to the north transept of the cathedral. The relationship between these two portals, aligned on the same city street, was not lost on the fifteenth-century viewer (Figs. 1, 21, 52, 53, 107).

The north transept of the cathedral, constructed by Jean Davi after 1280 and the south transept, completed shortly after, perhaps by 1300, mark the first major reaction in Normandy to Parisian rayonnant.[26] The melding of Parisian linear refinement characterized by the multiple gables, quatrefoil embrasures, and magnificent rose windows, with Norman sculptural plasticity, conveyed by multiple passages, and rich figurative sculpture, resulted in what Viollet-Le-Duc called the most beautiful of gothic portals.[27] The elegance, high quality of construction, and clarity of design of the rayonnant transepts represented the apogee of the craft of masonry before 1380, and must have served as a strong magnet for Robin. Robin repeated the same clear compositional components (a single gabled portal with interlocking balustrade before a passage, triforium, rose window inscribed by tall rounded arch, surmounted by a gable with interlocking balustrade before a passage, and a roof gable); he frames and buttresses the tall narrow wall of tracery and glass with two staircase turrets. Although Robin attenuated the balustrade and gallery windows to accommodate the narrower proportions of his facade, and transformed the self-contained geometric tracery into flowing and sinuous line, the presence of the high gothic model is unmistakable. The greatest discrepancy between the two facades is one of scale, and this relationship provides an explicit example of Robin's miniaturization of monumental architecture. The width of the cathedral transept (including aisles) is 24.6 m whereas the width of the transept of Saint-Maclou is 6.8 m.[28]

The south transept of Saint-Maclou provided access to the *petit aître*, the mason's lodge, and the presbytery; although it is identical in basic composition and scale, it was accorded less detail and decoration (Fig. 54). The portal lacks a gable, the roof gable lacks blind tracery, and less skillful masons executed the portal jambs.

The cathedral models that guided Pierre Robin in his design of elevation and transept facades were not suitable for the west facade of the parish church. Once liberated from a specific older compositional model, Robin was free to find a solution that showcased his mastery of drafting, geometry, and structure in order to "re-create" works of the past. His west facade may be considered a "masterwork" of late gothic architecture.

The towerless facade consists of two essential components, a five-gabled polygonal porch placed before a west-wall termination articulated with a rose window and gallery lighting the central vessel and flying buttresses above the aisles (Figs. 18 and 55). Characterized as a "perverse fantasy," or inaccurately described as having a compressed or bowed porch, the poor state of restoration, blackened stone, and visual complexity of the gables, irregular buttresses, and paneled flyers have obscured the actual clarity of the underlying geometric and structural scheme.[29]

Robin was faced with four possible models. The twin-tower facade associated with monumental high gothic cathedral architecture embodied meanings of temporal power and were likened to fortified city gates or entrances to ducal palaces. These associations were inappropriate to the function and meaning of a parish church facade. The miniaturization of the formidable twin towers would also have resulted in a "caricaturesque" solution reminiscent of Notre-Dame de l'Epine and would have detracted from the visual focus of the lantern tower.

The second, and most typical, solution for parish church facades was a pyramidal termination designed around a central gable, lower aisles, and usually a single tower to one side, creating a static and asymmetrical entrance. Robin would have been familiar with the fourteenth-century Norman facades of the parish churches of Saint-Pierre at Caen and Saint-Jacques at Dieppe. Earlier he had designed the facade of the *nef unique* chapel of Saint-Yves in Paris with its large single lancet window, but Saint-Maclou required greater imagination.

A third solution was provided by a number of early fourteenth-century churches in the Low Countries and Germany. Saint Bavo's in Ghent, for example, is preceded by a pyramidal facade dominated by an imposing central tower. At Saint-Maclou the central tower has been pushed back from the west facade to the lantern crossing. The fourth model for Robin was, once again, the cathedral of Rouen; unlike, however, the uniform and unambiguous model provided by the cathedral transepts, the west facade presented a complex multi-layered grid of architectural indecisiveness (Fig. 109).

The renovation of the cathedral facade begun by Jean Perier shortly after 1370 had been completed around 1406 by Jenson Salvart. In preparation for the burial of the heart of

Charles V in the choir of the cathedral, Perier, master mason of the cathedral from 1362 until 1388, had designed a new rose window to replace the triple lancet opening of the central vessel and a series of thin, multilevel gabled screens that would be superimposed on the four small thirteenth-century turrets rising above the three portals.[30] Perier also submitted plans for a new porch to the chapter and vestiges of the fourteenth-century shafts supporting the porch vaults can still be seen on the side portals attached to the massive buttresses added by Roulland Le Roux in the sixteenth century. Perier's porch does not survive today and it is not clear how much was actually constructed when Le Roux was commissioned to rebuild the center portion of the facade due to its imminent collapse aggravated by the construction of the Butter Tower by Guillaume Pontis after 1485.

The remaining porch vault springers indicate that Perier's porch may have been polygonal and it is easy to visualize a gabled porch that repeats the gables of Perier's upper facade design (Fig. 110). More important, from the middle of the fourteenth century, references are made to a *viri galilae* on upper parts of the cathedral west facade, where two canons ascend during the celebration of the Feast of the Ascension to sing a response that began "Men of Galilee, why do you stand looking up to heaven?" The *viri galilae,* a broad platform above the portal, is still mentioned in reference to Le Roux's new design and direct access to the nave through a small door below the rose and gallery.[31] Saint-Maclou has the exact disposition of the upper platform and small portal (Fig. 56). Thus, it appears that Robin combined the pyramidal arrangement of the traditional Norman parish church and the central emphasis of the churches of the Low Countries, with Perier's gabled porch and platform of the cathedral.

The polygonal porch at Saint-Maclou was not merely an ingenious formal solution; it satisfied both functional and structural demands. Function may have been the initial motivating factor, but the vaulted porch supported by deceptively massive and irregular masonry, provided efficient buttressing for the thin western wall and high vaults and permitted Robin to create a diaphanous entrance to this church. By eliminating a single offcenter tower or twin towers, Robin could also draw attention to the lantern tower through the careful orchestration of external massing. The polygonal porch set up a series of recessive diagonal planes, complemented by the diagonally faced buttresses, which visually climax at the lantern tower. In addition, by beveling the western termination, the church is more comfortably aligned to the disjointed north/south street, the rue Damiette—rue Malpalu running in front of the porch (Fig. 1).[32]

Structure

Just as the gigantism of Notre-Dame in Paris in the twelfth century forced architects to think about structure in daring and innovative terms, the diminution of scale of Saint-Maclou in the fifteenth century provided Pierre Robin with a new opportunity to manipulate traditional structural elements for illusionistic and aesthetic purposes. With a complete understanding of the structural problems of monumental buildings (experience gained as master mason of Notre-Dame in Paris), Robin maximized the illusory potential of the skeletal system by reducing the amount of visible supporting masonry without compromising the structural integrity.

The severe damage sustained by Saint-Maclou in 1944 revealed that the church was a true exemplar of gothic structural dynamics. Albert Chauvel's 1958 restoration report states that "the limits of the laws of equilibrium were reach with the construction of the church. There are numerous uses of *porte-à-faux*. Piers have been reduced to the minimum section while still maintaining stability."[33] The integrity of the entire structure is challenged if a single member is altered—as was the case in 1944. What was the supreme accomplishment of the late gothic architect became the bane of the twentieth-century restorer. Laquet wrote in his inspection report of October 1944, dealing with the question as to whether the lantern tower could be saved: "The operation is difficult not only because of the damages sustained by the bombing but also because of the defective manner in which the tower is constructed which defies all principles of statics and construction" (Fig. 57).[34]

The plan established by the 1988 survey offered a radically different picture of the structural system of Saint-Maclou (Fig. 76). When compared to Vincent's plan of 1899 (Fig. 20), which depicts the exterior walls and walls dividing the chapels of the same dimensions, the new plan indicates that, at least at the interior floor level, the interior chapel walls are twice the width of the exterior walls.[35] In addition, although the arcade piers are relatively slight, the piers at the chapel openings are massive. Thus, the structure of the building is dependent on a radial armature consisting of the interior chapel dividing walls and their attached piers. These walls extend above the aisle roofs to support the flying buttresses.

The interior space conveys the impression of lightness, verticality, and fragility. The average nave pier has a diameter of 1.510 m (north/south) × 1.630 m (east/west) at floor level, with a bay span of 6.034 m in the central vessel. Thus, the ratio of pier to span is 1:3.996 or 1:4. This might be compared to a building of similar scale, Saint-Urbain in Troyes, where the nave pier diameter to central vessel width ratio is 1:3.2.[36] The sharp unimpeded prismatic moldings underscore the vertical surge of movement, and the narrow central vessel, and expansive clerestory window, contribute to the sense of weightlessness.

While a basic precept of interior gothic space has been the creation of a weightless, vertical, and light-filled interior through the development of a skeletal system of structure, Robin has extended the illusion also to the exterior. He accomplished this by using several means to disguise the true structure on the exterior. The walls between the chapels are .93 m; as they extend to the exterior and become visible as spur buttresses, however, they are reduced by several centimeters and appear as thin, diagonally faced wedges that seem to frame the bay rather than support the wall. The chapel dividing walls are further reduced in thickness at the drip molding above the chapel roofs (Fig. 69). These single courses of stone abut the sticklike flying buttresses. To stabilize and strengthen these walls and to increase their function as buttresses for the central vessel, Robin has added reinforcing arches (or interior flying buttresses) below the roofs and above the aisle vaults that connect the central vessel with the salients (Fig. 58).

Robin understood the radial armature of the interior chapel walls and piers, concealed from both the interior and exterior, to be the true support system. He was thus able to make the walls of the central vessel and exterior walls exceedingly thin. As a conservative measure, he reinforced the central vessel wall with great relieving arches below the triforium and hides them from view (Fig. 59). The generous breadth of the chapel-opening piers demonstrates their importance in the structural system. In the central nave chapels, these piers average 2.463 m (east/west) in diameter while the chapel opening of the central nave chapel is 2.961 m creating a pier-to-opening ratio of 1:1.2. Few gothic buildings have such massive supports, yet few provide such an illusion of weightlessness. The illusionistic potential of the skeletal system that formed the basis of structural development in the thirteenth century, continued to be the object of experimentation in the fifteenth-century.

Robin may have compensated for the thin walls and arcade piers by choosing a blind triforium rather than a glazed one. He also designed a choir screen that was fully integrated into the design of the choir piers. The horizontal members of the choir screen and *jubé* would also have functioned as a brace for the exceedingly fragile hemicycle piers. Robin's use of other structural devices such as *porte-à-faux* (conspicuously present in the lantern tower) and the *tas-de-charge* of the high vaults, was, by the fifteenth century, good building practice (Fig. 60).

The support of the lantern tower masonry over the crossing bay had always been a challenge to the master masons of Normandy. A common solution was to transform the square bay into an octagon by using *écoinçons* or corbeled shelves constructed between the right angles of the bays and sometimes articulated with tracery, creating eight sides of equal length and reducing the size of the tower above (Fig. 61). This solution was first used as Notre-Dame in Coutances whose tower was erected soon after the completion of the choir under Bishop Jean d'Essey (1251–74) and served as a prototype for the flamboyant lantern towers of Evreux Cathedral and Saint-Pierre in Coutances.[37]

The alternative solution, the square lantern tower, presented problems at Rouen Cathedral.[38] The lantern tower, completed in the mid-thirteenth century began to fail and was significantly reinforced in the fifteenth century when additional buttresses were added and corbeled out above the roof. Saint-Ouen, which has a crossing tower, may have intended to have a lantern; because, however, of the major buckling of the crossing piers in 1441, a lantern was never executed.[39] Closest in scale and design to Saint-Maclou is the lantern of Saint-Germain, Argentan, although it was constructed on top of thick walls and dates to the mid-sixteenth century.[40]

Pierre Robin combined the structural soundness of the octagonal shape and the openness of the square lantern. Above the transept crossing arches he placed four semicircular relieving arches (visible on the exterior) obviating, to some degree, the large corbeled masonry wedges, which would diminish and transform the lantern into an octagon. Instead, only vestiges of the corner *écoinçons* remain, linking the interior triforium passages across the corners and stabilizing the flat walls. Therefore, the lantern tower remains square in the tradition of rouennais architecture but with the structural soundness of an octagonal design.

Pierre Robin's rejection of contemporary vaulting solutions may be as telling as his decision to adopt others. He chose to vault his entire structure with quadripartite vaults despite the fact that they must have appeared to be extremely conservative and backward-looking. Decorative vaults along with pendant keystones first appeared in Rouen on the Porch of the Marmosets at Saint-Ouen around 1400.[41] By the 1470s, the curved petal vault ribs often associated with the late gothic period were used by Guillaume Pontis, a mason from Saint-Maclou, for the chapel of Saint Etienne beneath the Butter Tower at the cathedral. However, decorative vaults nullify the form and function relationship of the rib and supporting member, and this solution would have been inconsistent with Robin's insistence on visual logic. He continued to improve upon the structural aspect of vaulting by reducing the vault thickness to 7−8 cm, evident in the exposed vaults of the chapel of Sainte Clotilde.[42]

As would be expected, Robin uses *tas-de-charge* throughout to transmit the collective vault pressures to the flying buttresses.[43] These massive blocks of masonry combining the springing vault ribs with the wall ribs and moldings of the adjacent clerestory windows vary between four and five courses. The complex steriometries must have required the most sophisticated and up-to-date methods of design and cutting that existed anywhere in France. The vault and roof forces are transmitted with pinpoint accuracy to the double-tier of flying buttresses on the exterior, indicated by their extremely thin profiles and emphasized by the Y-shape formed by separation of the upper and lower struts at the point of departure from the wall (Figs. 62 and 63). At the transepts, the two tiers of flyers virtually become four individual sticks of stone. A single course of masonry traces the line of force from the vault to the salient. Despite their insubstantial appearance, they are models of efficiency enhanced by their precise placement against the wall of the central vessel, by the angle of the slope, and by stability achieved through the insertion of iron rods joining the thin courses of stone.[44]

The complete coordination of all aspects of design and structure is revealed in one last detail. There are ten staircase turrets at Saint-Maclou that provide maximum access to the upper parts. Four turrets, two on each transept facade, provide access from the ground level while four turrets at the corners of the lantern tower and two turrets from the west facade above the porch provide vertical links at the upper levels. The staircase turrets that frame the steep, thin transept walls function as buttresses and provide access to the upper parts. They are relatively unarticulated at the lower levels; although they are fully integrated into the overall facade design (the repetition of diagonally set buttresses for example), they remain distinct forms and their function is always explicit. In much of late gothic architecture there is a tendency to integrate forms in such a way that they lose their individual identity: the triforium is absorbed into the clerestory; individual shafts and ribs either disappear into the pier or are blanketed in undulation; the ribbed vault becomes a decorative surface of calligraphic liernes, tierceron, and pendant keystones. Finally, as with the work of Martin Chambiges and Roulland Le Roux, the staircase turret is wrapped with vertical paneling that extends across the entire facade. In contrast, Pierre Robin struck a balance between individuality and continuity or visual integration and the integrity of each constituent architectural element—he maintained, in Panofsky's phrase, "distinctive and deductive cogency."

Clues, Mistakes, and Puzzles

The assiduous uniformity and geometric interrelationships that permeate every aspect of the design of Saint-Maclou were occasionally violated by small deviations from the established formula. These curious and almost imperceptible anomalies remain unexplained and, for the most part, unnoticed. Generally, rifts in the fabric are essential clues in unlocking the building history; there are, however, differences in opinion as to what claims may be made from the physical discrepancies.[45] The stylistic and archaeological inconsistencies observed at Saint-Maclou fall into three categories: some are intentional; some genuinely reflect changes over time and can be related to chronology of construction, stylistic development, and changes in master mason; and some can only be explained as mistakes or the expression of an inept or inexperienced mason.

Two inconsistencies in the architectural language—the varied window tracery patterns and the base profiles—have already been mentioned as examples of intentional or planned patterned diversity. A third visible deviation is seen in the change of elevation proportions between the clerestory window and triforium of the choir and nave on the one hand, and the transept on the other (Fig. 64). In the transept, the clerestory is enlarged by more than a meter while the triforium height is diminished by the same amount. In addition, the tracery pattern of the transept triforium is different from that of the nave and choir. The absence of the sloping roof over the aisle vaults of the transept and the resulting change in structural requirements permitted a taller transept clerestory. These discrepancies all appear in patterns and the patterns are consistent within themselves.

A number of other anomalies, however, indicate that slight deviations from the original scheme still occurred. These are relatively minor but when coordinated with written and design evidence, they provide clues that confirm a clear sequence of construction. Pierre Robin's distinct spur buttresses on the exterior chapel walls have diagonally set faces that are designed around two squares, one inscribed inside the other and then projected so that the diagonal of the inner square is aligned with the front face of the larger square. There is a small change in cross section between buttresses n2e1 and i (attached to chapel NIIEII, Figs. 65 and 66) and the complementary buttresses on the south side, s2e1 and x (attached to chapel SIIEII). These four buttresses lack the sharp groove that separates the two squares at the corners. This groove, found on all other exterior spur buttresses of the church, reappears in these four buttresses above the chapel wall (Figs. 67 and 68). The written sources and layout procedure of the plan (discussed in Chapters 1 and 3) indicate that these buttresses belong to the first phase of construction.

The most complex series of transformations occurs in the design of the upper portions of the buttress salients. The various solutions may be the result of a combination of intentional patterned diversity, changes in campaigns of construction, and attempts to correct structural deficiencies of an earlier buttress design. All the clerestory flying buttresses spring from salients formed by the extension of the chapel dividing walls rising above the roof line. These salients have four different types of termination. The salient extrados of the radiating chapels walls (n2e2, n2a2, s2e2, s2a2) form straight slopes surmounted by a single pinnacle while the salient extrados of the wall between the two choir straight bay chapels (n2e1 and s2e1) terminate with a curved slope (Figs. 69 and 70). The symmetrical appearance of the variations on the north and south are consistent with the idea of planned patterned diversity, the change also confirms the sequence of construction indicated by the spur buttress design of the same two buttresses.

However, a less subtle deviation distinguishes the buttress salients on the north side of the nave from their counterparts on the south side (Figs. 71 and 72). The slope of the salient extrados on buttresses s2w1, s2w2, and s2w3 is not so steep as it is on the north side—indicated by the fact that the salient extrados molding descends directly to the base of the pinnacle whereas, on the north, the salient extrados molding flattens out at the top of the outer salient wall before joining the pinnacle. There is no supporting structural evidence to suggest that the change in pitch of the slope was related to a desire to improve the structural efficiency of the buttresses but this seems the most likely explanation. As the accounts of Troyes Cathedral indicate, slope was a crucial consideration in design and structure.[46] Whatever the explanation, the three southern buttresses follow a different plan than the three on the north.

A cosmetic variation also occurs in the design of the triforium tracery of the choir. On the south side of the church in the straight bays and turning bays of the hemicycle, the blind triforium lancets continue behind the bay dividing shafts (Fig. 23). This small motif does not exist on the north side nor in the triforium of the transept and choir. Although these bays are all heavily restored, the design reflects the original triforium. As a comparison with earlier structures in the Norman Vexin will indicate (see Chapter 5), this detail can be linked to the early phases of construction at Saint-Maclou.

Regardless of how complete or detailed the drawings of Robin must have been or how insistent the treasurers were in adhering to them, occasionally subsequent master masons, particularly Ambroise Harel and Pierre Grégoire, were permitted to indulge in marginal deviations from the original plan in a style that reflected the contemporary and more fashionable trends of the late fifteenth century. It is precisely these superficial embellishments that undermined the clarity and integrity of Robin's vision. This is especially true for the west facade and certain details of the porch. Limp, low relief, blind tracery fills the space above the side portals, is squeezed between the spandrel gables of the porch, and agitates every available surface of the roof gable, while fragile crockets and delicate vertical paneling disguise the form and function of the westernmost flying buttresses (Fig. 73). A spherical triangle, banished by Robin from all window tracery, is embedded in the second gable from the north. This articulation is gratuitous, superfluous, and inconsistent with the vision that formed the precise and fully integrated interior elevation, pier design, and ground plan or that designed the basic plan and composition of the western facade and porch.

A last group of anomalies might only be categorized as mistakes. Because of the rigorous control provided by drawings over the execution, the number of "essai" forms is minimal. However, bizarre deviations appear on the south transept jamb bases and plinths and in the upper triforium elevation of the south transept. While the base profiles of the south transept jamb niches are identical to those on the north, the plinth cross section designs do not follow any identifiable formula (Figs. 24c [C and D] and 74). The plinths on both the east and west embrasures vary among themselves; although they support an equally eccentric molding, design has run amuck. How can these eccentricities be explained in light of the rigorous control evident in the rest of the building? Why did this master not use the same templates for the plinths used elsewhere? It is not similar to anything else in Rouen from the late fifteenth century nor does it appear to be intentional patterned diversity. We can only speculate that these jambs may have been the among the first to be constructed before the *appareilleurs* had good control and coordination of their templates for the complex and multilayered designs or perhaps, because of the lack of importance of the south transept portal, inexperienced masons or apprentices were assigned to its execution.

A second puzzle exists in the upper part of the south transept. Above the triforium at the end of the south aisle a large block of masonry is inserted (Fig. 75). It appears that a higher stringcourse or perhaps taller triforium was begun and then abruptly changed to the present proportion. It is even curious why this block of masonry was left remaining. Does this represent a change in plan, a mistake, or a joke?

Conclusion: Pierre Robin's Theory of Gothic Design

When the treasurers of Saint-Maclou first examined the drawings for their new church, they must have immediately been aware of the radical departure from conventional ecclesiastical forms that Robin's plans presented. Yet they wholeheartedly embraced his design. An axial pier, polygonal porch, continuous moldings, and a complete absence of capitals were unprecedented in any gothic monument. We should not view these forms as arrogant conceits reflecting the unrestrained imagination of the gothic draftsman; rather, they are perfectly understandable within the context of certain aesthetic aims inherent in the long tradition of gothic architecture.

Saint-Maclou can be considered a turning point in gothic design because Robin consciously breaks from his immediate past. Perhaps because of the absence of contemporary coherent models or perhaps because of retrospection fostered by a desire to reclaim an order and clarity of older models, Robin rejected foreign influence and the degenerative overrefinement characteristic of his contemporaries and chose high gothic models. He responded to the historical authority of the high gothic canon and attempted to reclaim certain design principles conveyed by these models, restating them with even greater clarity, and drawing attention to their underlying design principles through his powers as a draftsman and his faith in an uncompromising geometry. His piers far surpass the compound pier in "visual logic"; his elevation articulation and window tracery are perfect expressions of the "principle of progressive divisibility." By using quadripartite ribbed vaults, clearly defined pentagonal staircase turrets, and a blind triforium, his design is never gratuitous and thus strikes a balance between structure and articulation maintaining the "principle of deductive cogency."

Robin draws on specific models of the cathedral of Rouen including the interior elevation, transept facade, lantern tower, and possibly western porch, and his reference to the cathedral is unmistakable and clearly intentional. By pursuing even further the design logic inherent in his model, however, he arrived at unconventional solutions. Thus, absolute visual logic could only be achieved through the elimination of the capital; perfect regularity of the eastern termination, especially where turning bays of the hemicycle join the straight bays of the choir, could only be resolved with the introduction of an axial pier; inconsistencies between the desire for a elegant and pyramidal western entrance, the asymmetrical massing of a single tower and the structural problems of supporting the nave vaults inherent in parish church facade design were resolved by the design of a polygonal porch. Finally, the illusionistic potential of the skeletal system developed on the interior of the gothic church was extended to the exterior of the monument through a coherent and fully disguised radial armature. The degree of explicitness and precision in Robin's drawings could only have been achieved if he consciously sought to reclaim and perfect high gothic *manifestatio*.

While this dissection and analysis of the constituent architectural elements illustrates Robin's use and transformation of isolated parts of older models, a number of broader aesthetic aims guided his design and can be discerned from a consideration of the monument as a whole. An unflagging homogeneity, the miniaturization of monumental architecture, illusionism, and movement and diagonality, distinguish Saint-Maclou, and perhaps many late gothic monuments, from their high gothic models. The historical basis for these abstract principles will be explored in subsequent chapters, but suffice it here to provide a few observations.

Rigorous homogeneity is highly unusual in a gothic monument that has been constructed over a long period of time. The conditions that permitted, and indeed, insisted upon uniformity in construction at Saint-Maclou are linked to the presence of a corporate patron, the increased function of drawings, and a clearly defined workshop structure that provided a continuity over time that substituted for the presence of a single master mason. But there is also an unprecedented uniformity or harmony in design where one part of the building echoes or mirrors another part. For example, the articulation of the chapel windows and chapel dado reveal the same relationship as the clerestory windows and triforium; the core moldings of all the piers and shafts extend beyond themselves to form the wall moldings that wrap around the lower level of the entire church; all the profiles and forms of the arcade, vault ribs, and formerets can be read directly from the piers; and all the articulation systems are composed of the same set of five fillet bases, plinths, and moldings. This visual harmony was possible only with extensive advanced planning and detailed drawings.

Second, although Saint-Maclou is a small-scale building, and its dimensions indicate that it could literally be inserted into the transept of the cathedral of Rouen, it aspires to monumentality by borrowing architectural attributes normally associated with prestigious cathedrals and abbeys and not other parish churches. It features double-tiered flying buttresses, full-fledged transept facades with rose windows and sculpted portals, a spatially dominant lantern tower, three-story elevation, ambulatory and radiating chapels, and an elegant *clôture* and *jubé*. Its association with monumental buildings is even more closely approximated by the illusionistic manipulation of the perception and experience of space.

Robin was aware of the relationship between viewer and architecture: through carefully calculated visual effects, the manipulation of proportions, and an awareness of optical distortions he created the illusion of monumental space. The narrow proportions of the central vessel and unimpeded continuous moldings of the articulation convey a sense of unrestrained verticality. Optical illusions are created by the placement of pier bases 1.67 m above ground level or at approximately eye level (diminishing the size of the viewer in relationship to the supporting members), by enhancing the profiles of the bases at the upper level, and by projecting the transept keystones into three dimensions. The quiet stability and broad proportions of earlier monuments of identical size such as Saint-Urbain, Troyes, have been replaced by highly energized and emotive spatial environment that must be understood within the context of devotional and liturgical use of late gothic space.

Linked to illusionism of scale and proportions is the massing that adamantly rejects planar surfaces and self-contained forms in favor of movement and diagonality. Through the diminished diagonally-faced wall buttresses, polygonal porch, and pyramidal massing, the perception of the exterior massing is one of shifting, diagonal recessions that culminate in the lantern spire. On the interior, the absence of a flat eastern bay in the hemicycle does not permit visual resolution of the lateral movement of the arcade toward the east. Rather, it shifts the focus back to the transept crossing. In no gothic basilica, is a single focus or climax stated with such irresolute force.

This discussion of the relationship between the high gothic canon and the late gothic craft rests on a visual analysis of the constitute parts and broader aesthetic aims. But a more profound connection exists between gothic architecture of the high and late gothic periods: the underlying structure provided by the basic design tool of the medieval mason—geometry. Only through a careful examination of cross sections of parts as well as the geometric design schemes of plan and elevation (to be explored in chapter 3), can we fully understand the transformation between high and late gothic. A pervasive and uncompromising geometry contributes to the precision and idiosyncrasies of the architecture of Saint-Maclou.

3

"le parchemin ou leglise est gectee toute complecte"

Geometry, Design Schemes, and the Layout of the Gothic Church

When Pierre Robin arrived in Rouen sometime before 1437 and met with the treasurers of Saint-Maclou[1] to discuss the specifications for a new parish church he was to design, one of his first tasks must have been to survey visually the site of the new construction. The western end of the site would have been occupied by the thirteenth-century church described in the 1432 indulgence as collapsing in the transept and too small to accommodate the growing parish. Running along the north side of this chapel was a major artery of the city, the rue Martainville, the Roman *decumanum* as well as the primary east/west access to the medieval city (Fig. 1). Adjacent to the old church on the southwest side was an important piece of real estate in the parish, the Hôtel des Flagon, owned by Etienne Dufour. Facing the western entrance was the Grand Moulin, a symbol of the parish's cloth industry, and the Pont du Robec, which led to the archbishop's palace and the cathedral. To the south of the church stood the *petit aître* surrounded by a wall separating it from the king's street. Like most medieval buildings, the new church would be raised around the old structures, progressively demolishing them as the space was needed for the new construction. The treasurers, however, must have made it clear to Robin that, except for the rue Martainville on the north and the rue Malpalu on the west, all the urban impediments would concede to the new building and, once the initial dimensions were decided upon, no site adjustments would be needed to accommodate the plan on parchment.

The treasurers provided Robin with a rare opportunity to design an entire church. He had previously executed drawings of the facade of Saint-Yves in Paris and processional canopies for the funeral of Charles VI, but there is no evidence that he, or indeed, very many gothic architects, were given the task of designing an entire monument. He would have relied on the oral traditions of his craft that instructed him on how to use geometry to design a plan and elevation that would be structurally sound and properly proportioned. Robin must have relished the opportunity to give full expression to his talent as a draftsmen and to provide his patrons with "state of the craft" drawings. Saint-Maclou is uniquely a textbook example of late gothic design—a precise and accurate manifestation of the elegant, sophisticated, and deceptively simple drawings that Robin created on parchment. Pierre Robin left Rouen in 1437, long before most of the foundations were completed or the superstructure raised. But his drawings provided the coded instructions for everything from the design of pier templates to the setting out of foundations at the site, understood by the subsequent master masons such as Oudin de Mantes and Simon Le Noir, and followed by the *appareilleurs* such as Jehan Le Prevost and Friset Le Mestre.

Among the drawings of "the complete church" was, no doubt, a ground plan, the first and perhaps most fundamental step in the initial conception of the church. From the dimensions and configuration of the ground plan, the structure, the elevation, and the space were defined. Pierre Robin was perhaps his most innovative at the ground-floor stage in his visualization of the new church. He introduced an axial pier, a polygonal porch, polygonal interlocking radiating chapels, and unequal bay sizes (described in Chapter 2). Although a number of factors may have contributed to the inclusion of these architectural features, most likely they were the result of a priority given to geometry in design. Just as in the design of his keystones, geometry became the subject and not merely the underlying vehicle for design, so too in the ground plan the distinct prismatic character resulted from exposing the precise and uncompromising geometric scheme. Robin's plan represents a radical departure from traditional parish church or cathedral design in the degree to which its geometry is revealed in proportional and spatial divisions. Yet the design schemes and procedures are wholly within the gothic workshop tradition. Our explanation of the underlying geometric framework for Saint-Maclou also provides the most efficient and economic blueprint for setting out the foundations at the site. The interdependency between progressive squaring as a design tool and constructive geometry as a practical building procedure of the craft is especially evident in the plan.

The hemicycle of Saint-Maclou is designed around half an octagon, forming an axial pier and an even number of identical radiating chapels. The generous size of these four chapels compensates for the lack of an axial chapel, but this unorthodox treatment of the chevet is particularly puzzling at this time when many churches in Normandy were concerned with the enlargement and emphasis of the axial chapel.[2]

The polygonal porch that wraps around the western facade is perhaps the most celebrated feature of the exterior. Although a vaulted porch is found at the abbey of Saint-Ouen on the south transept and a triple portal porch was probably intended for the cathedral, these may have been constructed for specific royal and liturgical purposes, functions not applicable to the parish church.[3] The Saint-Maclou porch inspired a number of stunning variations found at Saint-Vincent in Rouen, Notre-Dame in Alençon, Saint-Germain in Argentan, and the western facade of the abbey of Saint-Ouen; the reason for its appearance at Saint-Maclou, however, is unclear.

Although Saint-Maclou is a basilica, the emphasis on the transept crossing is unmistakable. Placed midway between the choir and nave, the transept and crowning lantern tower, from both the point of view of external massing and interior space, provide the visual climax of the architecture. Despite the symmetry created by the transept, the straight bays of the choir and nave are of different dimensions, increasing in size from the western nave to the transept and then decreasing from the transept to the hemicycle (Fig. 77).[4] It seems unlikely that this lack of uniformity in a small-scale building is the result of continued readjustments in the laying out of the building.

Progressive Squaring and the Design Schemes of Pierre Robin's Plan

From the numinous locus of the transept crossing, space unfolds toward the east and west, and toward the north and south with the march of arcade columns, banded triforium, and glazed clerestory lights. One experiences the transept as a center stage under the spotlight of the lantern tower. The transept was the nexus of two distinct liturgical spaces within the church: the sanctuary, hidden behind the jubé and clôture and reserved for the clergy and the mysteries of the Eucharist; and the nave, where the parish laity would assemble. Thus, from the perspective of the spatial and visual experience as well as the symbolic meaning, the transept crossing is the generative center. It is not surprising then that the transept is also the fundamental design center, from which all other dimensions in the plan are derived.

The dimensions of the transept square have long been the key to the proportional systems in plan design. From the Saint-Gall plan of the ninth century to Cistercian churches of the twelfth century, a square module derived from the transept crossing served as an easily divisible unit that provided dimensions for aisles, chapels, and central vessel widths.[5] However, these dimensions are based on arithmetic relationships. At Saint-Maclou, the relationships are geometric, incommensurable, more difficult to recover, but exacting in their placement. The space defined by the unequal bays and subtle geometric dependencies is dynamic, integrated, and organic. Diagonality, implied from the very beginning of gothic architecture through the use of the ribbed vault and bias-set capitals, was at odds with a static and additive bay design. The subtle expansive and contractive relationship of the bays of Saint-Maclou extends the idea of diagonality to spatial experience.

In the thirteenth century, the transept crossing bay was often rectangular, but the bays adjacent to the transept on the east and west, formed a square used to determine other dimensions.[6] Perhaps because of the small size of Saint-Maclou, Pierre Robin was able to use the transept geometry to control all other significant dimensions including the length of choir and nave, the individual bay size, and the polygonality of the eastern hemicycle and chapels and the western porch.

The crossing bay of Saint-Maclou when combined with the adjacent bays, which are of equal dimensions, forms a square of 18.474 m (Fig. 78a). When rotated, the diagonal of the square identifies the width of the church at the transept crossing (26.126 m). This simple module sets up the relationships that will be used throughout the church.

Dimensions of 5.411 m and 7.652 m are created by a grid formed at the intersection of these two squares. The larger dimension determines the width of the transept; the smaller dimension, the width of all the straight bays in the choir and nave. Although the bay dimensions, when measured from the pier centers, appear to be of different sizes, increasing toward the transept, they are actually all derived from 5.411 m (Fig. 79). An elastic spatial progression is achieved by varying the placement of the pier centers in relationship to the grid established by the unit of 5.411 m.

The transept module designed around a point in the center of the transept crossing (0) also provides the basic dimension for the length of the choir with its center in the middle of the hemicycle (0′) and the length of the nave with its center in the middle of the central nave bay (02). Thus, the overall proportional ratio of length of the church to its width is 1 : 2 (the width of the church is 26.126 m and the overall length is 52.252 m, Fig. 80).

Using the fundamental design tool of the master mason—progressive squaring—Robin arrived at a supremely elegant and uncomplicated solution for the radiating chapels, ambulatory and hemicycle. The placement of the hemicycle piers is determined by a single rotated square based on the width of the hemicycle, 7.574 m (Fig. 81a).[7] A second pair of rotated squares based on the width of the central vessel and aisles determines the centers of the chapel-opening piers with the first rotation and the depth of the chapel-opening piers with the second rotation. A third pair of squares in this same progression but rotated 22.5 degrees, located the outer chapel walls.

The individual radiating chapels were also designed around a single rotated square (Fig. 82a). They appear to be irregular or compressed hexagons but the depth of the chapel (to the outside wall) is equal to the width of the chapel, a formula frequently repeated in gothic monuments.[8]

As we have seen, the length of the nave and the dimensions of the nave individual bays were determined by the transept module. Despite the visual complexity of the western porch with its five gables and three-sided polygonal plan, the design, once again, was arrived at through a simple manipulation of the transept module. Just as a 22.5 degree rotation of the macromodule generated from the center of the hemicycle determined the outer walls of the radiating chapel, a 22.5 degree rotation of the same macromodule generated from the central nave bay established the polygonality of the western porch (Fig. 83a). Although the ultimate appearances of the eastern and western ends of the church are distinct, their underlying geometries are complementary and provide a unity to the overall space and form.

Constructive Geometry and Setting Out the Plan at the Site

The apparent simplicity and clarity of this plan design conceals the actual complexity of the geometric relationships in the placement of walls, piers, and chapels. It is difficult to imagine that masons would have laid out the foundations of the church according to progressive squares or 22.5 degree rotations. However, the same abstract design schemes that facilitated the conceptualization of the plan on parchment by Pierre Robin, also provided the most efficient, practical, and economic blueprint for the setting out of the foundations at the site. Pierre Robin may have visualized his plan in terms of progressive squaring, but the master masons and *appareilleurs* who carried out the execution of the plan understood the same design in terms of constructive geometry.

The written sources and stylistic evidence make it clear that work began to the east of the old nave, probably with the straight bay chapels of the choir (NIIEI and SIIEI) as well as part of the second straight bay choir chapels (NIIEII and SIIEII) as a coherent unit. Although a number of different methods may have been used to "construct" the placement points for this portion of the church, the procedure outlined in Figure 78a that required only the use of a cord and the knowledge of how to construct a right angle provides a possible scenario. This construction captures precisely the same relationships expressed in the geometric schemes of Figure 78b.

Pierre Robin's first decision would have been to pace off the width of the new church just to the east of the old nave. This dimension may have been symbolically derived from another structure or simply determined by the availability of land at the site.[9] Thus, this dimension (*AB*) equals the width of the church with the center of the transept a *0*. Through a series of simple constructions using a cord, the construction of a right angle, and the intersection of arcs, the placement of the key points for the two straight bays of the choir chapels can be established.[10] It is important to note that the walls dividing the turning bays from the straight bays could not be laid out from the center point of the transept. The difference in spur buttress design at this juncture and discussed in Chapter 2, confirms this sequence in setting out the foundations.

Variations of this procedure were also used to locate the placement of the hemicycle piers and radiating chapel walls (Fig. 81b).[11] The design scheme demonstrates that the exterior radiating chapel walls were located by the macromodule rotated 22.5 degrees The late gothic mason had neither the tools, knowledge, or need to use degrees in setting out masonry. A more direct method was used to "construct" the placement points of the walls and exterior chapel buttresses. The walls between the chapels were established by the octagon generated from the center of the hemicycle as already demonstrated. The outer wall was located by the construction of a hexagon generated from a centerpoint 03 within the chapel (Fig. 82b).[12]

The placement of the massive irregular west facade porch buttresses was achieved in a similar fashion using the centerpoint 02. Although the diagonal planes of the porch can be explained in terms of a 22.5 degree rotation, they can be constructed using a varia-

tion of the same procedure that determined the foundations of the transept and choir
(Fig. 83b).[13]

Thus, there existed a direct relationship between the abstract design schemes based on
progressive squaring and root 2 relationships suggested in the plan of Saint-Maclou and the
practical constructive geometry needed to lay out a foundation. A clear, precise, and elegantly simple geometry governs the design of the axial pier, the polygonal porch, and bay
dimensions. The absence of Pierre Robin from the site beyond the first year of construction
necessitated an expedient geometry that could be clearly communicated in drawings, easily
translated by the subsequent master masons, and efficiently executed at the site.

Conclusion: Pierre Robin and the Theory of Plan Design at Saint-Maclou

Both the extensive use of drawings and the absence of the master mason/draftsman from
the workshop distinguished the construction of Saint-Maclou from thirteenth-century traditions of gothic building. These conditions necessitated and allowed for an expedient
geometry in plan design. The most unorthodox features, the axial pier and absence of an
axial chapel, demonstrate that the uncompromising geometry of Saint-Maclou may have
been too radical, even in the fifteenth century. While a number of collegiate and parish
churches copied the axial pier—Notre-Dame at Caudebec-en-Caux (Fig. 131), Saint-
Germain at Argentan, Saint-Paul at Le Neuberg (Fig. 132), and Saint-Pierre at Caen
(Fig. 130), to name a few—none continued to eliminate the axial chapel, thereby negating
the benefits of the perfect harmony and regularity achieved in the chevet of Saint-Maclou.

From this analysis of the plan design, it is also possible to revise an earlier attribution of
the polygonal porch. Paul Frankl suggested that although Pierre Robin drew up the plans
for the entire church in the 1430s, the porch was redesigned by Ambroise Harel, who was
master mason between 1467 and 1480.[14] Because the overall length of the nave and western
porch was determined by the transept module and because the design of the porch is a variation of the same theme expressed in the choir, it seems likely that Robin was responsible
for its unusual form. Ambroise Harel, like the other masters associated with Saint-Maclou,
merely followed the drawings left by Robin.

In light of our analysis, the unequal size bays gain new meaning. Their dimensions are
generated geometrically from a common design center and impart an organic unity to mass
and space. Bays in this late gothic building are not self-contained, independent units added
to one another , but imperceptible and powerfully linked to the whole. The geometry sets
up an integration or spatial movement through diagonality. Thus, diagonality is not only
conveyed by the ribbed vault and diagonally set capitals and bases as in early and high gothic
architecture; it is also applied to the relationship of bays, of parts to the whole, of mass and
space. Diagonality resonates at Saint-Maclou in every aspect of Pierre Robin's design: the

axial pier, the polygonal porch, the diagonally faced wall buttresses, the pier design of flat-nosed fillet moldings, and the fundament integration of mass and space through geometry. Once again, Robin seems to take a principle expressed in earlier gothic architecture and assiduously applied to the whole.

This analysis also reestablishes the transept as the generative center for the design and links late gothic plan design to a long tradition beginning in the Carolingian period. Although there is a major shift from arithmetic to geometric procedures between the ninth and fifteenth centuries, these results suggest that there may be a common language or theory of design underlying many medieval buildings as yet unexplored.

It is surprising that there is no evidence of a "foot" in the large overall dimensions. Scholars have been preoccupied with discovering the unit of measure used to layout churches by identifying a seminal unit based on a linear measurement.[15] Although the fabric accounts of Saint-Maclou frequently mention units such as the *tonneau, toise, quartier, parpain,* or *carreaux* in the purchase of stone, these refer to cubic measurements or sizes and shapes of stones.[16] In his study of fifteenth-century monuments in Rouen, including the Tour de Columbier, the Hôtel du Four, the Grand Moulin, and the Palais de Justice, Raymond Quenedey has identified a unit of measure in common usage.[17] The Rouen foot varied between .311 m and .328 m with the average unit of measure equal to .324 m. Thus, the *toise* was equal to 1.944 m or six feet and the *perche* equal to 7.776 m or twenty-four feet. To support this conclusion he cites a bronze sixteenth-century folding foot marked off to .325 m and in the collection of the Musée des Antiquitiés in Rouen.

Although this "foot" is not present in any large dimension, it is clearly the unit used in the design details, including buttresses, walls, and staircase turrets. Three faces of massive and irregular masonry that frame the central portal, buttresses the west facade, and supports the vaults of the western porch were cut from templates designed around a dimension of .325 m (Fig. 84a). Despite the complexity and asymmetry of these buttresses, the masonry between the inner and outer walls is seamless, and were therefore constructed as single units. While the irregular faces respond to a complex set of demands imposed by the vaults, jamb pedestals, and moldings, the basic dimensions of the pier (at least three of the four faces) were determined by the simplest of all mason's design procedures: a progression of inscribed squares with the first dimension laid out using the king's foot of .325 m (Fig. 84b).[18]

The clearest example of the use of geometry to determine structural sizing is found in the design of the transept staircase turrets (n2w, n2e, s2w, s2e). On each side of the north and south transepts there is a complex mass of masonry that includes a polygonal staircase turret attached to diagonally set door embrasures. The interior chapel walls adjacent to the transepts on both the east and west become thicker and the four lancet windows have been reduced to three (the same solution was used at Saint-Urbain, Troyes, one hundred and fifty years earlier to accommodate the support for the transept facades). The geometry of the staircase turrets reveals how the dimension of the chapel wall and the size of the small spur buttresses of the turrets were determined (Figs. 85a and b). Master 2 in Villard de Honnecourt's portfolio describes "how to trace a five cornered tower." An 18 degree rotation is achieved by using the marks on a mason's square to determine the width of the spur but-tresses.[19] The pentagon as a geometric form fascinated late gothic masons and is pre-dominantly displayed on the north rose of the abbey of Saint-Ouen, in the dado spandrels of Lisieux; it was also the basis for design for a number of the keystones at Saint-Maclou (Fig. 47). Unlike the layout of the plan of the church, these details would have been exe-cuted with the use of templates and the unit of measure or "foot" was a convenient way to control the design.

It is impossible to determine exactly how the massive irregular exterior supports and em-brasures were designed. A number of incompatible solutions with arbitrary relationships are revealed using progressive squaring (Fig. 86). Yet a crisp, precise polygonality pervades every form. Pierre Robin's approach to design stands at the end of a long formal and tech-nical evolution. He shared with his predecessors, the builders of thirteenth-century cathe-drals, the mental processes involving the use of geometry to provide coherency, harmony, and structure to their monuments. He departed from them in his assiduous application of geometry and by making explicit the basis of his craft.

PART II

THE CONSTITUENCIES
Interpretations

4

The Mercantile Patrons

The Impact of the Hundred Years' War on the Economics and Ideology of Building in Fifteenth-Century Rouen

Although the records are far from complete, the funds for the construction of Saint-Maclou, as indicated by the building accounts and cartularies, originated almost entirely from within the parish, were in the form of relatively small donations made over a long period of time, and involved the participation of virtually every parish family.[1] The leading parishioners, the merchant families that eventually created an aristocratic bourgeoisie of the city, through their charitable gifts and through their positions as church treasurers collected, managed, and generated revenues for construction of the new church. In addition to marshaling the needed resources over several generations, they played a crucial role in the conception and design of the church. The primary meaning of the architectural form of Saint-Maclou resides in the vision of these leading parish families and that vision was forged in the economic uncertainty and political instability of the 1430s during the last two decades of the English occupation of Rouen and the end of the Hundred Years' War.

Those social groups that traditionally played a significant role in medieval church construction are conspicuously absent in the documentation of Saint-Maclou. Ecclesiastical aid was limited to several indulgences granted in 1432, renewed in 1433, 1452, 1500, and 1511. These letters only served to generate money from within the parish. Official aid from both the English and the French was equally insubstantial.[2] Despite the fact that the duke of Bedford was known as a great builder, he showed no interest in the initial stages of the construction of the most lavish monument in Rouen.[3] The letters of amortizement of his king, Henry VI, provided only nominal sums but offered encouragement to parishioners to participate in the construction by their gifts and donation of properties. Only Louis XI in the second half of the fifteenth century conceded small amounts of tax money to be taken on properties on his streets in the parish. These royal and episcopal gestures carried no obligations and the formation and control of design resided wholly within the parish in the hands of the leading parish families.

The Parish and the Patrons

The demographic makeup of the parish, from the time it was enclosed within the city walls in 1258, was one of contrasts. Of the thirty-three parishes located within the walls of the fifteenth-century city, Saint-Maclou was second in size, and along with Saint-Nicolas and Saint-Vivien, was one of the three poorest parishes in the city. The accounts of rents for the city of Rouen during the period of the 1460s indicate that of the 166 rents collected within the city, 47 (or 28 percent) were located in the parish of Saint-Maclou.[4] However, these rents constituted only 11 percent of the total revenues collected with properties averaging only 1 livre 1 sous in comparison to the rents of richer parishes such as Saint-Candre-le-Vieux at 9 livre, Saint-Martin-du-Pont at 5 livre 18 sous, or Saint-Denis at 5 livre 3 sous per property. This indicates that the parish was densely populated but the value of real estate was among the lowest in the city. On the other hand the tax records indicate that wealthy individuals, although densely clustered in the affluent parishes, also lined the major streets of the parish of Saint-Maclou along the rue Malpalu and rue Damiette that ran in front of the church and perpendicular to the rue Martainville.[5] The mixing of rich and poor can be attributed to the expanding cloth industry centered in the parish. Mills needed to dye, weave, and produce cloth were located on the Robec and Aubette Rivers that circumscribed the parish. Thus, both the wealthy cloth merchants and *chefs des métiers* as well as artisans working as weavers (*tisseurs*), fullers (*foulons*), shearers (*tondeurs*), hatmakers (*bonnetiers*), and dyers (*teinturiers*) lined the banks of the rivers and were employed by the heads of the commerce of the *draperie*.[6] However, the poorest parishioners, not listed in the tax rolls, but described by the chroniclers of the day, were migrants from the countryside who had settled in the numerous *place vydes* or open places of the parish. With the renewed efforts of Henry V after 1417 to claim the French crown and the uncontrollable devastation of the *routiers* or roving bandits in the countryside, large populations sought protection inside the Porte Martainville of the parish.

In this environment the merchant families of Saint-Maclou acquired and exercised power within the city. The most prosperous corporation benefiting from the commercial privileges secured by the merchant bourgeoisie were the cloth manufacturers or *drapiers* centered in the parish of Saint-Maclou. They were politically powerful and initiated major riots over taxation in 1382 and 1417. The earliest mention of the *draperie* in the parish of Saint-Maclou is recorded in 1360, although the industry probably existed well before this date.

After a large number of *drapiers* sought refuge in Rouen during the war in the first two decades of the fifteenth century, conflict arose between the *draperie foraine* and the *grande draperie* composed of the Rouennais bourgeoisie, who possessed exclusive right to the production of high-quality cloth. In 1424, Henry VI combined the two industries under a single set of statutes outlining the strict rules of the guild and conditions of apprenticeships.[7] Apprentices obtained the right of master at Saint-Maclou, and the building accounts of 1436–37 show twenty-seven *droits du meister* while the account of 1443–46 list forty-two. The *draperie* continued to flourish after the recapitulation and under the protection of the French kings. In 1458, an ordinance established by Charles VII and confirmed again by Louis XI in 1474 and Charles VIII in 1490, continued to privilege the Rouennais *drapiers* with the exclusive right to manufacture high-quality cloth. The revenue records of the vicomte d'Eau showed that the volume of wool sold in the city doubled from the mid-fifteenth century to 1475 and that the quantity of cloth measured by the *courtiers* (the intermediaries between the buyers and the manufactures) quadrupled.[8] Although the statutes assured careful control over quality and maximum employment, the refusal of the Rouennais *drapiers* to abandon traditional methods in favor of newer, more efficient ones eventually caused the collapse of the industry. Subsequently the production of cloth was transplanted from Rouen to the suburbs of Longpaon and Darnétal in the beginning of the sixteenth century where the forbidden spinning wheel and mill fullers were used to make the same cloth more economically. The conservative attitude of the parish *drapiers* also finds expression in the architecture of Saint-Maclou. In the second half of the fifteenth century, the patrons refused to concede to popular taste and the more fashionable trends of building expressed in the richly decorative work of Guillaume Pontis and Jacques Le Roux. Rather, they insisted on the design, and tradition established in the 1430s by Pierre Robin.

Thus, a large percentage of the population of the parish of Saint-Maclou was made up of artisans of this craft and related crafts.[9] The master *drapiers* and cloth merchants who headed the guilds formed an elite aristocratic bourgeoisie who gained increasing power and wealth in the course of the fifteenth century. The most prominent and successful among this group were the Dufour and families related to them through marriage such as the Croixmare, Grenouville, Basin, and Masselin. Over several generations, the heads of these families served as the temporal administrators of the parish, often functioning as parish treasurers and major patrons for the construction of the new church (Table 3). Because of the new wealth secured through successful commerce and trade, they passed through successive social levels ascending from middle-class merchants to city counselors and finally to lords and *parlementaires* by the end of the century.[10]

Etienne Dufour played a decisive role in the conception and initial funding of construction during the English occupation of Rouen.[11] He is listed as a church treasurer in the 1436–37 fabric account and in February 1441 he established two masses "en l'autel derrière le choeur" through the donation of rents from the Hôtel des Flagons, a property on the rue Malpalu joining the church near the *petit aître*. This property provided the considerable rent of 25 livres 10 sous per year to the church treasury. In 1444 he gave rents from

Table 3 Genealogy of the Dufour Family

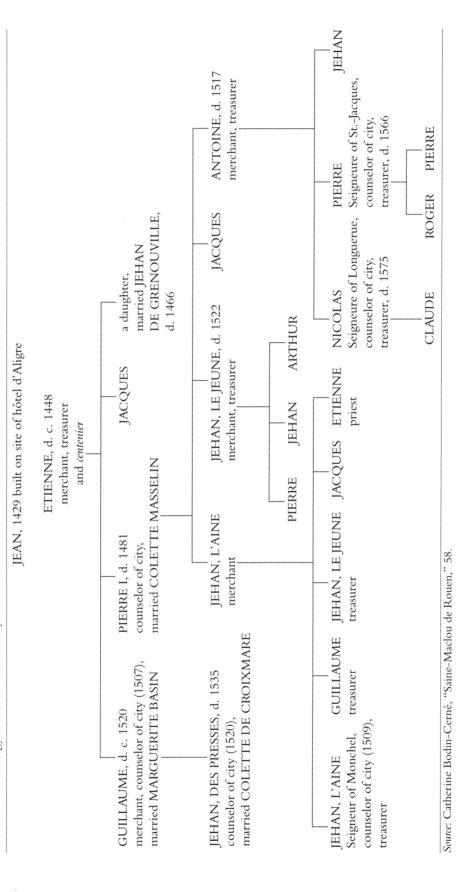

Source: Catherine Bodin–Cerné, "Saine–Maclou de Rouen," 58.

additional properties on the rue de la Mielle in the parish.[12] As one of the leading members of the notable parish families, Etienne served as *centenier* for the church, and participated as a collector of donations for a parish subscription for funds toward the construction. This archival document is undated, but since Etienne died before 1448, the subscription must date to the years before. The document records the names of more than four hundred and fifty families in the parish, almost the entire population, excluding those that were not taxed such as the poor, Jews, and clergy, and it demonstrates the broad base of support for construction. Etienne's personal commitment to the construction is evident not only in his gifts, rents, properties, and foundations, but also in his efforts in the administration and collection of parish revenues designated for the new work. Familial continuity in the project over several generations was provided by a similar participation of his two sons, Pierre and Guillaume, as well as his son-in-law, Jean de Grenouville.

While Etienne acquired considerable wealth through the manufacture and trade of cloth, Pierre acquired new social prestige through his appointment as a city counselor in 1463, an administrative post reserved for men of important social rank. This may have been bestowed on him as the result of the title of nobility he received from Charles VII for his role in the recapitulation of Rouen in 1449.[13] In 1471, Pierre gave to the treasury the rents from the property called the *l'hoste des Estuves Saint-Maclou* or the *Neuves étuves* to complete the work on the nave.[14] Although Pierre died in 1481 and was buried along with his brother Guillaume in the newly completed chapel of Saint Léonard, his wish to complete the church was carried out by his widow, Colette Masselin. In 1487, she established a mass in the chapel of Notre Dame and in the nave before the crucifix to be paid for by rent on "l'Image Saint Claude" on the rue Malpalu near the Pomme d'Or.[15] In this same foundation, she promised to pay for the pavement of the chapel Saint Symon and Saint Jude, and the western rose window and triforium.

Etienne's second son, also a cloth merchant, married a noblewoman, Marguerite Basin, and served as city counselor in 1507. In their capacity as cloth merchants, the Dufour traveled extensively and frequented the fairs of Lyons and Geneva. In 1460, Jean Dufour was recorded to have taken a gold brocade cloth from Florence and Geneva to Rouen for the archbishop, and in 1466, he forwarded 1500 ecus d'or to the archbishop in Rome.[16] In 1510 Guillaume endowed a mass with rent from a house outside the parish on the rue Gros Horloge.[17]

Despite the frequency of various gifts of rents, properties, and donations listed by Loth and Bodin-Cerné, most are for endowment of masses and only a few are earmarked for the fabric of the church. In addition, the individual amounts are insignificant when compared to the actual cost of construction. For instance, the rent of the Hôtel des Flagons, the most lucrative property donated to the parish, would scarcely pay for the salary of a master mason for a single year. On the other hand, the claim that the Dufours were the major patrons is substantiated by two documents. Etienne's son-in-law, Jean de Grenouville, also a cloth merchant, is identified with the work of Saint-Maclou. He provided a lifting machine, referred to as the "engin grenouville" in 1445.[18] More important, however, his tomb inscription of 1466, found in the chapel of the Virgin, describes Jean as having made "le plus de cette église." At this time, the choir and transepts were completed and possibly vaulted and the nave was under construction. The inscription and the prestigious location of the tomb confirms Jean's participation as a major patron although the extant building accounts and cartularies make no mention of significant donations.

The second piece of evidence confirms the Dufours role as primary patrons is their depiction in the *Grand Chartrier*. This lavishly illuminated manuscript was assembled sometime between 1531 and 1535 at the request of Nicolas Dufour. It contains lists of documents relative to foundations, rents, and properties in the possession of the parish. The manuscript begins with a full-page illumination of the patron saint presenting three members of the Dufour family to the seated Virgin and Child (Figs. 87 and 88). Each Dufour holds a gift— the cartulary itself, a charter (probably referring to rents, properties, and foundations given to the parish by the family), and a reliquary, most likely meant to represent the church itself—paid for by their generosity. A cityscape of Rouen can be seen in the background. The coat-of-arms of the newly nobled family, three gold crescents surrounding a gold *molette* or star wheel on a blue ground, appears six times in the manuscript (Fig. 89).

Between the first mention of Etienne Dufour in 1436 and the completion of the cartulary after 1531, several generations of Dufour are listed as treasurers and patrons of construction; usually, however, their gifts are relatively small and inconsistent. Pierre Dufour and Colette Masselin had at least three sons who played an active role in parish business. Jean Le Jeune and Jean L'Aîné, listed as treasurers in the 1514–17 account, lent large sums of money to the treasury when expenses for construction exceeded revenues.[19] The tomb inscription of Jean L'Aîné dated 1514 in the family chapel of Saint Claude and Saint Léonard also acknowledges his patronage.

> In the year 1514
> The 27th day of June
> For Jean Dufour the eldest son
> Of the noble Pierre Dufour the younger
> The notaries of the church council
> For land taken by him
> Agree by a letter passed
> The day after his death
> To have said in this chapel
> A mass and *de profundis*
> Praying God that in heaven
> He will take all the souls
> Of the Dufours and their wives.[20]

The son of Guillaume and Marguerite Basin, Jean des Presses, was the wealthiest Dufour. Like his father and cousins, he served as a city counselor and married into a noble parish family, the Croixmare. In addition to his contribution of rents he gave furnishings for the church and most of the interior decoration including an altar for the family chapel, an organ, a bench for relics and statues of the apostles to be placed on the piers around the choir. A foundation contract of 1527 indicates that a mass was to be said perpetually in the chapel of Saint-Léonard where his father Guillaume Dufour, his wife, and his uncle were buried.[21]

The *Grand Chartrier* displays the coat-of-arms of other merchant families and patrons of the church. Nicolas de la Chesnaye, also identified in the building accounts was a merchant and *seigneur de tot*, lord of a fief within the parish. As receiver of the Domaine in the Viscountcy of Rouen, a city counselor, and deputy of the state in 1515, he was among the highest-ranked parishioners. His coat-of-arms is found adjacent to the Dufours.

Like the Dufours, the Amyot family must have been benefactors over several generations. In 1434, Tassio Amyot (Amiot) and his wife paid for a mass in the newly completed chapel of Notre-Dame and by the 1460s, his coat-of-arms, a silver ground with three red hearts, appeared in the vault keystone of the first northern nave aisle bay adjacent to the west facade. The same coat-of-arms appears again in the cartulary of 1531 (Figs. 45 and 90).

Building Revenue and Economic Trends in Fifteenth-Century Rouen

Although the Dufours were the most generous in their gifts, the accounts indicate that the most reliable source of steady working capital used for construction came from ordinary church revenues. Enough money was amassed through small regular contributions to maintain a mason's workshop, purchase construction materials, and cover the costs of daily building activity. While the pace of construction over a span of fifty years seems brisk, when compared with cathedral construction, it must be remembered that Saint-Maclou was approximately equal length and width to that of the transept of the cathedral of Rouen. During the most intensive building activity of the 1470s when the nave was being completed and the vaults installed, the mason's workshop consisted of only nine men. The slow steady pace of construction is mirrored by the small amounts but consistent availability of revenue for construction.

The nature and amount of funding for construction can be gleaned from the building accounts. As described in Chapter 1, four sets of accounts survive for the years 1436–37, 1443–46, 1476–79, and 1514–17 with an additional summary of expenses for the years 1465–69. The accounts of 1517–20 and 1520–23 provide additional information on the decoration of the church in preparation for its dedication. However these accounts make no mention of extraordinary revenues such as parish subscriptions, royal property taxes, money collected for indulgences, or most rents and foundations. This income must have been recorded elsewhere and is only partially identified in the cartularies or loose parchment of the archives.[22] Thus, a complete picture of church finances including extraordinary and ordinary revenue is impossible to reconstruct; the few extant building accounts, however, provide a glimpse into a narrow range of expenses and receipts related to the daily activity of the church treasury for specific moments in the building history.

The church treasurers functioned as the building contractor for the project and oversaw the administration and control of funds. In Rouen, church treasurers who served as temporal administrators within the parish had existed since 1235 when the statutes of the synod of the diocese of Rouen reorganized the administration of parish churches. The treasurers were chosen from the notable families in the parish and, with the approval of the curate, would oversee the daily operations of parish business, usually for a period of three years.[23]

The categories of revenues listed in the extant building accounts are similar, although the amounts collected in the last account are far more substantial. With total receipts of 578 livres for the year 1436–37 (compared to expenses of 582 livres), the treasurers, including Etienne Dufour, Colin Le Roux, Pierre Le Coq, Guillaume de La Mare, Colin Le Febvre, and Cardinot Coquin, recorded the largest income of 141 livres under the heading of "cuilly a leuvre de leglise." Money collected in front of the church amounted to only 12 livres and money found in boxes located in the church, 17 livres. Collections made for relics on nineteen feast days of the year totaled 47 livres with the largest sums collected on the feast day of Saint-Leu (7 livres) and Easter (21 livres). Substantial sums are recorded for burials in the church (98 livres), burial in the small and large cemetery (16 livres) and other burials (19 livres), the rights of masters of the cloth and bakery crafts (20 livres), rents on properties (51 livres), nuptials (3 livres), and the sale of unwanted construction materials including lead, wood, and stone (25 livres).

A separate miscellaneous category identified as gifts to the church (totaling 113 livres) lists a variety of entries including a gift of 4 livres from Jean Boissel, curate of the church, and 100 sous to help pay for a room where the brothers of the confraternity of Saint Leu could make "neufvaines de mess Sainct Leu." These receipts were balanced against the expenses for the new construction and repairs on the old church (as discussed in Chapter 1) as well as the normal costs incurred in the daily operation of the parish.

By 1443, the treasurers, including Pierre Le Gay, Henry Le Houppeur, Jacquet La Hoteron, Cardin Fessart, Thomas Fugart, and Jehan Conlombel, were supporting a workshop of five masons who were completing the choir. The increased activity is provided for by the expansion of sources of revenue and the intensified efforts on the part of the treasurers to secure funds. Under the category of relics, 26 feast days are listed for the year 1443–44 with a total of 52 livres collected.[24] Jehan Dufour gives the lucrative rents for two properties including the "maison hugnete deminelles" at 40 sous and the "lostel des Flagons" for 10 livres.[25] Because of the incomplete record for this period the total receipts are not known but the expenses total 1258 livres or approximately 419 livres per year, slightly less than those of 1436–37.

The purchase of large quantities of building stone and the presence of a workshop of nine masons who are completing the nave suggests that work has accelerated by 1476–79.[26] The expenses of 1893 livres or approximately 631 livres per year are slightly greater than the receipts of 1742 livres (or approximately 580 livres per year). It is surprising that these amounts are close to those recorded in the 1436–37 account when work was just beginning and the expenses were directed to repair work on the nave roof as well as setting out the choir foundations. The registers for these three years indicate steady small amounts collected from individual parishioners. Rents are also charged to shops that have clustered around the newly completed entrances to the church including "daupres du portail Saint Cler," "derrier la chapelle Saint Cler," and in the large cemetery.

By the early sixteenth century, the modest sums and balanced accounting of the building records changes. The 1514–17 account describes the completion of the lantern tower (a project that seems relatively minor when compared to the completion and vaulting of the nave) but lists receipts of 4161 livres (or approximately 1387 livres) per year and expenses of 4810 livres (or approximately 1603 livres per year). These revenues were three times greater than the yearly receipts and expenses of the fifteenth century, apparently because of higher construction costs. For example, Etienne Cauchée, an *apparailleur*, is paid 102 livres for making a spiral staircase for the tower, Jehan Le Preux is paid 207 livres for roofing lead; Symonet Le Cousterier, a quarrier from Vernon, is paid 158 livres for stone that he delivers to the church; and Martin Le Bourc, an ironworker, is paid 73 livres for an iron cross weighing 756 pounds. The treasurers, headed by Jehan Dufour and Jean Le Jeune, and Louys Orel attempt to offset the high expenses by borrowing money from Jehan L'Ainé. Etienne Caucheé's income for one project, based on piecework rather than daily wage, is considerably greater than the *appareilleur*, Jehan Le Prevost, working in 1444. Prevost was paid 5 sous per day or approximately 65 livres per year.[27]

Despite the tedious character of these details, a number of general conclusions can be made about sources and nature of building revenue. The fabric accounts indicate that from the beginning of construction until the completion of the nave around 1480, church revenues were relatively small, averaging around 500 livres per year. These funds were sufficient to maintain a small workshop, including four to six masons in 1443–47 and six to nine in 1477–79. The steady supply of funds, albeit in small amounts, was enough to finance an unbroken sequence of construction throughout the fifteenth century.

Second, the documents clearly indicate that revenues for construction originated almost exclusively from within the parish. The largest receipts were collected by various methods for donations and relics; the second largest source was through extraordinary revenues provided by a number of the most notable parishioners or the curates through foundations, rents, properties, loans, and outright gifts. These parishioners were predominately from the merchant-class families who made their living through the manufacture and trade of cloth and who paid for the privilege of becoming a master of that craft to the church. The participation of families such as the Dufour and the allied families through marriage is substantially documented in the building accounts, cartularies, chapel inscriptions and manuscript illuminations.

What distinguishes the Dufours and the other parish families as patrons is that they not only provided the money for construction but played a direct role in controlling costs, soliciting funds from other sources, and making decisions that directly affected the construction process. They exercised civic and Christian responsibility by serving as *centeniers* or *dizaniers* in parish subscriptions, and by their role as treasurers. The commitment of the treasurers to the project at Saint-Maclou is also illustrated by the loans made by the treasurers Jehan and Antoine Dufour in 1514–17 accounts when expenses exceeded receipts.[28]

However, the steady financing of construction from the 1430s to the 1470s does not coincide with the general economic contours of Rouen during the fifteenth century. In his seminal study of Norman commerce during the fifteenth century, Michel Mollat, points out that from the 1430s until the end of the English occupation in 1449, Rouen passed through a severe economic depression from which it only gradually emerged by the 1470s.[29] To chart the economic recovery, Mollat cites the records of salt ships entering the port at Rouen.[30] In 1458–59 there were 43 salt ships; 1461–62, 184 ships; 1472–73, 199 ships; 1478–79, 283 ships; and 1514–15, 430 ships.[31] Thus, by the time Rouen was entering into a period of prosperity in the 1470s, the significant superstructure of the church of Saint-Maclou was completed. The decades of the 1430s and 1440s were the most difficult for the merchant patrons, yet this is the moment they decided to undertake the construction of a lavish and expensive monument unlike any other gothic church that existed in either Paris or Rouen. The letter of amortizement of Henry VI of 1448 confirms that the church was begun without "*deniers* or materials of good stone," yet the treasurers, at considerable sacrifice, invested their personal fortunes in its construction.

Thus, it cannot be assumed that building activity always corresponds with general economic trends.[32] Because of the unsympathetic economic conditions, these patrons must have been strongly motivated by forces other than the need to replace an old building. The priority given to building by the Dufour must be examined against the events of the 1430s during the last two decades of the English occupation of Rouen.

Rouen at the End of the Hundred Years' War

After 1380 the collective consciousness of the merchants and artisans of the parish of Saint-Maclou was partially shaped by three historical events that had a direct bearing on the economic and commercial prosperity of their city. This period also coincides with distinct changes in architectural style. From 1380, gothic architecture as represented by the major projects of the period, the new facade of the cathedral of Rouen and the completion of the transepts and southern porch of the abbey of Saint-Ouen, had become more fragmented, more receptive to a range of outside influences, and more preoccupied with refinement of detail. These new stylistic impulses appeared at the beginning of the reign of Charles VI. Because he was a weak ruler, suffering from intermittent illness, political power resided with his uncles, preoccupied with their own interests or aggrandizement. The decentralization of administrative control diminished the influence of Paris and decreased the prestige of the French king; at a time of great vulnerability to English forces, France floundered without decisive leadership.

In order to finance war efforts due to renewed claims to the French throne by the English king, Charles VI levied additional taxes on already overburdened urban middle classes. Additional taxes on wine and salt voted upon by the Estates of Normandy and encouraged by the king's royal officers, brought about riots in many cities throughout the realm and in Rouen resulted in the devastating riot in February 1382.[33] Led by a large number of the cloth workers from the parish of Saint-Maclou, the rioters looted houses of the wealthy bourgeoisie and royal collectors, attacked the chateau of the king, priests, Jews, and money-lenders, released prisoners, and invaded the abbey of Saint-Ouen that had traditionally been exempt from heavy taxation. Charles VI entered the city in March and responded to the rebellion with repressive actions. He imposed heavy taxes (*aides* and *gabelles*), silenced the bell named Raoul—a symbol of communal authority—and reorganized the communal government.[34] Three hundred bourgeoisie were arrested and the city was assessed a fine of 60,000 livres. By replacing the mayor with his own representative, the bailiff, Charles effectively put an end to the communal autonomy that had controlled the city since the twelfth century.

Thus, along with the other royal representatives in the city, including the captain of the chateau, the viscount de l'Eau and the viscount de Rouen, the king was able to manipulate municipal institutions, especially concerning future taxation. Perhaps the most devastating repercussions of the Harelle for the cloth merchants of Saint-Maclou was the loss of the "compagne normand" in favor of the "compagne français," or the subordination of Rouen to Paris in control over the lower Seine and the right to tax ships in and out of Rouennais ports. Although some of the communal liberties were restored by 1391 (for example, the city council elected six counselors and "Raoul" was remounted in a new belfry in 1389) the loss of the mayor, resentment from heavy fines as well as new taxation, and subordination of Rouen to Paris in trading privileges, defined politics and conflicts between the Rouen commune and outside authority, be it French or English, well into the sixteenth century.

By the early fifteenth century internal conflicts left France vulnerable to English invasion.[35] The prolongation of the Hundred Years' War was due not only to the unresolved claim of two sovereigns to the French throne but also to complications brought about by a French civil war between the Burgundian house and those surrounding the dauphin, Charles VII. Divided by internal conflict, France could offer little resistance to a renewed English invasion in 1417. Domestic hostilities were accelerated by the Burgundian/Armagnac conflict and political assassinations. In 1407, Louis, duke of Orléans, and brother to the intermittently mad Charles VI, was murdered by John the Fearless, duke of Burgundy. The duke of Berry, uncle to Charles VI and Charles, son of Louis and the new duke of Orleans, were joined by Bernard, count of Armagnac, against Burgundy. Although the Orléanists or Armagnacs, aligned with the aristocracy, retained control of Paris until 1418, popular opinion resided with the duke of Burgundy, who, through timely propaganda, promised reorganization of the administration and the reduction of taxes. This conflict, fueled by resentment deeply rooted in the riots of the Harelle, emerged in Rouen in 1417. According to Monstrelet, partisans of the duke of Burgundy encouraged the populace, led by a large number of cloth workers, to rebel as a protest for a new tax recently levied under the king.[36]

Under the leadership of Alain Blanchart, they murdered the king's bailiff, Raoul de Gau-
court, an Armagnac noble, and several other officers. The dauphin, preceded by the archbishop of Rouen, Louis d'Harcourt, entered the city to extinguish the riots and find resti-
tution for the murder of his representative. However, prominent bourgeoisie and cathedral
canons aligned themselves with the rioters and the king was forced to pardon all but those
directly responsible for the revolt.

Henry V of England resumed his claim to the French throne and, seizing upon the opportunity afforded by the distraction of French forces in a civil war, he invaded Normandy
at Harfleur in 1417. In light of the repressive action of the French king in Rouen in both
1382 and 1417, it is difficult to understand the degree of resistance Henry V confronted in
overtaking Rouen in 1418 but the suffering of the Rouennais during the ten-month siege
is recorded in contemporary chronicles and poems.[37]

Henry began the siege in August 1418, cutting off all traffic on the Seine and surrounding the city with thirty thousand men.[38] The inhabitants, unable to solicit aid from either
King Charles VI or the dauphin Charles VII, were encouraged by the Burgundian partisans
to capitulate. The isolation was particularly devastating for the parishes of Saint-Maclou,
Saint-Vivien, and Saint-Nicolas. Located near the city walls and with abundant "places
vydes," large number of refugees from the countryside had sought safety from the English
forces inside the city. These were the first casualties of the famine brought about by the
siege. The population of Rouen dwindled to fifteen thousand from approximately thirty
thousand. With the surrender of the city, the greatest burden fell on the bourgeoisie. Eighty
hostages from this group were taken to England to assure the payment of a ransom of
375,000 livres to be paid in écu d'or before January 1419.[39] To raise the money, the bailiff,
ordered the confiscation of wealth of the church, widows, minors, and absentees. In return
for their submission, Henry V allowed the inhabitants to maintain their privileges, posses-
sions, and their communal government, now headed by the bailiff of the English king.

From the point of the capitulation, a new era began in Rouen politics and commerce.
While nineteenth-century scholars such as Albert Chéruel describe this period as one of
foreign oppression, recent studies suggest—at least for the twelve years of administration
under the duke of Bedford, regent to the young king Henry VI—a period of comparable
peace and commercial rejuvenation.[40] The willingness of the Rouennais to function under
a so-called foreign power can better be understood if the occupation is viewed as a return
to ducal Normandy, part of the former Anglo-Norman empire, with political boundaries
similar to the period prior to its absorption into the royal domain by Philip Augustus in
1204.[41] With a decentralized French administration, regional factionalism, and the absence
of a powerful French king, temporary rule by an English king was a viable alternative and
provided the opportunity for a stable government not achieved under Charles VI. In addition, the Treaty of Troyes in 1420 legitimized the English claim to the French throne
through the betrothal of the young Henry V to Catherine, daughter of Charles VI and Is-
abeau of Bavaria.[42] At the same time Charles VI disinherited the dauphin, Charles VII, for
the murder of John, duke of Burgundy. Henry V now referred to himself as heir and regent

of France.[43] An Anglo-Burgundian alliance was formalized by the Treaty of Amiens in 1423 contracting the marriage of the duke of Bedford to Anne, sister of the duke of Burgundy.

Despite the overwhelming burden of ransom on the merchant class and the extension of oppressive tax policies, especially the hearth tax and tax on commodities of wine and beer, Henry V provided a stable government in Normandy and initiated a policy of reconciliation that was carried out by the duke of Bedford. As a "benevolent conqueror," Henry returned the keys of the city of Rouen to the municipal government and allowed it to continue as it had before the siege. Englishmen were appointed only to military positions, although the bailiff, viscount de Rouen, and viscount de l'Eau were still responsible to the king. Confiscation of ecclesiastical benefices and properties of the absentee nobility were not given for the most part to English but were used as rewards for submission of prominent French clergy, bourgeoisie, and nobility. Bedford, cultivating the Norman identity of Rouen, reestablished Norman institutions and called the Estates of Normandy.[44] The Estates, composed of French nobles, clergy, bourgeoisie, viscounts, and lieutenants of the bailiff was presided over by Bedford, met on a regular basis during Bedford's lifetime, and was primarily concerned with the administration of Normandy, ratification of treaties, and the approval of taxes. After the final victory of the English over Charles VII at Verneuil in 1424, the entire territory of Normandy fell under Bedford's control and he turned to the Estates for 240,000 livres tournois.[45]

However Bedford also took steps to curry favor of the bourgeoisie, to encourage commerce, and counteract the heavy burden of taxation. He attempted to stabilize currency, forbade circulation of base French currency, and fixed a standard value for new gold and silver coinage.[46] He passed statutes regulating weights and measures in Normandy, confirmed commercial privileges, granted tax exemptions, and attempted to regulate the crafts.[47] Special legislative statutes were passed to favor Rouennais merchants on shipping of the Seine; with the English control of Paris, Rouen, their administrative capital, regained control over shipping in the lower Seine.[48] The direct effect of these measures on the prosperity of the Rouennais merchants is indicated by the lavish home constructed by Jean Dufour on the site of the Hôtel d'Aligre in 1429, only ten years after the siege.[49]

All this changed in the 1430s. The bourgeoisie of the parish and of Rouen were content with English rule as long as the reform policies and trade privileges proved beneficial to commercial interests. Initially they seemed unswayed by nationalistic allegiances and failed to become politicized at the martyrdom of Jeanne d'Arc, who was tried in 1431 and burnt at the stake in the Vieux Marché. Bedford had pressured for her execution and, although a majority of the judges at her trial were French, there was little popular support for her. The sacrifice of Jeanne as a martyr for French nationalism did not become an issue until her rehabilitation in 1452. The chronicler Pierre Cochon, describes an enthusiastic welcome given to the young king Henry VI as he made his entry into the city in August 1430.

However, the shift in sympathies of the Rouennais from reluctant tolerance to conscious resistance in the 1430s was gradual, steady, and spearheaded by the merchant class. Due to increased activity of Charles VII in the Pays de Caux and to the unrelenting pillage of the *routiers* and brigands in the countryside, regions around Rouen were becoming unsafe for trade and travel. In 1433, the abbot of Saint-Ouen made a request to Henry VI to transfer the "plaid" normally held in the Forêt Verte outside the city walls to the cemetery of the abbey because the country was infested with enemies of the English. The archbishop also asked the king to authorize the holding of the litigation of the Lord of Deville in his own palace for the same reason.[50]

The territorial insecurity was followed in 1434 by a severe famine and clearly marked the decline of the economy. An anonymous chronicler described it as "L'yer dura depuis la Sainct André jusques à Pasques, et de ce commença la et durant cest cherté mesure de Rouen, valoit quatre salutz d'or. A Rouen, grand nombre de peuple mourut par guerre, après par famine et tiercement par la mortalité."[51]

The most significant event of the decade and the ultimate factor leading to the expulsion of the English from Rouen was the Treaty of Arras in 1435. Encouraged by his adviser, Nicolas Rolin (probably under payment from Charles VII), Philip the Bold recognized Charles as king of France in exchange for the territory of Macon, Auxerre, and Ponthieu. The Armagnac/Burgundian civil war was ended and the Continental ties with England were severed. Bedford, who had committed his life to establishing English rule in Normandy, had died a week before the treaty was signed, and was buried near the organ of the cathedral of Rouen where he had served as a canon.[52]

While Bedford had always sought to respect the customs, rights, and properties of the Normans, upon his death, the weight of English oppression grew more apparent. "The idea of the conqueror and the conquered again revived."[53] There was a fundamental change in policy: "the French having been rebels to Henry VI must in no wise be spared," and troops were now to "burn and ravage the country as they go, sparing nothing." This was applied to districts from Normandy to the Loire. Churches, which had been spared under the more benevolent Henry V and Bedford, were not exempt from destruction and now "no sanctuary should serve traitors, conspirators or rebels."[54]

By 1435, England could no longer finance military operations on the continent to the same extent. English garrisons with five thousand men-at-arms had been reduced to fifteen hundred.[55] As a result, Paris was easily taken by Richemont in April 1436. The insurrection of Paris had a twofold effect on Rouen. The English withdrew from the French capital to Rouen, making it the center of their administrative and military arm on the continent. With Paris cut off from Rouen, the large volume of trade between the two cities ended abruptly, damaging Rouen commerce. Economic isolation was further increased by the insurrection of the Pays de Caux that was given impetus by the return of Paris to Charles VII. In 1436, in less than six weeks, the major cities of upper Normandy, including Dieppe, Fecamp, Harfleur, Lillebourne, and Tancarville, returned to French hands. Navigation on the Seine from Rouen to the sea was kept open only by armed vessels that assisted the transportation of troops and supplies from England to Rouen.[56]

Insecurity around Rouen had increased to such a degree that requests were made by the duke of York for more men to guard the city walls. To support the intensified defense ef-

forts of the English in Rouen, additional taxes were levied on the bourgeoisie, already bur-
dened by the atrophy of trade. Except for the initial meeting in the first decade under Bedford, the Estates of Normandy voted upon taxes ranging from 120,000 livres tournois to
200,000 l.t. but this amount was steadily increased after 1431 to 220,000 l.t. in 1433 and
340,000 l.t. in 1434.[57] The repercussions of these events are reflected in the commercial activity in Rouen ports as recorded in the accounts of the viscount de L'Eau. In 1445, the accounts show a deficit of 600 l.t.; by 1446 it had risen to 1,000 l.t. indicating that despite the
tentative Truce of Tours in 1444, which allowed the Rouennais merchants to continue trading on the Seine between Paris and Dieppe, these routes were still dangerous.[58]

Despite the deplorable state of economy and government during this period, Rouen had
the potential to grow, develop its industry, and extend its trade. All that was needed was a
political situation to nurture the commercial interests. With the absorption of Normandy
back into France in 1449 and the end of war, Rouen began its economic recovery. Mollat
points out that because of the economic depression that resulted from the monetary and
price fluctuations, disorganization of markets, insufficient production, the absence of capital, and depopulation, it took several decades to return to conditions conducive for a
healthy commercial activity. Only by 1470 can one talk about a thriving economy in
Rouen.[59]

Thus, the conception and initial construction as well as the completion of Saint-Maclou
is circumscribed by these events. The merchant families whose livelihood was most directly
affected by the economic contours of the period fashioned, financed, and fostered the construction of a new vision of gothic architecture. It is extremely difficult to probe the psychological and emotional sentiments of the patrons of Saint-Maclou. No explicit documentation exists that confirms their political sentiments, and their allegiances seem to be
determined by economic and commercial factors. However, historians have pointed out a
number of emerging characteristics unique to this period that may provide an explanation
for the retrospection of the architecture of Saint-Maclou and the pervasive nostalgia in late
gothic architecture that distinguishes it from merely borrowed forms or categories of regional stylistic schools.

Retrospection, Architectural Models, and Meaning

It has already been established that Saint-Maclou references specific parts of the cathedral
of Rouen and miniaturizes attributes of monumental architecture. Parish church architecture had always mined its local cathedral and abbey buildings for motifs, vocabulary, and
ideas; prior to the fifteenth century, however, these humble gothic structures never had the
resources to rival their more prestigious models. Saint-Jacques in Reims or Saint-Paul in
Rouen scaled down and simplified aspects of their local cathedral. In Rouen, one monument frequently exercised influence over another for a variety of reasons. Inspired by a

sense of competition, the inner south transept wall of the abbey of Saint-Ouen under construction around 1350 was a more fashionable version of the inner south transept of the cathedral, completed around 1300. On the other hand, the small boxy porch planned for the west entrance of the parish church of Saint-Vivien, the small hall church of the poorest parish in Rouen, was modeled on the Porch of the Marmousets of the abbey, to mirror the temporal association of the two monuments. Precise models were sometimes specified by the patron. In 1420 the merchant Robert Alorge constructed a chapel at his own expense in the church of Saint Martin-du-Pont and gave instruction to two painters to paint the vaults, aisles, and piers in imitation of those at the abbey of Saint-Ouen.[60]

Although the specific vocabulary of moldings, piers, and shafts of Pierre Robin is a reflection of his individual artistic language and is not related to anything in Rouen, he clearly uses the cathedral triforium/clerestory elevation, the cathedral transepts, the cathedral lantern tower, and possibly the cathedral western porch, as a point of departure for much of his design. It is curious he did not chose Parisian monuments such as the transepts of Notre-Dame or the elevation of Saint-Denis that may have been more familiar to him. Since there is no indication that Pierre Robin ever spent any time in Rouen or worked on any other Rouennais monument, the indebtedness of Saint-Maclou to the cathedral was most likely initiated by the patrons rather than a choice of the architect. The most contemporary and fashionable architecture expressed in the work of Pierre Robin's Rouennais contemporaries, Jenson Salvart and Alexandre de Berneval, has no resonance in the style at Saint-Maclou. The rejection of these models may be as important as the selection of the cathedral in understanding what motivated the patrons.

In 1431, Jenson Salvart, master mason of the cathedral of Rouen, had just undertaken the redesign of the cathedral choir clerestory windows in order to continue the enlargement of the clerestory windows begun in the nave in the mid-fourteenth century.[61] Salvart's clerestory windows combine geometric and double-curved tracery forms supported on lancets defined by thin almond-shaped shafts and fragile rows of capital leaves—characteristic of the overrefined vocabulary of "proto-flamboyant" architecture in late fourteenth- and early fifteenth-century Rouen. His work is indistinguishable from the work of his predecessor, Jean de Bayeux, who along with Salvart, completed screens on the west facade of the cathedral. Alexandre de Berneval, master mason of the abbey of Saint-Ouen, was probably completing the south transept rose at the same time that Robin arrived in Rouen. Both Jenson and Alexandre were in the employment of the English king and worked together on a new palace to be used by Henry VI and Bedford after the siege of 1419. Although the cathedral facade screens, the choir clerestory, the south transept chapel of Saint-Ouen and its facade are indicative of the highly refined and fragile style of the early fifteenth century, they are also laced with English influence. The chapel window in the south transept of Saint-Ouen, adjacent to the transept on the western side, is a literal copy of an English perpendicular window, with its mouchettes and soufflets conforming to the supermullions that rise above the lancets. This window has been attributed by André Masson to Alexandre de Berneval on the basis of a trip Alexandre made to Nottingham. Jenson Salvart, although he accomplished little in his tenure as master mason of the cathedral, continued the varied and highly refined style of his predecessor Jean de Bayeux, who has been credited with importing English perpendicular paneling to the facade of Rouen cathedral in the form of the great transomed screens that articulate the upper parts of the cathedral.

These foreign influences are conspicuously absent in Pierre Robin's design. Nowhere do we see rectilinear paneling, tiers of vertical niches, or perpendicular tracery. In addition, the parts of the cathedral that served as a source of inspiration for Saint-Maclou all date to the period prior to 1380 and reflect strong ties to Parisian architecture. Marcel Aubert has pointed out that the cathedral transept facades executed between 1280 and 1300, the most significant model for Robin, are elegant interpretations of those recently completed at Notre-Dame in Paris. The enlargement of the nave clerestory and redesign of the triforium of the cathedral were undertaken in response to the stunning new choir of Saint-Ouen, but the architectural forms that stress linkage and four pairs of lancets is ultimately derived from Saint-Denis. On the other hand, the porch and the lantern tower are connected to strong local traditions specifically associated with the cathedral. The porch, designed perhaps with the approval of Charles V, incorporated an upper platform necessary for the "viri galilae," performed on the special feast days at the cathedral. The lantern tower had long been a feature of prestigious Norman buildings and virtually every Episcopal see in the archdiocese of Rouen had a lantern at its crossing.

Thus the relationship of Saint-Maclou to earlier gothic monuments takes three forms. It involves the miniaturization of attributes of the cathedral architecture including the double-tiered flying buttresses, the full-fledged transept facades, the ambulatory and radiating chapels. Second, there are specific references to Rouen cathedral including updated versions of the transept facades, the triforium/clerestory elevation, the western porch, and the lantern tower. Finally, the architecture of Saint-Maclou mined only the parts of the cathedral that dated prior to the 1380s; that is, before foreign influence, especially English Decorated and Perpendicular architecture, first appeared in Rouen. The patrons of Saint-Maclou rejected the contemporary Rouennais style expressed in the work of Jenson Salvart and Alexandre de Berneval and chose a non-Rouennais architect, a Parisian who had formerly been in the employment of the French king.

Given the extraordinary historical circumstances surrounding the construction, we can assume that these forms carried a specific meaning for the parish families and that the ultimate character of Saint-Maclou was not accidental or merely the result of fortuitous aesthetic decisions. It was a conscious attempt on the part of the Dufours, the Grenouville, the Amyot, the Croixmare, and the ordinary parishioners, who made tremendous financial sacrifices in undertaking this lavish construction, to convey an essential message. The retrospection of Saint-Maclou becomes ideological when it can be linked both to their nationalistic sentiments and the perceived propagandistic power of architecture. On the one hand, the architectural forms of Saint-Maclou echoed older models that carried desired associations for the new patrons, and provided a public and visible vehicle for new social self-definition. Although more tentative in its conclusions, it may also be possible to probe layers of meaning by exploring the psychological and emotional repercussions of the Hundred Years' War and the English occupation of Rouen on the merchant-class patrons of Saint-Maclou.

Rolland Sanfaçon identified retrospection as a prevalent feature of late gothic architecture. He points out that "toutes les régions ont retrouvé à l'époque flamboyante leur passé artistique."[62] This is certainly true for a number of ambitious parish church projects. Saint-Séverin, Paris with its double ambulatory and continuous radiating chapels echoes Notre-Dame; Saint-Pierre, Coutances is a smaller version of the cathedral of Coutances; and in Rouen, the choir of Saint-Vincent, completed in 1480, copies the choir of the cathedral of Rouen.

Two subthemes may be linked to the retrospective character of Saint-Maclou: a new sense of French nationalism that arose out of the antagonism over the English occupation of Rouen and/or a desire to recover an order and sense of civic duty lost in the social upheavals at the end of the war.[63] The architecture of Saint-Maclou is associated with architecture of the *époque communale* in Rouen; that is, prior to 1380, prior to the loss of communal autonomy, prior to the influence of English Decorated and Perpendicular style at the cathedral and Saint-Ouen, and prior to the English occupation of Rouen. Historians such as Kenneth Fowler have pointed out that one of the repercussions of the prolonged conflict between the French and English was a polarization of the population that forged a national identity.[64] Nationalistic sentiments also came into focus as the Valois Charles VII attempted to legitimize his claim to the throne over the Plantagenets. The historical episode of Jeanne d'Arc, who rallied support around the dauphin by proclaiming him the true and legitimate heir to the French crown, "fanned the flames of patriotism and xenophobia."[65] The duke of Bedford found it necessary to alter the genealogy of Henry VI in order to justify the title of King of France, and England used both painting and poetry as a propagandistic tool.[66] Englishness versus Frenchness was a conscious tool wielded by the royal houses for propagandistic purposes in the Hundred Years' War as is evident in both the war literature and production of art.[67]

Can the decidedly French and Parisian flavor of Saint-Maclou be attributed to the nationalistic sentiments of the Dufour? Historical evidence suggests that not only did the political events of the last two decades of the English occupation affect the general economy of Rouen; the reaction to the situation arose specifically from the merchant classes within the parish of Saint-Maclou. The bourgeoisie were directly affected by the loss of trade routes between Paris and the sea. They were also saddled with the burden of the ransom still left unpaid by 1430 and by additional taxes imposed by the Estates of Normandy. In addition, as Le Cacheux points out, the major attempts to overthrow the English, were all initiated by the bourgeoisie and principal families of the city. The wealthy bourgeois Robert Alorge in 1421, Richard Mites in 1424, and Richardville in 1432 all led unsuccessful conspiracies to return Rouen to French hands.[68]

Within the parish itself, there is clear evidence that the clergy remained loyal to

Charles VII. Jean Mercier, the curate of Saint-Maclou, headed the list of persons whose properties were confiscated in 1420 for failing to pledge allegiance to the English king.[69] Mercier remained curate until 1436, although he spent little time in Rouen after the siege. As a canon of the cathedral, Mercier was appointed to accompany Archbishop Hughes d'Orgues to the Council of Basel. It is his close relationship with Hughes that may account for the indulgence granted to the church in September 1432 that provided the initial funds for construction of the new church. However the most direct evidence of the Dufours' political sentiments is provided by the titles of nobility they received from Charles VII for their role in the recapitulation of Rouen in 1449.[70]

Despite this circumstantial evidence, it is difficult to argue for a national consciousness with regard to architectural style. It seems unlikely that the Dufours would have associated the Perpendicular tracery in the chapels of Saint-Ouen or the facade of the cathedral of Rouen with foreign occupation. The Dufours and allied parish families seem generally ambivalent about national identity, especially in the 1420s and 1430s. Likewise it is doubtful that they designed their parish church with the idea of constructing a monument proclaiming a national or royal French sentiment regardless of how disgruntled they were with the English government of the 1430s. It is unlikely that Henry VI would have written the letters of amortizement contributing to the construction in the late 1440s if the architectural forms were resonant with the fleur-de-lis of Charles VII. After all, Henry himself had been crowned king of France and England in the cathedral of Notre-Dame in Paris, which had been draped with the lion and fleur-de-lis.[71] Economics, not politics motivated the Dufour.

In one of the few attempts to associate the construction of Saint-Maclou with the political events of the decade, Elizabeth Chirol claimed that the conception of a new church was directly related to the retrenchment of the English in Rouen after the fall of Paris to Charles VII in 1436.[72] The English then decided to enhance their new administrative center with lavish new monuments. To sustain this argument, she dismissed the work recorded after 1432 as mere repairwork, stating that any new construction was dismantled in 1436 when Pierre Robin submitted his plans for the new church. Pointing out that Pierre Robin had been working in Paris under Henry VI she claimed that he was forced to retreat to Rouen along with the English government at this time. However, there is no evidence that Bedford, the duke of York, or Henry VI contributed to the new church during the crucial period of its design and initial construction. Other evidence also confirms that artists seemed to operate outside of political alignments and were more often guided by the availability of work than by national ties. Both the master mason of the cathedral of Rouen, Jenson Salvart, and the mason of the abbey of Saint-Ouen, Alexandre de Berneval, continued to serve in their respective positions before and after the siege of Rouen.[73] Likewise, Pierre Robin was employed by Charles VI before the occupation of Paris but most likely continued to work for Henry V and Henry VI.[74]

If political reasons did not underlie the recovery of architectural forms of the past, then how else might it be explained? The strongest argument for retrospection lies in the restructuring of the social order brought about through changing patterns of wealth and power after the war. Historians are in general agreement that the nobility experienced a considerable decrease in resources as a result of the war.[75] Revenues from properties outside the cites fell due to a variety of reasons, including low grain prices, rising wages, shortage of laborers, and devastation of the brigands.[76] Many of the great Norman families—the Harcourt, the Tancarville, and the Granville—had hereditary palaces in Rouen but resided there only occasionally; during the English occupation most remained loyal to the dauphin, refusing to return to the city and swear allegiance to Henry V, thereby having their properties confiscated and redistributed.[77] New wealth, however, secured through the commercial success of the Rouennais merchants and accumulated in the course of the fifteenth century permitted the purchase of properties, fiefs, and estates. In addition, increased social status was achieved through *lettres d'enoblissement* issued by the king. An act of November 1470 by Louis XI collectively granted titles of nobility to all non-nobles who had acquired fiefs in Normandy.[78] The titles given to the Dufour from the parish of Saint-Maclou were gestures of appreciation by Charles VII for their assistance in returning Rouen to the Dauphin. Jonathan Dewald suggests that the *noblesse de robe* in Rouen of the late fifteenth century had benefited from both the commercial success of their bourgeoisie parents and their backgrounds, which had provided them with the skill to administer landed properties successfully.[79] The purchase of estates was only one way in which the commercially successful class sought to establish themselves as a privileged order through the imitation of nobility.

As Philippe Contamine points out, the most common method of ennoblement was by positive prescription. In the 1376 poem *Le Songe du Vergier*, the anonymous author maintains, "those who have always performed noble deeds and acted like nobles for as long as it can be remembered should be known as such."[80] The imitation of noble deeds by the merchant class must also have included the construction of religious monuments. The resonance of older architectural forms—associated with the socially elite classes in the new architecture—would have contributed to the appearance of prestige and social responsibility adopted by the nouveau riche. The backward-looking aspect of the architecture of Saint-Maclou discussed in Chapter 2 and expressed as a reclamation of the high gothic canon seems primarily motivated by (1) the master mason's desire to reestablish a lost order or coherency in design, and (2) the patrons' desire to enshrine elements of the pre-1380 cathedral of Rouen. This conservative backlash may be particularly poignant on the eve of the recapitulation of Rouen in 1449. P. S. Lewis writes:

> Perhaps it is from the other side that one should look at later medieval French society: as a society in which change was undesirable, novelty synonymous with illegality, and reform reaction to present decay and a return to the golden ages of the past. It was not therefore . . . from social upheaval that French society had to recover in the fifteenth century. . . . It was revolt against the failure of the latter to do their social duty rather than revolt against society as it was—or should be. Privilege was respectable: as long as those who received it did the duty for which they received it.[81]

The order and clarity as well as the meaning provided by the older model of the cathedral touched both the architect and the patron. In the politically and socially fragile time of the 1430s, the architecture of Saint-Maclou provided a visual link to an era of order, peace, and prosperity. Through the acquisition of new wealth through commerce, the Dufours and other merchant families began to acquire the visible symbols of social status: coats-of-arms, fiefs, estates, positions as city counselors and *parlementaires*. They also created for themselves, in miniature, architecture that had traditionally been associated with the social elite.

The association of their church with the cathedral of Rouen is made unmistakable in a miniature in the *Grand Chartrier*. In the background of a scene illustrating the life of Saint-Maclou, a cityscape depicts the newly dedicated church of Saint-Maclou alongside the cathedral (Figs. 91 and 92). Equal in size but more dazzling with its pinnacles, flying buttresses, gabled roofs, and tower, Saint-Maclou rivals and surpasses the cathedral. This exaggeration becomes evident when the scene is compared to a contemporary cityscape in the *Livre des Fontaines* (Fig. 93).[82] The latter artist had no vested interest in his depiction of Saint-Maclou, and the parish church blends into the forest of spires of city churches surrounding the cathedral. Thus, the form of the architecture of Saint-Maclou was both linked to the old social order, prestige, and power of the past, and emblematic of the status, wealth, and power of the new commercial class.

5

Pierre Robin

His Career and His Contemporaries

Pierre Robin in Written Sources

The sophistication of his articulation, the supreme confidence in his management of structural forces, and his knowledge and use of architectural models, suggest that Pierre Robin was a master mason of great experience and celebrity. Unfortunately, scant documentation leaves us with little knowledge of his life, training, or work, and no other monuments have been attributed to Pierre Robin on a stylistic basis. The terse entry in the Saint-Maclou building accounts provides no clues concerning his career or personality. He is mentioned in a single entry of 19 May 1437 when he receives a payment of 43 livres 10 sous for the drawing of the complete church and for his work from the beginning of the year. This entry makes it clear that he was paid on a different basis than the other master masons of Saint-Maclou, who received wages of 5 sous per day. It is reasonable to assume that during his short stay in Rouen, he executed the drawings and oversaw the setting out of the earliest foundations. Although nothing else is known of his life or activity in Rouen, a number of sources suggest that he was a renowned Parisian architect, perhaps the most famous of his day.

Citing the 1436–37 fabric account, Ouin-Lacroix, in *Histoire de l'église et de la paroisse de Saint-Maclou de Rouen* (1846), was the first to identify Pierre Robin as the architect of Saint-Maclou. Thirty years later, the Rouennais archivist, Charles de Robillard de Beaurepaire, associated the master mason of Saint-Maclou with the Parisian "maître Pierre Robin sergent d'arms et macon général du Roi notre Sire" listed by the prevost of Paris in the 1429–31 accounts and first published by Adolph Lance in his 1872 dictionary.[1] Subsequent scholars have never questioned Pierre Robin's Parisian origins despite there being no surviving monuments in Paris that are stylistically linked to Saint-Maclou. A further complication is that the name "Robin" is extremely common: Charles Bauchal lists at least five masons with this name who were active between 1378 and 1450.[2] Another Pierre Robin appears as a laborer in the documents of Troyes Cathedral in 1484–85.[3] However, the Saint-Maclou master's Parisian origins are corroborated by an account for the confraternity of Saint-Yves in Paris. On 8 February 1412, the master mason of the chapel of Saint-Yves, Benôit de Savoye, presented a drawing executed by Pierre Robin for the new construction of the west facade gable to the confraternity of Saint-Yves.[4] Working with Robin at this time were three other masons including Simon Le Noir, Jean James, and Geoffroy Sevestre.[5] The former, Simon Le Noir, arrived in Rouen along with Pierre Robin and took over the Saint-Maclou workshop from Oudin de Mantes sometime in the early 1440s. This document confirms Robin was from Paris; in both cases, however, his name appears only in connection with a payment for drawings. Although he is a master mason (referred to in the documents as master), the workshops of both Saint-Maclou and Saint-Yves were under the direction of a second master mason.

With a confirmation of the Parisian origins of Pierre Robin, other sources permit us to establish his reputation. Pierre Robin held several prestigious positions in Paris during his lifetime. He was master of the king's works for Charles VI and master of the works of the cathedral of Notre-Dame. The earliest record of his name dates from 1412 in connection with Saint-Yves but he succeeds Henry Bricet as the architect for Charles VI and was appointed "maistre des oeuvres du roi au vicomté de Paris" on 7 March 1422.[6] In this capacity he executed drawings for ceremonial furniture needed for the royal funeral of Charles VI, who died on 21 October 1422, including two wooden processional canopies to cover the body of the king that would be placed in the choirs of the cathedral of Notre-Dame in Paris and the abbey of Saint-Denis.[7] The litter, used to transport the king's coffin, constructed by the king's carpenter Sanson Hubon, in a procession from the Hôtel Saint-Pol to the cathedral, was also executed after plans by Pierre Robin.[8] For this work he received 189 francs.[9] There is no evidence to connect Pierre Robin with Charles VII; after 1422, however, he was retained by the city of Paris as the master of the works of masonry[10] and was named by the chapter of Notre-Dame, as master mason of the cathedral.[11] The reference to Pierre Robin as sergeant at arms and general mason to the king in 1429–31 in Paris cited by Lance must have applied to the English king Henry VI, as Paris was occupied by the English between 1417 and 1436.[12] In this capacity, Robin may have designed the architectural paraphernalia needed for Henry's coronation at the cathedral of Notre-Dame in 1431. Thus, in every documented reference connecting Pierre Robin to a specific work, Saint-Maclou, Saint-Yves, the funeral canopies and litter for Charles VI, he is paid for drawings alone. Robin's reputation was as a draftsman and the daily work of overseeing the construction of a monument at the site fell to other master masons. The complex and sophisticated drawings needed to execute Saint-Maclou bear this out. Thus, the specialization among master masons between "architect/designer" and "general contractor" may have existed as early as the fifteenth century.

Pierre Robin and Paris

We can assume that Pierre Robin was a young man in 1412 when he designed the gable of Saint-Yves. The history of Parisian architecture of the late fourteenth and early fifteenth century that stimulated, influenced, and gave shape to the artistic language of Pierre Robin has yet to be written.[13] Almost nothing survives from this period and the fragments of Saint-Séverin, Saint-Nicolas-des-Champs, and Saint-Gemain L'Auxerrois that can be dated to the early fifteenth century have nothing in common with Saint-Maclou.[14]

The chapel of Saint-Yves, sold and demolished in the Revolution is known only through written sources and engravings. The first stone for the wooden vaulted nef unique chapel was placed by Jean Le Bon on 30 May 1337.[15] However the west facade was not constructed until the early fifteenth century when work came under direction of the Parisian masons, Henry Bricet and Benoit de Savoye. Soon after, Pierre Robin was asked to supply a drawing for the gable. The 1751 engraving from Du Chemin de Carpentier provides a detailed view of the portal with the sculpture of Jeanne de France and her husband Jean V of Bretagne installed in the adjacent niches in 1413 (Fig. 94).[16] The architectural details of the portal including bases, jambs, molding profiles, and voussoirs are comparable to the 1441 portal of the priory of Saint-Lo in Rouen and displays none of the streamlined vocabulary of Pierre Robin (Fig. 95). An earlier engraving of 1702, although not so precise, was executed before the modifications of the upper portions of the facade and provides a glimpse of the gable designed by Robin (Fig. 96).[17] The portal is surmounted by a vast double lancet window set into a gabled facade. The drawing is probably an unreliable indicator of specific tracery patterns but unusual quinquepartite cusping articulates the lancets and no geometric forms are readily discernible. A large single freestanding sculpture replaces the *fleuron* at the peak of the gable and stands before a complex screen of tracery, a device used for all the portal gables at Saint-Maclou. Although this is scant evidence indeed, the revolutionary style of Saint-Maclou may have its origins in the lost works of Paris. Destroyed monuments such as the parish church of Saint-Jean-en-Grève, begun in 1326 on a five-aisle plan with double-tiered flying buttresses, 29-meter-high vaults, and three-story elevation (including a blind triforium) provide important Parisian prototypes for the miniaturized monumentality of Saint-Maclou.[18] However, until the history of Parisian architecture from 1380 to 1450 is written, the formation of the specific vocabulary used by Robin must remain open.

On the other hand, the cathedral of Paris had a profound impact on Pierre Robin. Although he was master mason of Notre-Dame from 1422, there is no evidence of fifteenth-century masonry in the present fabric of the cathedral. Yet this early gothic structure, completed and updated in the high gothic period, and overlaid with rayonnant articulation finds unexpected resonance in the late gothic parish church of Saint-Maclou. Some of Robin's most unconventional features have their roots in the archetypal cathedral.

The first master of Notre-Dame placed an axial pier in the ambulatory aisle in order to permit a uniform and elegant pattern of Y-shaped vaults. Taken up again by the anonymous late gothic master of the choir of Saint-Séverin, the axial pier was showcased by giving it a new twist using continuous fillet moldings (Fig. 133). Robin's axial pier was dictated by the geometry of his choir plan, but permission to plant a support in the axis of the arcade may have been granted by the venerable Parisian model.

The nonprojecting aisleless transept of Saint-Maclou, related to the creation of chapels between the buttresses of the nave and choir, is an uncommon solution in parish church design. Robin's prototype may have been the transept of Notre-Dame, created by the second master mason of the cathedral.[19] However, it is difficult to appreciate the compact form and abstract spatial relationships from visual observation and experience alone. A plan drawing similar to the Notre-Dame choir plan at Strasbourg and dating to 1300 may have captured Robin's attention and made apparent the streamlined design cohesion of the nonprojecting aisleless transept.[20]

Finally, the redesigned cathedral choir with its new chapels and aristocratic decoration provides several points of reference for Robin.[21] When seen from the eastern exterior, the choir chapels created by the extension of the choir wall to the outer surfaces of the buttresses, ring the east end in a series of beveled surfaces elegantly capped with gables and divided by pinnacles (Fig. 97). The same visual effect is achieved by the equally anomalous porch of Saint-Maclou that wraps around the western end of the church in a series of flat, angled and gabled surfaces. The earliest precursors of Robin's diagonally faced wall buttresses divide the chapels of the choir of Notre-Dame. The structural support provided by the radial walls dividing the chapels are swallowed by the outer chevet wall, which has been pushed to the exterior and made invisible. Although the large scale, sprawling mass, and the vocabulary of forms are quite removed from the precious scale and descriptive architectural language of Robin's flamboyant church, the two monuments are kindred spirits in these details. In his capacity as master mason of Notre-Dame, Robin must have been intimately familiar with the forms, design, and structure of the cathedral. It seems appropriate that a monument with its pedigree and prestige should be his teacher and source of inspiration.

Pierre Robin, Chartres, and the Vexin

Robin had no opportunity to craft a unique style in his work at Notre-Dame. Glimpses of Robin's unconventional vocabulary of forms expressed at Saint-Maclou are evident elsewhere in the area around Paris. Working alongside Pierre Robin at Saint-Yves was Geoffroy Sevestre, best noted for his design of the chapel of Vendôme at Chartres Cathedral begun 1417.[22] Constructed for Louis of Bourbon, count of Vendôme, the chapel was tucked between two buttresses of the easternmost bay of the south nave aisle. Sevestre uses trumpet bases and geometric tracery combined with curvilinear tracery but creates a fluid linear continuity reminiscent of Saint-Maclou by using continuous prismatic moldings. The chapel vault keystone, based on a disc of openwork tracery with a coat-of-arms in the center, is a close parallel to Robin' design.

Reflections of early fifteenth-century Parisian architecture can be seen in churches along the Seine river valley between Paris and Rouen. While the direct hand of Pierre Robin is not discernible, one witnesses sequential design changes that were to lead to his particularly "modern" vision expressed in the dynamic forms of Saint-Maclou. The two best examples of this transitional style are to be found at the collegiate churches of Notre-Dame, Vernon and Notre-Dame, Le Grand Andely.

An intimate connection between the workshops of Rouen and Vernon existed since the fourteenth century when architects such as Jean Auxtabours worked in both locations.[23] The subterranean quarries for the Saint-Maclou stone were located just outside of Vernon. The church of Notre-Dame in Vernon had been under construction since the twelfth century when work began on the choir, but there is little documentation to provide an absolute chronology for construction of the nave, transept, chapels, and facade.[24] A building account of 1432–39 indicates unspecified minor work in a chapel adjacent to the chapel of Sainte Marguerite. This later chapel can be dated between its foundation in 1441 and the burial of Jean de Bordeaux in the chapel in 1446. The molding and pier base designs of these two chapels are related to the nave arcade and triforium, which were executed prior to the chapels in the 1410s and 1420s.

Like the Saint-Maclou piers, the nave arcade piers of Vernon are fashioned from clusters of shafts that rise from bases placed at eye level (Figs. 98 and 99).[25] Like the contemporary Parisian compound piers, however, these rounded shafts spring from trumpet bases and terminate with foliate capitals. The arcade shaft is reconfigured to form a flat-nosed fillet molding and springs from a fillet plinth and base identical to those of Saint-Maclou. The fillet base and molding provides a bold linear underscoring of the arcade profile, just as it does in the chapel-opening piers of Saint-Maclou. This appears to be the earliest example of a fillet base and molding and may have evolved from what might be termed inner-directed impulses, or new solutions arrived at through an aesthetic decision.[26] The tall and narrow fillet bases and plinths are clustered together and connected by a deep concave scoops at the core; they rise from a socle defined by concave scoops. The Vernon fillet base has a profile similar to the exterior and upper fillet bases used by Pierre Robin with a upper and lower torus roll (Fig. 100). The similarities between the Saint-Maclou and Vernon piers are particularly evident in cross section and their overall dimensions are strikingly close: 1.52 m × 1.66 m at Vernon and 1.51 m × 1.63 m at Saint-Maclou. Although Vernon still retains capitals on every shaft, these intrusions appear at odds with the fluid continuous moldings of the concave scoops that connect the shafts. The small, unconnected capital perched on the fillet molding seems particularly tentative and vestigial. It is not surprising then that the capital block remained uncarved on the molding of the chapel of Sainte Geneviève and then was eliminated altogether by 1441 in the adjacent chapel of Sainte Marguerite (Figs. 101 and 102).

In addition to the pier design, the nave triforium at Vernon belongs to the same family as Saint-Maclou although their relationship is not entirely clear.[27] Even though Pierre Robin used the cathedral of Rouen as the model for the triforium/clerestory elevation at Saint-Maclou, other flamboyant versions of the cathedral model may have existed, and may predate the one at Saint-Maclou. The Vernon blind triforium screen is composed of six pairs of lancets linked to the clerestory with continuous moldings and balanced by a horizontal balustrade identical to Saint-Maclou (Fig. 103). However, the flamboyant tracery of the lancets is closer to the cathedral's rayonnant formula and the Vernon master retains the traditional polygonal plinths, trumpet bases, and almond shafts rather than the fillet plinths, bases, and shafts of Pierre Robin. A small detail links this portion of Vernon directly to the early work of Saint-Maclou. In the first campaign of the choir of Saint-Maclou a modification was made in the lancet tracery between the straight bays on the south side and the hemicycle and the north side of the choir. Blind tracery of the lancet molding continues behind the formerets dividing the individual bays. This motif is dropped on the north side of the choir elevation and is not found in the transept or nave. On the other hand, the motif is used throughout the nave elevation at Vernon. Thus, Vernon may be contemporary or earlier that the first campaigns at Saint-Maclou.

The collegiate church of Notre-Dame, Le Grand Andely, situated midway between Vernon and Rouen on the Seine River more closely anticipates Pierre Robin's vocabulary of forms.[28] Work on the transept is undocumented but the forms of the piers and elevation are similar to Vernon and Saint-Maclou. A tall freestanding pier base on the east side of the south transept is composed of a combination of trumpet and fillet plinths, bases, and moldings (Figs. 100 and 104). To underscore and soften the profile of the arcade molding, the designer used a "triplet" similar in geometric composition to the "triplet" used in the arcade of Saint-Maclou but composed of trumpet bases rather than fillet bases. The socle designed around a combination of deep concave scoops and small flat faces places the pier in the immediate family of the Saint-Maclou pier type; the deep concave scoops of the pier core that connect the individual fillet and trumpet bases link the two monuments in a very direct way. The blind triforium grille and paired lancets defined by a combination of fillet and trumpet bases is similar to Vernon but the triple foliage bands (beneath the balustrade, above the truncated lancets, and between the clerestory and triforium) are characteristic in composition if not in style, to those of Saint-Maclou (Fig. 105).

Because of the lack of precise dates, it is difficult to know exactly the relationship among Vernon, Le Grand Andely, and Saint-Maclou. The collegiate churches employ a mélange of Robin's radical forms and the more conventional polygonal plinths, trumpet bases, and almond shafts. By 1450 in Rouen all hints of the latter were discarded as virtually every active workshop came under the influence of the new work at Saint-Maclou. It is also difficult to reconstruct the stylistic roots of Pierre Robin out of fragments of other monuments.

Robin's creative genius is expressed in his ability to integrate parts of the monument with overall design: the resonant diagonality, the complementary east and west ends, or planned and patterned diversity in tracery. It may have been only through the unique convergence of circumstances at Saint-Maclou that Robin was given the freedom to forge a highly original and creative vision of architecture.

Pierre Robin and His Rouen Contemporaries: Salvart and Berneval

To fully appreciate the unconventional character of Robin's architecture, it is useful to survey the work of his contemporaries (Table 4). Rouennais architecture from the first few decades of the fifteenth century seems to differ little from contemporary Parisian architecture as defined by the lower portions of the chapel of Saint-Yves built by Henry Bricet. When Pierre Robin arrived in Rouen, he must have visited the workshops of Rouen's most celebrated masters, Jenson (or Jehan) Salvart, master mason of the cathedral, and Alexandre de Berneval, master mason of the abbey of Saint-Ouen. Salvart had just finished work on the cathedral facade and in 1431 he had begun a project to enlarge the clerestory windows. The abbey of Saint-Ouen, which had served as a garrison for English soldiers and was passing through a period of notorious corruption, was in a drastically incomplete state. Although the brilliant rayonnant choir of Marc d'Argent had been completed in a relatively short period of time between 1318 and 1339, work on the transepts lingered and proceeded in a piecemeal fashion for the remaining century. The transepts display a great range of foreign influences and experimental motifs that reflect the transitional nature of fourteenth-century architecture. When Alexandre de Berneval took over the workshop sometime before 1422, the bankrupt abbey had little money to sustain major construction; he managed, however, to continue work on the south transept.

Salvart and Berneval had been master masons of their respective monuments both before and during the English occupation, and the change in administration in Rouen after the siege of 1419 had no effect on their employment.[29] Alexandre de Berneval was appointed to the position of master of the work for the king in the bailliage of Rouen, and Salvart was hired to construct a new royal palace for Henry V near the Seine even though he had recently supervised the construction of fortifications at Harfleur prior to the English invasion.[30] Working with Salvart as the *magister novi palacii Rothom*, were two English master carpenters, Thomas Matthew and William Reyner, the latter of whom was commissioned to bring sixty carpenters from England in March 1421.[31] In 1427 Salvart and Berneval were implicated in a plot to overthrow the English by assisting in the recapture of the king's palace and castle; neither suffered any consequences from their involvement.[32]

The cathedral west facade, new clerestory windows, the transepts of Saint-Ouen and south porch, as well as the portal of priory of Saint-Lo are virtually indistinguishable in their vocabulary of forms and constitute what has been called proto-flamboyant style.[33] Salvart's

Table 4   Positions held by Master Masons associated with the work at Saint-Maclou, Rouen

Jean II de Bayeux
   master mason of Saint-Maclou (1399)
   master of the works of the abbey of Saint-Ouen (1399, 1411)
   master of the works in the city of Rouen (1398)
   master of the works of masonery in the bailliage of Gisors (1390–95)
   master of the works of masonery of the Comte d'Eu and of Perche (1409)

Jenson Salvart
   master mason of Saint-Maclou ? (1414)
   master of the works of the cathedral of Rouen, 1398–1447
   master of the works in the city of Rouen (1447)
   ordonneur of the chapel of the Cordiers of Rouen (1402)
   Magistre novii palacii rothom (for Henry V)
   master of the works of the Lord of Tancarville

Pierre Robin
   master mason of Saint-Maclou, (1436–37)
   master of the works of the viscount of Paris, (1422)
   master of the works of the cathedral of Notre-Dame, Paris (1422)
   master mason of the king of Paris (1429–31)

Simon Le Noir
   master mason of Saint-Maclou, 1443–46
   master of the works for the king in the bailliage of Rouen (1436, 1438)

Guillaume Pontis
   mason, Saint-Maclou (1443–46)
   master of the works of the cathedral of Rouen, 1462–97

Jacques Le Roux
   master mason of Saint-Maclou, (1492)
   master of the works of the cathedral of Rouen, 1496–1510

Jean Le Boucher
   master mason of Saint-Maclou, (1508)
   master of the works for the king in the bailliage of Rouen (1490)

Roulland Le Roux
   master of the works of the cathedral of Rouen, 1508–26
   master of the works in the city of Rouen, (1510–26)

work on the facade is not easily separated from his predecessor's, Jean de Bayeux, and Alexandre de Berneval's work is confused with that of both his son's, Colin de Berneval, and his predecessor, Jean de Bayeux.

In 1398 Salvart replaced Jean de Bayeux as master mason of the cathedral of Rouen, a position he held until his death in 1447.[34] Despite the longevity of his career, the turbulent economic and political times in the city did not permit any major new construction. Between 1406 and 1421 he completed two of the great screens for the west facade, begun by Jean Perier in the 1370s and continued by Jean de Bayeux. In 1406 and 1407 he executed repairwork on the portal of Saint Jean and after 1431, he undertook the enlargement of the choir clerestory windows.

Salvart, like all the major masters of his day, held several positions simultaneously. At the cathedral he was retained on a yearly pension of 17 livres per year and paid 5 sous per working day in the summer and 4 sous 6 denier in the winter. References to Salvart from 1406 to 1409 describe him as a juror or participant in an expertise to verify work on the city gates and the Pont-de-Seine.[35] In a contract of 1402 between Robert Alorge (a bourgeois of Rouen), and Thomas Gaignet (a mason from Saint-Ouen), Salvart served as *ordonneur* (overseer) involved in the rebuilding of a chapel for the monastery of the Cordeliers.[36] From 1409 until 1412, he was occupied on the château of Tancarville, at first working with the master of the works of masonry of the city of Paris, Robert de Hellebucerne, and then qualifying as the sole master of the works of the lord of Tancarville.[37] As architect for Guillaume de Melen, the count of Tancarville, he received an annual pension of 25 livres per year plus 5 sous per working day. The Tancarville accounts provide abundant information as to the duties of the master masons. In the year 1410–11, Salvart spent forty-five days traveling; during this time he consulted with the count in Paris, hired masons, carpenters, plasterers, roofers, and various other workers in Rouen, and visited the quarries of Saint Leu d'Esserent to choose the "banc" or stone layer for the best stone to cut the machicolations for the tower. He was also engaged in drawing up the plans for the carpentry as well as the masonry.[38]

Salvart's career is of particular relevance to Saint-Maclou because he had entered into a contract with the treasurers for a considerable sum of money. The tabellionage records for March 1414 notarize a payment of three hundred ecu d'or by the treasurers of Saint-Maclou to Salvart and the master carpenter, Martin Le Roux, for unidentified work.[39] On the basis of the celebrity of Salvart and his 1414 contract, Beaurepaire suggested that Salvart may have been responsible for the design of Saint-Maclou.[40] Frothingham further suggested that the payment of three hundred écu d'or was for the specific project of building a model of the new church; this model has survived and is now found in the Musée des Beaux-Arts in Rouen (Figs. 5a and 5b).[41] The doors on the model are guarded by iron grilles that were replaced in 1541, thus suggesting that the model was executed before the mid-sixteenth century.[42] However, the elaborate exterior spur buttresses with sculptural niches set into the diagonal faces, are unlike those of Saint-Maclou but copy those of the nave of Saint-Ouen, which was under construction only in the second half of the fifteenth century. Although it cannot be stated with any certainty when the model was executed, it must date after the dedication of the church in 1521.

The cathedral facade is one of the most complex stylistic and chronological puzzles of the gothic period (Fig. 109). The facade underwent at least four major transformations between the twelfth and sixteenth century, and since the nineteenth century, it has been in a constant state of restoration. The result is a chaotic display of niches, canopies, gables, tracery, screens, and sculpture spanning four centuries. However, the primary cosmetic work in the fourteenth century involved an appliqué of seven multitiered tracery screens stretched between the four small thirteenth-century turrets. Salvart's contribution included the completion of the last two screens based on the general formula established by Jean Perier in the 1370s.[43] At Rouen, Perier combined repetitive rectilinear paneling popular in England with the elegant niches, gables, and tracery found on the south transept of the cathedral of Rouen, the Portail de la Calende, completed around 1300. The result was a complex and unconventional facade unlike anything in France. Although Camille Enlart connected Perier's work to English facade design, especially to Wells and Salisbury, and identified it as the first major example of English Perpendicular architecture on the continent, the paneling owes more to the problematic design of the thirteenth-century facade, which necessitated the use of screens, than the desire of Perier to use English models.[44] Scholars generally agree that Salvart completed the two middle panels above the portal of Saint Jean. The same vocabulary of forms, including fragile almond shafts, trumpet bases, and capitals repeat the vocabulary of Jean Perier and Jean de Bayeux; however, the tracery of the gables combines geometric and flamboyant tracery absent in the work of Perier, and beginning to appear in the work of Bayeux.

In 1430 Salvart was contracted by the cathedral canons to enlarge the choir windows. The new windows of the choir straight bays reproduced the rayonnant forms of the nave clerestory that had been rebuilt one hundred years earlier. The hemicycle clerestory windows, however, illustrate a very restrained form of double-curved tracery. The triple lancets are surmounted by two large *mouchettes* and a fat *soufflet* at the apex (Fig. 111). Geometric cusping persists and mingles with double-curved forms. The lancets are defined by thin round shafts, with capitals and trumpet bases. Thus, in 1430, gothic architecture in Rouen was following a conservative and unimaginative path employing exceedingly refined and uninspired articulation.

The most celebrated master in Rouen at the time of Robin's arrival was Alexandre de Berneval. His fame is attested to by his burial in the choir of the abbey of Saint-Ouen marked by a tomb slab with his portrait and an epitaph (Fig. 137) reading: "Here lies Master Alexandre de Berneval, master of the works of masonry of the king our sire, in the bailliage of Rouen, and of this church who died 1440 the 5th day of January, pray to God for his soul."[45] He is shown in a robe holding a compass and tracing out the south transept rose window, which is generally attributed to him. In 1409 Alexandre de Berneval first appears as a simple mason in Rouen; by 1413, however, he enters into a contract with Estaud d'Estouteville, abbot of Fécamp, to construct an unidentified monument for the abbey. He was sent to Newcastle-on-the-Tyne in England to purchase alabaster for this project.[46] Several years later, in 1420, he was again called to Fécamp to execute a masonry tabernacle to be placed in the choir to display the relic known as the Pas de l'Ange or Pas au Pélerin.[47] According to legend, the relic was an impression, preserved in sandstone, of the footstep of an angel, who was present at the dedication of the new church. The tabernacle, standing at present in the south transept of the abbey, provides the earliest extant example of Alexandre de Berneval's work (Figs. 117 and 118).

In 1417, Alexandre was master of the works of masonry in the baillage of Rouen; in 1419, soon after the capitulation of the city to the English, he was contracted by Henry V to work with Salvart in the construction of a new palace. In 1431, in a report of the English sergeant-at-arms, he is referred to as "master of the works of masonry and general master of the works of our Lord the Regent of France, the duke of Bedford for the realm of France."[48] By 1422 he is master mason of the abbey of Saint-Ouen, although it is not clear what work is being executed. During the English occupation, the abbey was used as an English garrison, and owing to the complete lack of discipline within the monastery, the archbishop of Rouen, Hugues d'Orgues, condemned and imprisoned the abbot. Some work must have been carried out on the crossing tower due to structural problems that were revealed in a 1441 expertise but it is possible that the only major work carried out during this period involved the completion of the south transept chapels and rose window.[49]

Both the Pas de l'Ange tabernacle and the south transept rose have all the same characteristics of the work by Jenson Salvart: combinations of geometric and double-curved tracery, and the same basic vocabulary of thin almond or round shafts and minuscule capitals. However, because of Alexandre de Berneval's documented trip to Northumberland, scholars have also attributed two transept chapel windows to him (Fig. 123). Both are examples of pure rectilinear window tracery using supermullions and quinquepartite cusping typical of English Perpendicular tracery. In addition, the inner south transept wall of Saint-Ouen, possibly attributable to Alexandre, is copied from the same wall of the cathedral of Rouen, but has been transformed by a grid of Perpendicular paneling (Fig. 122).

Thus, Rouennais architecture of the first half of the fifteenth century, as practiced by its most famous architects, was in no sense a harbinger for the forms introduced by Pierre Robin. A systemic overrefinement of shafts, bases, and capitals, and an imprecise but experimental use of double-curved forms mixed with geometric shapes was frequently made to conform to organization formats of rectangular grids. In addition, both the cathedral and abbey architecture provide evidence for the direct influence of English Perpendicular vocabulary in Rouen.

Pierre Robin and the Master Masons of Saint-Maclou

Pierre Robin's drawings, carefully guarded in the lodge of the *petit aître* served to inspire and define the careers of the master masons who followed him at Saint-Maclou. Of the seven masters who directed the Saint-Maclou workshop after Robin's departure, five (Oudin de Mantes, Simon Le Noir, Jehan Chauvin, Jean Le Boucher, and Pierre Grégoire) are known to us only through documentation while two (Ambroise Harel and Jacques Le Roux) were instrumental in introducing Robin's ideas into mainstream architecture of the city in the second half of the fifteenth century. In addition, Guillaume Pontis, recorded as an ordinary mason in the Saint-Maclou building accounts of 1444, was master mason of the cathedral between 1462 and 1498 and, along with Roulland Le Roux, the nephew of Jacques Le Roux, elaborated upon Robin's basic articulation and design systems, creating the rich, decorative, and opulent masonry characteristic of the last phase of flamboyant architecture in Rouen. Robin's vocabulary of forms was disseminated into local architectural tradition very directly by masters who had pondered the complex geometries of the architectural drawings and instructed the execution of templates. The moldings, bases, and traceries of the lower portions of the Butter Tower or the Palais de Justice appear to have been cut from the same templates used at Saint-Maclou.

It is also clear that many masters who did not have privileged access to the drawings, could only marvel at the wondrous complexities and elegance of Robin's work. Without the internal cohesion provided by Robin's elegant linear geometry, their imitations based on visual observation were often awkward, bizarre, or misinterpreted tributes to the original model. This is especially true for late gothic architecture outside of Rouen in upper Normandy. The overlay of the brittle linear fillet moldings, shafts, and bases on indigenous cylindrical piers in the nave of Saint-Germain, Argentan or Notre-Dame, Alençon, provide an uneasy combination of styles (Figs. 127 and 128). The syncopated quality of piers with "fillet fan" bases defy any rational geometric coherence.

In 1437 Robin left the Saint-Maclou workshop in the hands of Oudin de Mantes. Oudin's natal region of the Vexin fostered the style that came to fruition in Rouen, but nothing is known about his brief tenure at Saint-Maclou. By the next decade, the workshop was under the direction of Robin's companion, Simon Le Noir. Simon worked at Saint-Yves in Paris along with Robin, but his reputation was to be made in Rouen. In the same year he appears in the 1436–37 building accounts of Saint-Maclou as a mason earning 4 sous 2 denier per day, he was also appointed master of the works of the masonry for the king in the bailliage of Rouen, a position that he held until 1448.[50] As with Oudin, no work survives that can be attributed to Simon, but an outline of his career indicates that he held several positions at the same time and normally worked only one day per week at Saint-Maclou between 1443 and 1446.[51]

A clearer picture of the role that Saint-Maclou played in defining Rouennais late gothic can be surmised from the life and work of Ambroise Harel, Guillaume Pontis, Jacques Le Roux, and Roulland Le Roux. Although Harel never attained the celebrity of his contemporaries he directed the Saint-Maclou workshop from 1467 until 1480. During this time the nave, west facade, and western porch were completed and the nave vaulted.[52] An entry in the cathedral chapter deliberations of 1467 refers to him as "Ambroise de Saint-Maclou." In this year he participated in an expertise to evaluate the structure of the tour Saint Romain.[53] More important, however, Harel supervised the completion of the parish church of Saint-Vincent, a project of equal size and sophistication to that of Saint-Maclou. Between 1468 and 1480, Harel is referred to in the accounts of Saint-Vincent as "maître machon de l'oeuvre Saint Maclou," and is paid a pension of 6 livres per year.[54] Unfortunately, Saint-Vincent was a victim of the 1944 bombing of Rouen, but Pugin's drawings of the porch and prewar photographs provide visual records of his work (Figs. 125 and 126). The nave, transept, chapel of Saint Nicolas, and northern portal, of Saint-Vincent were constructed between 1458 and 1471 under Harel's direction. In 1471 when the crossing piers of the transept were being placed he was responsible for "gecter les moules sur les deux premières pierres."[55] Even though there are some similarities in vocabulary, the results were emphatically different. The fillet base was used in the main arcade of the nave, but the short two-story elevation is more typical of parish church design in Rouen, before the construction of Saint-Maclou. Only the choir, which was constructed much later (between 1511 and 1530), bears some resemblance to the tall narrow proportions and three-story elevation of Saint-Maclou. The tall cylindrical columns, however, suggest that the direct model was the choir of the cathedral of Rouen.

Although Saint-Vincent was begun in 1458, after the completion of the choir of Saint-Maclou, scholars have incorrectly insisted upon its influence on the work at Saint-Maclou exercised through Harel.[56] The parish of Saint-Vincent had obtained the privilege of the salt tax in a letter from Charles VI dated 4 July 1409 on the occasion of restoration work, but like most of the parish churches, did not have sufficient funds or incentive to rebuild until after the recapitulation of Rouen in 1449.[57] Work was begun in the nave and completed by 1471, including the chapel of Saint Nicolas and the portal on the north side toward the cemetery and presbytery. The accounts from this period identify two brother masons, Regnaud and Gillet Faucon working with their valet, Massinat. During this period, expenses accrued for "roseau" to cover the mason's lodge, vaults, and new masonry; in 1458, expenses for carpentry in the side aisles; in 1459, purchase of stone for "arcs" and an expense of 76 sous 6 denier for "bors d'illande" for making templates; in 1462, wood purchased to cover the tower; in 1463, reconstruction of the *jubé* by Jean Beauvoisine; and in 1468, work on construction of the chapel of Saint Nicolas.

In 1469, a second right to the salt tax was obtained from Louis XI and renewed for one year, yielding an income of 350 livres (nearly two-thirds of the yearly income during construction for Saint-Maclou). A new contract was made by the treasurers with the Faucon brothers and Ambroise Harel. Harel drew up the plan and executed the templates for the first two stones of the transept. Throughout the accounts of 1475, he is acting as "directeur ou surveillant des travaux"; in 1475 he receives a pension of 1 ecu d'or and was paid 32 sous 6 denier in 1479 and 1480 for overseeing the work for which he is given a robe by the treasurers indicating a position of distinction.

On 5 September 1480, the first stone of the west portal was placed and Harel was employed for one and a half days. Harel's distinguished position suggests that he was the author of the elegant western porch at Saint-Vincent (Fig. 125). The plan analysis proves that the porch of Saint-Maclou is intimately linked to the overall design by forming a geometric and spatial complement to the eastern end; therefore it must have been designed by Pierre Robin in the 1430s. Although some of the superficial flourishes of the upper elevation of Saint-Maclou may have been embellishments added by Harel, he was following the drawings of his eminent predecessor. Thus, the porch of Saint-Vincent is derived from Saint-Maclou and Harel, who must have been privy to the drawings, used the same crisp polygonality, elegant proportions, and streamlined vocabulary (fillet plinths, bases, and continuous moldings, geometric disc keystone, and simple quadripartite vault) as the basis for his design at Saint-Vincent. The additive quality of Harel's pentagonal porch is revealed in its abrupt projection from the western facade wall.

The greatest impact of Pierre Robin's influence, however, is found in the work of the cathedral master masons, Guillaume Pontis (master mason of the cathedral from 1462 to

1497), Jacques Le Roux (master mason of the cathedral from 1497 to 1508) and Roulland Le Roux (master mason of the cathedral from 1508 to 1527). In the 1444 account of Saint-Maclou the name of Guillaume Pontis appears, working as a simple mason between March 1444 and April 1444. Eighteen years later, he is appointed as master mason of the cathedral, and through his innumerable projects at the cathedral, Robin's unique vocabulary of forms becomes permanently infused into local building style. During his thirty-four years as master mason of the cathedral he accomplished considerable work despite the perpetual contention with the chapter, who exercised tight control over funds, the size of the workshop, and the designs for projects.[58] During this time he completed the crown of the tour Saint-Romain (Fig. 115), the library on the west side of the cour des Libraires before the north transept, the celebrated stone staircase within the north transept that gave access to the library (Fig. 113), the stone *clôture* in the choir and before the vestry (Fig. 114), and the *avant-portail* or gate before the cour des Libraires facing the rue Saint Romain (Fig. 112). All but the choir *clôture* are extant. He was not to see the completion of his most-celebrated work, the tour de Beurre or Butter Tower. Begun in 1487, the upper termination was finished by his successor Jacques Le Roux. Pontis's earliest work at the cathedral involved the termination of the tour Saint Romain (Fig. 116).[59] He made "les gests, traiz, moules et mesures" for the tower, but at the request of the chapter, which was under financial stress, he minimized the amount of decoration and was permitted a workshop of only two masons. The chapter had opted for the less costly termination of a terrace; after the insistence of Pontis, however, the present pavilion plan was adopted and completed by 1470.[60]

Pontis incorporated the fillet bases and continuous moldings, the lozenged balustrade, and diagonally set buttresses, all borrowed from the work at Saint-Maclou. He harmonized the articulation with the existing cathedral facade using tall double-tiered lancets under triangular gables and sculpture niches in the pinnacle buttresses. The syncopated rhythm of the lower balustrade is not present in either Saint-Maclou or the earlier cathedral facade. This same vocabulary is the building block for his other projects; because, however, these projects tend to be additions to an existing whole, it is difficult to get a sense of the internal coherency of design that distinguishes the plan, elevation, and pier forms of Saint-Maclou. Rather, the influence is limited to surface articulation that becomes increasingly dense and refined. Pontis's screen before the southern radiating chapel provides perhaps the closest surviving parallel to Robin's destroyed choir screen and *jubé*.

With the design of the Butter Tower, Pontis had more of an opportunity to exercise his knowledge of the design schemes of Robin. As early as 1479, the cathedral chapter had solicited aid from Pope Sixtus IV in the form of indulgences for the dioceses of Rouen and Evreux for an exemption during Lent for the consumption of butter and milk.[61] Through the successful intervention of Cardinal d'Estouteville in Rouen, the papal bull was obtained in 1484. For two years debates over the location of the tower and how it was to accommodate the parish of Saint-Etienne situated near the entrance of the cathedral slowed initial progress of the construction. The plans of Pontis were finally adopted and the tower rose opposite the tour Saint Romain on the south side of the church. The first two bays of the nave on the south side of the cathedral would provide the access into the parish church, which would occupy the lower level of the tower.

The later work of Pontis, although based on the same forms used as Saint-Maclou, became increasingly complex and refined in detailed. The gateway to the cour des Libraires replaces the traditional triangular gable preferred by Robin with the double-curved gable, and endlessly multiplies the lancets, moldings, fillets; the portal jambs are fragmented into tiny fillet bases too numerous to reflect their supporting function clearly (Fig. 112). The Butter Tower, the most lavish of all of Pontis's constructions, uses double-curved nodding ogee crowns above the numerous sculptural niches—a nonstructural formula inconsistent with Robin's canonical tastes.

The tendency toward dense lush decoration and overrefinement, evident in the rayonnant-based architecture of proto-flamboyant in Rouen, also contributed to the transformation of the more "classic" vocabulary of Pierre Robin in architecture during the second half of the fifteenth century. The climax of these tendencies is expressed in the work of Jacques and Roulland Le Roux. Jacques Le Roux may have been master mason of Saint-Maclou from 1480 until 1494. By 1496 he had signed a contract with the abbot of Fécamp to construct the Virgin Chapel at La Trinité. He was also occupied between 1496 and 1507 with the completion of the Butter Tower. Along with Roulland, he submitted plans for the construction of a new cathedral portal that went on display in the city hall in 1508, a few months before he died (Fig. 109).[62] Roulland became master mason of the cathedral after the death of his uncle, completed the center portal of the cathedral, restored the crossing tower, continued work on the Palais de Justice, and designed and constructed the first Renaissance building in Rouen across from the *parvis* of the cathedral, the Bureau des Finances in 1510.

While vestiges of Pierre Robin's vocabulary are still evident, the relationship between articulation as a expression of canonical rules and an expression of structure has changed. The Le Roux portal is based on the west facade of Saint-Maclou (and also on its own north transept) but the stylistic exuberance inherent in the sophisticated craft of masonry, once held in check by the discipline of older models, is abandoned as sculptural virtuosity is flaunted at the expense of visual clarity. Once articulation ceased to function as an expression of structure, the basis for gothic as a style was threatened. Three general observations can be made concerning this last phase of flamboyant in Rouen.

Although Jacques, Roulland, and their contemporary at Saint-Maclou, Pierre Grégoire, used Robin's vocabulary—the fillet base, plinth, continuous molding, lozenged balustrade—they placed greater priority on decoration at the expense of coherent system of articulation. The willful assertion of the autonomous architect is suggested in the chapter deliberations of 6 July 1512. Roulland Le Roux is criticized by the dean of the chapter for his work on the upper parts of his west facade portal. He states that the time and expense to carve sculpture with such meticulous perfection placed too far from the viewer's eye to be appreciated or noticed could not be justified. Although the canons were concerned primarily with the time and money it took to carve the upper portions of the portal, they were equally critical of his style. They were aware that the overrefinement of stone was confusing and disguised the structure.[63] The virtuosity achieved in the technique of stonecutting may have been perfectly suitable for small-scale objects but was inappropriate for monumental architecture.

Architects of this period also seemed to have a different perception of themselves in relation to the use of older models. Deville points out that Roulland had surreptitiously begun to increase the height of the lantern tower after the fire of 1514 by adding another level without authorization from the cathedral chapter. After nine feet had been added, the canons called him before the chapter and asked for an explanation, to which he replied "ad sumptuositatem et decorem ecclesie" and then placed a self-portrait of himself in the niche of the corner pier.[64] Unlike Robin, who was acutely aware of traditions, especially of thirteenth-century models, Le Roux made no attempt to harmonize his new work with the lower levels of the thirteenth-century tower. The point of reference for this new generation of architects was not the past but the current work of foreign masons working for the archbishop of Rouen, Georges D'Amboise, at his new chateau at Gaillon. Their Renaissance vocabulary gradually began to replace the gothic structural articulation and putti. A new relationship of decoration and structure appears on Le Roux's central portal jambs and is given full expression in his design of the Bureau des Finance.

Conclusions: The Legacy of Pierre Robin

As we become chronologically removed from the 1430s and the inception of Saint-Maclou and direct links to the workshop, tracing motifs becomes meaningless and unsatisfying. Although the search for borrowed motifs illustrates that Saint-Maclou was one of the most stylistically emulated models for master masons, a conveyor of urban taste and sophistication, and an exemplar of "Parisian" modernity, the reflections of fillet moldings and diagonally set buttresses contribute little to our understanding of the unique histories of individual buildings. The real frustration in seeking a constellation of monuments that provide insights into Pierre Robin as a draftsman, designer, and master mason, is the complete absence of examples that would confirm and examine the most brilliant aspect of his talent: his ability to coordinate and integrate all aspects of gothic design around an all-embracing, comprehensive, and fluid geometry.

Outside of Rouen, echoes of Saint-Maclou are present in fragments of new constructions. Polygonal porches appear at Notre-Dame at Louviers, Notre-Dame at Alençon (Fig. 129), La Trinité at Falaise, and Saint-Germain at Argentan. Axial piers provide unconventional choirs at Saint-Pierre at Caen (Fig. 130), Saint-Paul at Le Neuberg (Fig. 132), Saint-Germain at Argentan, and Notre-Dame at Caudebec-en-Caux (Fig. 131). Pierre Robin's vocabulary of forms articulates the choir chapels of Caudebec-en-Caux and the straight bay choir chapels of Evreux Cathedral. The resonant polygonality recurs in the transepts of Saint-Germain at Argentan; the conservative three-story elevation framed by continuous moldings is used in the new choir of Mont-Saint-Michel and Saint-Jacques at Dieppe; and the diagonally set spur buttresses articulate the exterior walls of Evreux Cathedral choir and axial chapel, Mont-Saint-Michel choir, and Notre-Dame at Caudebec-en-Caux.

However, we are struck by the rare convergence of circumstances at Saint-Maclou and the uniqueness of the opportunity afforded the master mason. Only a handful of gothic monuments embody the unaltered vision of a single master mason. This task demanded control over every aspect of design and tapped the limits of the creative imagination of the architect, drawing on his full range of skill and knowledge of the craft of masonry. Late gothic architecture is known to us primarily through fragments of buildings: towers, chapels, facades, or choir screens.

A situation was created at Saint-Maclou that was rarely duplicated. Opportunity to give shape to a single vision was not enough. Because of the lengthy construction period, continuity had to be maintained by factors perhaps unique to the late gothic period: the use of the original drawings and a corporate patron who, over successive generations, insisted on the adherence to these drawings. Finally, one needed an architect that was up to the task. Pierre Robin provided us with a complete and consummate expression of the late gothic craft of masonry.

6

The Craftsmen

*Flamboyant Architecture as an Expression
of Cultural Values*

The earliest description of late gothic architecture in Rouen is found in the travel diary of
Don Antonio de Beatis who accompanied the cardinal of Aragon on his episcopal visits
across Northern Europe in 1517–18.[1] Upon viewing Roulland Le Roux's newly completed
central portal at the cathedral, he comments not on the symbolic or evocative aspects of the
architecture, the unique portraits of the Rouennais archbishops in the niches, or the magnificent Tree of Jesse in the tympanum; rather, he notes the height of the towers, the quality of material, and the technical skill and craftsmanship of its masons.[2] Three hundred and
fifty years later John Ruskin is still fascinated by the dexterity and sophistication of the
craftsmen in fifteenth-century Rouen. On Guillaume Pontis's *avant portail* or gateway to the
cathedral's north transept executed in 1481, Ruskin writes,

> The exhibition of technical dexterity in work of this kind is often marvelous, the
> strangest possible shapes of sections being calculated to a hair's breadth, and the oc-
> currence of the under and emergent forms being rendered even in places where
> they are so slight that they can hardly be detected but by touch. It is impossible to
> render a very elaborate example of this kind intelligible, without some fifty mea-
> sured sections.[3]

Since the sixteenth century, Rouennais flamboyant architecture has consistently evoked
responses of awe, disbelief, or even repulsion and has dazzled the viewer with the apparent

transformation of stone into fine fabrics or tongues of flame. In the earliest nineteenth-century study of the architecture of Saint-Maclou, Charles Ouin-Lacroix compares the upper parts of the church with delicate threads of a silk web and ornaments of rich lace.

> Who does not contemplate with admiration this slender lantern, these daring piers, these thin vaults, these thousand curved moldings which ramble and interlace in all parts of the church like delicate threads of a silk web, these long galleries so delicately wrought which unrolls around its flank like an ornamental belt of the richest silk?[4]

For Ruskin, the mason's technical proficiency gave late gothic architecture its expressive power, where the "true workman paints with his chisel, does not carve the form of a thing, but cuts the effect of its form."[5] He was most eloquent on the transformational potency of the porch of Saint-Maclou.

> He (the gothic designer) makes the fire as like real fire as he can; and in the porch of St. Maclou at Rouen the sculptured flames burst out of the Hades gate, and flicker up, in writhing tongues of stone, through the interstices of the niches, as if the church itself were on fire. . . . For in representing the Hades fire, it is not the mere *form* of the flame which needs most to be told, but its unquenchableness, its Divine ordainment and limitation, and its inner fierceness, not physical and material, but in being the expression of the wrath of God.[6]

The artisanal values identified by Beatis, Ouin-Lacroix, and Ruskin have historically been defining characteristics of flamboyant style. Other scholars have provided a variety of explanations for the shift in focus in the late gothic period to craftsmanship and the celebration of physical properties of materials. Huizinga considered extravagant display, whether it be in theatrical performance, expression of religious piety, costume and fashion, manners and protocol, or architecture as "a reaction to the crushing misery of daily life."[7]

> The flamboyant style of architecture is the late postlude of an organist who cannot conclude. It decomposes all the formal elements endlessly; it interlaces all the details; there is not a line which has not its counterline. The form develops at the expense of the idea, the ornament grows rank, hiding all the lines and all the surfaces. A horror vacii reigns, always a symptom of artistic decline. . . . The further we get away from pure plastic art, the more this rankness of formal decorative motifs is accentuated.[8]

More recently, art historians who have escaped the subjective tyranny of stylistic analysis by contextualizing style, have associated the new priority given to the craft with a historical evolution of technology: the increasing importance of the drawing, the specialization of labor within the workshop, greater control of quality through statutes and guild regulations, and an assiduous application of geometry as the primary design tool.[9] Rolland Recht adds that "the absence of pure theoretical preoccupation demonstrates that (late gothic) architecture rests profoundly on the artisanal craft."[10]

The fluorescent character of flamboyant architecture has also been connected to the improved economic fortunes of France following the Hundred Years' War. Indeed, the commercial prosperity in Rouen, due in large part to the expansion of trade and growth in the cloth industry, underwrote the rapid expansion of the building industry during the period from 1450 to 1520. Michel Mollat's magisterial study of fifteenth-century maritime commerce in Normandy declared that the city of Rouen had become "a vast workshop" where "ornamental exuberance and flamboyant affectation in architecture expressed the opulence of the bourgeoisie."[11] The link between the expression of artisanal values in architecture and economic prosperity of the merchant class was suggested by Dieter Kimpel, who illustrated that as early as the thirteenth century, advances in efficiency in production and an entrepreneurial spirit of the bourgeoisie contributed to the prefabrication and increased planning that made construction of the high gothic cathedrals possible.[12]

An exploration of the cultural forces that contributed to the display of artisanal values in late gothic architecture is particularly relevant to a discussion of Saint-Maclou. First, there is reason to believe that the professional identities of the masters and masons in Rouen were linked specifically to the architecture of Saint-Maclou, which could be construed as their corporate "masterpiece." Second, both the cloth industry represented by the patrons and the building industry represented by the masters and masons were primary constituents of the parish and had professional ties to Saint-Maclou. The social distinction between patron / cloth merchant / city counselor and master mason / entrepreneur was not so clearly defined as it was in the thirteenth century, suggesting that both groups shared cultural values that served to reinforce taste, style, and production method.

The building industry and the parish. In his 1610 history, *Antiquités de la ville de Rouen*, Taillepied reported that the masons of Rouen had their confraternity dedicated to Saint Simon Saint Jude in the church of Saint-Maclou.[13] The exact date of the foundation of the confraternity of masons at Saint-Maclou is not documented but a feast day to their patron saints was included in a contract made between the cathedral masons and chapter around 1445.[14] More important, a chapel dedicated to Saint Simon Saint Jude is mentioned in the earliest fabric accounts. In 1443–46, 30 sous were paid for the burial of a body in the chapel of Saint Jude and a chapel with the dual dedication to Saint Simon Saint Jude existed in 1489 when the wife of Pierre Dufour paid for the pavement in front of the chapel.[15]

According to the records published by Beaurepaire, Rouennais masons lived primarily in the eastern parishes of the city including Saint-Nicaise and Saint-Vivien, but were concentrated in the parish of Saint-Maclou. Some of the most important late gothic master masons including Jean de Bayeux, Geoffroy Richer, Jacques Le Roux, Pierre Le Signerre, Girard Le Vanier, Jean Trouve, Robert Trouvey, Simon Vitecoq, and Pierre de Lorme, owned property or lived near the church.[16] In addition, Geoffroy Richier, master mason of the cathedral of Rouen between 1451 and 1452, and the wife of Simon Vitecoq, master mason and *imagier* at Saint-Maclou and master mason of the cathedral from 1524, were both granted the privilege of being buried in the church of Saint-Maclou.[17] The question is then raised, were the professional identities of the masters and masons somehow expressed in the architecture of Saint-Maclou? The high degree of regulation of the craft, indicated by statutes, contracts, and competitions, continually defined what was valued and self-selected what was culturally important. Therefore, specific aspects of material, form, and design expressed or even elevated the social and professional status of these craftsmen.

The cloth industry and the parish. The second social group with greatest representation in the parish of Saint-Maclou was the cloth makers. The parish was bordered by the Aubette and Robec Rivers and the seven mills used for dyeing ringed the streets of the parish including the Grand Moulin, located directly in front of the church and attached to the bridge that led to the cathedral and archbishop's palace. The various artisans belonging to the cloth industry including the fullers, weavers, dyers, and so forth, established their confraternities in the poor parishes adjacent to Saint-Maclou, but the master *drapiers* and apprentices paid their fees to Saint-Maclou.[18]

Thus the entire social spectrum of two key Rouennais industries, the building and cloth industries, were concentrated within the parish and had professional affinities with the parish church. The church of Saint-Maclou was directly linked to the professional status of the cloth merchants and master *drapiers* as well as the lowest fullers, weavers, and dyers of the cloth industry on the one hand, and the master masons / architects, stonemasons, and laborers of the building industry on the other. Chapters 4 and 5 have discussed the form and meaning of Saint-Maclou from the perspective of the patrons, the Dufour and allied families, and from the perspective of the master mason, Pierre Robin. Equally important are the shared social and cultural values of the parish craftsmen in the cloth and building industry that governed aesthetic decisions in fashioning and financing church construction. An understanding of the unique relationship between the two groups—the cloth merchants and master *drapiers*, the Dufour and related families on the one hand and the master mason, Pierre Robin on the other—the agents of control exercised by one over the other, and the shared social and cultural values is essential for an explanation of the character of Saint-Maclou and for establishing criteria distinct from those of the thirteenth century.

The overlapping of class values between patron and architect is indicated by a variety of evidence. When Jean de Bayeux was elected by the city counselors of Rouen to oversee the building and repair of public construction in 1389, in addition to his title "maitre des ouvrages de maconnerie" and yearly pension of 10 livres, he was exempt from city taxes of the *guet*, *tutelle*, and *curatelle*, given a seat on the municipal council, and was permitted to wear a costume similar to that of the *échevins* or city counselors.[19] These were also privileges highly sought by the new merchant class in order to achieve new social standing for themselves.

The social boundaries between professions were perhaps more fluid than supposed. For instance, the son of Jenson Salvart, master mason of the cathedral, is identified as a *drapier* in a local account.[20] Although the entrepreneurial spirit and political savvy of the cloth merchants enabled them, unlike the master masons, to rise to positions of nobility and to func-tion as *parlementaires* by the end of the fifteenth century, the lower levels of cloth makers and masons shared similar incomes and social rank.[21] It was common for the master mason to own property in the city. During the English occupation of Rouen, the master mason of the cathedral, Jenson Salvart was granted the fiefs of Bourdeny and Saint-Aubin-la-Rivière and Cailly by Henry V as well as 275 sous of rent on several houses in Rouen.[22] Thus, the Dufours as master drapiers and merchants and Pierre Robin, Jenson Salvart, or Roulland Le Roux as specialized master masons can be considered as social equals who had risen to the highest ranks of their own respective industries. Although patrons exercised great control over the construction, a shared concern for a visible and public display of craftsmanship as an expression of newly acquired social status reinforced the underlying artisanal quality of Saint-Maclou.

If the preoccupation with artisanal values (that is, materials, display of skill, dexterity, or-nament and sophistication in technique), is a fundamental quality of late gothic architecture, then it can be assumed that the form, visual language, or "style" of flamboyant architecture is an expression of what is valued in society. Fundamental cognitive shifts that underlay chang-ing cultural values are influenced by a wide range of historical developments, including po-litical events, religious or philosophical trends, or technological inventions. To contextual-ize the stylistic developments of flamboyant architecture and to link ornament and artisanal display to forces other than Huizinga's generic "misery of life," Mollat's economic expan-sion and commercial prosperity, or Kimpel's technological evolution, it is necessary to focus on specific changes in methods and techniques of production and design and in the regula-tory relationship between patron and master and workshop. Although any number of changes in the cognitive makeup of the fifteenth-century master and patron could be identified, the emergence of individual expression within the arena of the architectural drawing and pro-ject competition and the recalibration of worktime—due primarily to the introduction of the mechanical clock—had a direct impact on form in late gothic architecture.

Individualism, the Architectural Drawing, and the Construction of Professional Status

Christopher Wilson has pointed out that loosening of the late medieval social order brought about "an explosion in cost, elaboration and variety" in dress as a way of asserting new social status. "Ostentation in dress was also a sign of the increased individualism which showed itself in religion as a preoccupation with the welfare of the individual soul."[23] The recognition of individual expression as a key factor in late gothic architecture has long been part of the debate. Casting a broad net that included all regional variations of French flam-boyant architecture, Roland Sanfaçon found an analogous development between the ex-pressive power and autonomy of individual decorative details and a preoccupation with liberty and personal expression.[24] For Sanfaçon, individualism resided within architectural form and its expressed deviation of established rules and conventions. Novel regional solutions contributed to the rich variety found in late gothic; decorative details became freewheeling and independent vignettes against a loosely organized architectural composition. More important, Sanfaçon situated this formal development within the larger artistic landscape of "flamboyant humanism" that included sculptors such as Claus Sluter and painters such as Jan van Eyck.

At the other end of the debate, Stephen Murray's more telescopic approach focused on individualism of specific master masons and their unique artistic identities expressed through form and approaches to geometry.[25] For him, the definition of individualism resided within specific artistic personalities and, as was the case with Pierre Robin, these individuals had tremendous abilities to redirect and influence architectural development over several generations. The refocusing on artisanal qualities of materials, craftsmanship, and visual and intellectual delight associated with late gothic is dependent on this new individual freedom.

The fundamental changes in attitude, however, that permitted new freedoms of expression and the social or cultural forces that served as the mechanism for these changes has yet to be examined. Although such profound social changes are dependent on numerous convergent factors, one specifically related to the master mason can be explored. Individuality was felt in the relaxation of class distinctions and the new social mobility experienced after the Hundred Years' War. Personal abilities, talents and skills of individuals, whether they be political, commercial, or artistic, became primary vehicles for the construction of new social and professional status. The wanton expression of individuality in gothic building had always remained in check by the rigid controls of the workshop traditions; the corporate nature of design, building, and the decision-making process; and the demands of structure and function. Yet from the first gothic buildings, the individuality of masters is readable in the details of molding profiles, pier designs, and geometric configurations. Due to increased specialization in the workshop and the competitive environment in which drawings were evaluated, and despite the increasing number of statutes and regulations that attempted to constrain imagination, the architectural drawing became the primary expression of professional status for the master mason.

An abundance of research in the last fifty years has demonstrated that the architectural drawing played an increasingly important role in the design and construction of late gothic buildings. Key studies by François Bucher, Hans Koepf, Peter Pause, Sergio Sanabria, and Michael T. Davis have discussed the various relationships of late gothic drawings to existing buildings or to the design and construction process.[26] It is possible to discern a shift in the functional role of the architectural drawing that may have contributed to a change in the character of architecture.

The use of architectural drawings at all stages of construction in fifteenth-century Rouen is well documented. The story of the flamboyant church of Saint-Maclou begins with the payment by the treasurers to Pierre Robin for a drawing on parchment of "l'église toute complecte." Although none of the drawings mentioned in any Rouen accounts have survived, two Rouennais drawings help to visualize the character of Pierre Robin's work. Two of the four extant French gothic drawings identified by Robert Branner may have a Rouennais provenance.[27] A drawing on parchment 1 m 91 and now in the cathedral treasury is most likely the study of a spire for the archbishop's chair constructed for Guillaume d'Estouteville by Philippot Viart and Laurent Adam d'Auxerre, master *huchiers* between 1457 and 1469 (Fig. 134).[28] A much smaller cropped drawing on parchment measuring 1 m 448 × 0 m 30, at present in the Cloisters, depicts a late gothic portal and has been identified by Branner as stylistically similar to a number of monuments, including Saint-Maclou (Fig. 135).[29] Precisely calculated relationships of verticals, horizontals, and arches are laid out with compass and straight edge and exquisitely embellished with ornamental detail at every opportunity.

Brush or silver point on parchment was far more receptive to flourishes of the hand or provocative complexities of geometrical constructions than the unforgiving insistence of limestone carved with chisel and hammer. When the drawing became the chief mediator between the idea and the execution, new liberties and freedoms were possible. Two pieces of evidence suggest that by the late fourteenth century, the architectural drawing rather than the monument itself was the primary expression of professional status and individual achievement.

An explicit shift in professional identity is indicated by changing representations of master masons in tomb monuments. Luc Mojon's study of Saint-Jean de Cerlier in Switzerland demonstrates that the early mason's tombs dating from 1110/20 are engraved with depictions of the mason's pick and square.[30] By the thirteenth century, the portrait of the mason is added along with representations of his tools, such as the well-known portrait of Hugh Libergier at Saint-Nicaise, Reims or William of Wermington at Crowland from the early fourteenth century. However, by the mid-fourteenth century in Rouen the emphasis shifts once again; the tomb portraits contain not just tools and portraits but also drawings, and the focus is on the activity of drawing. The anonymous master mason of the choir of Saint-Ouen, in Rouen from around 1340/50 and the double-portrait of Alexandre and Colin de Berneval from around 1440 illustrate Rouennais masons holding drafting tools and engaged in the act of tracing out an architectural detail (Fig. 136 and 137).[31] Their legacy is attached not to the monuments they constructed—illustrated a century earlier by Hugue Libergier holding a small model of a church—but by the drawings they executed. Their professional identity and sense of authorship is best captured by their display of drafting skill.

Another contemporary tomb epitaph from Normandy makes this association quite clear. Guillaume Le Tellier, the master mason of Notre-Dame at Caudebec-en-Caux, and the designer who imported many of the ideas of Pierre Robin to this part of Normandy, is remembered by a tomb plaque that included not a portrait but a distinct reminder of the mortality of his body (represented by a skeleton) and the immortality of his creative work (illustrated by a plan drawing) (Fig. 138).[32] The curled edges of the parchment suggest that Le Tellier's achievement was to be remembered by his designs on parchment as well as the portions of the church he completed.

Perhaps the most convincing evidence may be suggested by presenting a new solution to an old art historical problem. The idea that fifteenth-century architectural drawings are self-referential, independent, and representative of the most prestigious and highest achievements of the craft of masonry is best illustrated by a nonmason: the painter Jan van Eyck, a contemporary and kindred spirit to Pierre Robin. Panofsky's characterization of van Eyck's work, which "emphasized and glorified the materiality of the picture," and his description of van Eyck's architecture, which was created through "an imagination controlled and disciplined by geometry," underscores fifteenth-century artisanal values. These statements are equally applicable to Pierre Robin.[33]

The controversy surrounding the small painting of Saint Barbara in Antwerp over the state of completion of the work is resolved when the painting is considered within the context of architectural drawings, the construction of professional status, and competition (Fig. 139).[34] The small panel executed in brush point on a white ground illustrates Saint Barbara seated on a small foreground hill before an immense tower under construction. In the background, dozens of masons, carpenters, and laborers re-create the activity of a contemporary workshop. The emphasis on building activity suggests that van Eyck made the painting for a confraternity of masons, whose patron saint was Barbara. What has been disturbing to historians of painting is the grisaille treatment of the subject, which is unlike any other of van Eyck's paintings or even those of his contemporaries; the disproportionate size of the tower, which normally functions as an attribute to Saint Barbara; the inconsistencies in the representation of the architecture with other van Eyck paintings; and the presence of a signed and dated frame on a seemingly unfinished painting.[35] These anomalies are easily explained if we consider not only what is represented but how it is being represented.

Van Eyck creates, in the medium of paint, the illusion of an architectural drawing of a tower on parchment just as he creates the illusion of other media (such as the gem-encrusted metalwork of a goldsmith's reliquary in the Deëis of the Ghent altarpiece or the freestanding limestone sculpture placed in niches in the Thyssen Annunciation diptych or outer wings of the Dresden triptych). The goldsmith and sculptor are measured by the objects of their creation (their "masterpieces") just as the highest achievement or indicator of professional status of the master mason is measured by the architectural drawing and not by the constructed monument. Considering the lengthy duration and corporate nature of construction, the architect or master mason exercised complete control only in the drawing, and only the drawing is a representation of his individuality. Thus, van Eyck presents the masons not just with a representation of the activities associated with their craft but a visual equivalent of the highest achievement of their masters: the architectural drawing.

It is not a coincidence that the tower is the most common type of surviving architectural drawing. The tower attribute of van Eyck's Saint Barbara is comparable to the tower and spire drawings of the cathedral of Strasbourg by Hans Hammer before 1490; the Ulm tower drawings (project A and project B), attributed to Ulrich of Ensingen around 1399 and Moritz Ensingen in 1476; and the Saint Stephen's town in Vienna, attributed to Hans Puchspaum.[36] Van Eyck's medium of brush point on a white ground approximates the visual appearance of the architectural drawings of ink on parchment. Although dramatically different in scale, van Eyck's painting chooses a vertical format dominated by the octagonal tower under construction and raised to the third level. A peculiar perspective appears in both to indicate the space enclosure, especially in the lower levels of the Ulm porch and van Eyck's porch (Fig. 140).[37]

More important, van Eyck's tower is the only architectural depiction in his oeuvre that is designed consistently using a contemporary vocabulary of architectural forms. His painted versions of architecture always express a mixed and timeless version of various gothic and Romanesque styles.[38] The tower of the Antwerp panel, however, represents the most current and fashionable vocabulary of forms found in contemporary buildings and architectural drawings: tall, thin, rectilinear paneling covering buttresses and wall surfaces, screening, gables articulated with *soufflets* and *mouchettes* (not present in any other van Eyck depiction of architecture), combinations of ogees and gables with bells, gables surmounted by *fleuron* and crockets. Van Eyck captures the same style, vocabulary, and spirit of the contemporary professional architectural drawing.

The self-referential aspect of the craft and clear authorship of the drawing are made explicit in van Eyck's panel by his inclusion of the master mason, standing on a limestone block, wearing the robe of his status, and gesturing toward the tower, or the architectural drawing of the tower. To understand artistic intent one must make a methodological shift from concern with "what images mean," (that is, the tower as an attribute of Saint-Barbara, patron saint of masons), to "how images mean" (that is, van Eyck's reference through illusionistic imitation to status and achievement of the master mason).[39] The final irony common to van Eyck paintings is a visual play of authorship within a depiction of authorship: van Eyck signs and dates his frame. If competition and artistic rivalry were a key element in late gothic drawing, then van Eyck surpassed his competitors by the ultimate trompe l'oeil: his mastery of the materials and subject of craft to the point of illusion. If van Eyck was concerned only with iconography and historical description, he would have painted an illusionistic likeness of a limestone architectural tower; instead, he outdraws the draftsman.

A new sense of authorship associated with the drawing also contributes to its role as the primary conveyor of professional status. The fabric accounts of the cathedral of Rouen for 1430 record a contract made between the cathedral canons and the master mason Jenson Salvart on 29 May 1430 for the enlargement of the choir windows.[40] In addition to signing the written contract, Salvart places his signature on the parchment drawing of the proposed clerestory windows. From this period on, signatures of master masons become more frequent in Rouen documents.[41]

Throughout the fifteenth century, the show drawing, presentation drawing, or competition drawing—the most visually seductive of architectural drawings—was crucial in securing projects for master masons. It also became the primary point of intervention on the part of patrons to exercise their control over costs and design.

In his design and construction of the termination for the tour Saint Romain, Guillaume Pontis was required to submit drawings to the chapter for review and approval at virtually every stage of the project.[42] Although the chapter had authorized funds for the construction of the termination of the tour Saint Romain in 1468 and Pontis began making "les gests, traiz, moufles et mesures pour l'eglise" in preparation, the chapter was still undecided about the form of the termination. Originally the chapter had wanted a terrace and not a pavilion (as exists today). Going over Pontis's head, the chapter solicited an opinion from the city viscount, Guillaume Gombault, and the city architect, Guillaume Duval, who approved the work that Pontis had begun. It appears however, the chapter pressed for a termination of a terrace over the recommendation of the outside advisers and their architect. Perhaps in protest, Pontis became uncooperative and slowed the work pace. The chapter insisted that he work more diligently; more important, they demanded that he renounce the excessive ornament, which could not be seen from the ground anyway. Once again they consulted with "les bourgeois de la ville, échevins, ou personnes connues pour leurs goûts artistiques," and once again the recommendation was for a pavilion, the original plan of Pontis.[43] Although drawings are not specifically mentioned in the accounts, the conflict shows that chapters were increasingly willing to exercise authority over design as well as construction.

For the construction of the library staircase, on 27 April 1479, the chapter requested specifications from Pontis, which they approved. A few days later they asked for "un plan en règle" and it was also approved. In the course of the execution, however, Pontis made several changes and embellishments for which he was severely criticized, and the chapter demanded that he return to the original plan. Perhaps to impress upon their willful architect the need to control costs, or perhaps to punish him for his liberties, on 10 July the chapter reduced the number of workers.[44]

A new series of drawings was presented to the chapter for the construction of the tour de Beurre. On 6 October 1485 Pontis submitted a drawing on parchment of the tower that he proposed to construct. The chapter communicated this document to master experts for advice. The following December they requested from Pontis a *trect* or *giest* again for referral to other experts. Tension continued between Pontis and the chapter the following year. In September 1488, the master was called before the chapter and criticized for his lack of supervision of the workers; the result was the reduction of workers' salaries. This wrangling over design, worker productivity, and costs continued under his successor Jacques Le Roux.[45]

Jacques Le Roux was entrusted with the completion of the tour de Beurre.[46] Le Roux was required to submit two versions of the tower termination: one a terrace and one a spire to the canons who then consulted the experts of the city as to its "utility, magnificence, beauty and structure." Three years later in 1504, work had not yet begun and a third version was requested by the canons. Finally after another consultation with experts, the crown terminal was accepted.

The public debate and complexity of the decision-making process contributed to increasing importance being placed on the drawing. This is perhaps best illustrated by the fierce competition surrounding the construction of the western central portal of the cathedral. In 1506 Archbishop Georges d'Amboise sent Nicolas Biart and Guillaume Senault, two of his architects from the château at Gaillon, to inspect the collapsing western nave vaults and western rose. Plans for the reconstruction of the portal were submitted by Biart and Senault in addition to plans from the cathedral architects.[47] On 28 January 1508 the presentation drawings by Jacques Le Roux and his nephew Roulland Le Roux were put on display in the Hôtel de Ville and comments were invited from two other city architects, Jean de Boucher and Pierre Le Gallois.[48] Additional input was solicited from virtually everyone of importance in the city.

Although none of these drawings survive, it seems logical that the winning drawings needed to persuade, impress, and convince a wide audience. Roulland Le Roux's portal testifies to its winning visual appeal, although its visual complexity and delicate minutiae of sculpture, niches, fillets, and foliage were perhaps more impressive as a drawing than as a carved reality.

Thus, by the beginning of the sixteenth century the role of the architectural drawing evolved from a visual record that, along with the specifications, provided the patrons with a clear idea of what they were getting, to the primary basis on which commissions or projects were assigned and status was identified. The choice of a master mason for a project was no longer based solely on an individual's reputation, titles, and the prestige of his projects; the mason was now required to impress a vastly expanded public with his drafting skills.

Since the thirteenth century the architectural drawing played the role as an intermediary between conception and execution, between design and material. François Bucher's seminal study on gothic micro-architecture argued that the exchange of architectural vocabulary and forms across scale between cathedrals and abbeys and ivories and metalwork was possible by the use of drawings as a medium of communication.[49] The increased linearity and academic Scholasticism associated with rayonnant can also be linked to the role of the drawing in development of design. By the fifteenth century, however, new pressures were placed on the architect. The increased value of the drawing as an expression of professional identity and status and the demand for competitive distinction laid the ground for technical display of individual skill, exuberant artisanal dexterity, and in the end, visual seduction.

The Clock, Measured Time, and Productivity of Labor

Another major cognitive shift affecting the formation of cultural values in the fifteenth century was due in part to the appearance of the mechanical clock and the impact of measured time on the productivity of masons. The conflict between the cost of time and the value of invested time contributed to a new relationship between patron and mason and between mason and material.

Jacques Le Goff has pointed out that the regulation of time in the fourteenth and fifteenth centuries was a natural outgrowth of increased commercial activity.[50] Greater precision was needed in all facets of manufacturing and trade whether it be in standardization of weights and measure, increased precision in recordkeeping, or regulation of time. The building activity at Saint-Maclou was governed by the same bourgeoisie businessmen who demanded drawings that required precision in execution, who carefully controlled receipts and expenses by using fabric accounts recorded on paper, and who installed a clock in the church to keep track of time (and hence, "costs"). The precise form and impact of increased regulation of time on architecture and what this might have contributed to the artisanal quality of late gothic architecture has never been discussed. In addressing the general results of this cognitive shift, Le Goff suggests that "art's new function . . . was not to capture the eternal essence but rather to immortalize this ephemeral being of the individual in a particular space and time."[51]

The exact moment when the mechanical clock replaced the sundial and the water clock is not clear, but around 1300, with the invention of the escapement mechanism that permitted the exertion of a constant force on the gears, the passage of time could be divided into identical units. The earliest weight-driven clocks were far closer in mechanics to the geared astrolabes than the water or sun chronometers; hence early timekeeping was linked to the exhibition of patterns of movement of the universe.[52] The first monumental public clocks appeared in northern France around the mid-fourteenth century, such as the communal clock in Strasbourg of 1352 that included a moving calendar, astrolabe, and carillon.[53] Rouen's first communal clock was erected in 1389 upon the request of the city counselors. It was placed in a new tower constructed by Jean de Bayeux on the site of the old bell tower that was destroyed by Charles VI after the "Harelle" in 1382 (Fig. 141).[54] From the very first moment of its installation, the communal clock was used by the city to exercise greater control over the worktime of the masons employed in the construction of the belfry. This more precise regulation replaced the less rigorous structure provided by the bells of the cathedral.[55]

The first clock in Rouen, however, appears to have been installed in the cathedral sometime before 1372 when the cathedral accounts mention the presence of a clockmaker.[56] Clearer references are found in subsequent accounts of 1414–15 and 1431–32 when the chapter paid Raoul de Carville for adjusting the weights in the clock.[57] Considering the relative novelty and expense of clocks in the first few generations of its appearance, it seems significant that cathedral chapter fabric accounts record a portable clock being placed in the lodge of the masons on 14 November 1430 in order to "regulate their hours."[58]

Next to the cathedral, Saint-Maclou had the most active mason's workshop in the 1430s; it is thus not surprising that it also had the only parish clock.[59] Significant sums of money were used for the maintenance and repair of the clock throughout the fifteenth century. In 1436 Guillemin Ausoult was paid 70 livre tournois for lead for the counterweights and by 1445 a *gouverneur* was paid on a yearly basis to make frequent adjustments to the weights. The *appareilleur*, Friset Le Mestre, who was occupied with considerable construction during that year was paid an additional 40 sous "pour atrempé l'auloge." In 1479 a parish subscription including seventy-nine contributors underwrote the construction of a new clock that was finally installed in 1490. This was apparently an elaborate painted clock with expensive carpentry and a clock face. Although the clock was located in the north transept, the ropes for the weights were suspended from the lantern tower vault.[60]

Prior to this period, the workday of masons and other workers in the building industry was of flexible and varied duration, controlled by natural cycles of the rising and setting sun, the light of summer and winter, the ringing of bells for canonical offices, with frequent intrusions of feast days, celebrations, and religious activities. The concern over masons' productivity supplied the motivation for the installation of the clock and was addressed in an entry in the cathedral chapter deliberations of 1446, where the workers are called before the canons, reproached for their negligence, and instructed to apply themselves more earnestly in the future.[61] Not surprisingly, an undated contract between the canons and masons appears inserted into the deliberations at this time (Fig. 142). Salary, work conditions, quality of craftsmanship are not addressed; the sole subject of the two-page document focuses on the regulation of working hours based on the precise times provided by the city clock and supplemented by the bells of the daily offices.[62]

Clearly measured time became an increasingly valuable tool for the control of efficiency and costs in building. But how was this new tool perceived by the workers? Masons unfortunately did not leave written statements concerning their views about this new demand for increased productivity. It is difficult to imagine that rigorous regulation was greeted with little resistance; nonetheless, it appears that, perhaps due in part to a successful campaign of propaganda, time was equally valued by the community of masons.

There is an intriguing coincidence in the appearance of a new iconography in Rouen at this moment. In 1452 the city counselors of Rouen commissioned an illustrated translation of Aristotle's *Ethics, Politics,* and *Economics.* In addition to the intrinsic commercial interest of the texts for the patrons, the work was a translation provided eighty years earlier for Charles V by Nicole Oresme, a celebrated natural philosopher, adviser to the king, and dean of the cathedral chapter in Rouen.[63] The manuscript is accompanied by eleven miniatures depicting scenes of contemporary Rouennais urban life and a novel representation of the virtue of Temperance (Fig. 143). She appears centrally placed among other personifications of cardinal and theological virtues with a clock balanced on her head, and associated with other recent inventions, the windmill, eyeglasses, bit and bridle, and spurs.

The development of this iconography in Rouen stems from two sources. Because the mechanical clock evolved from the astrolabe and the chronometer rather than the sundial and water clock, it carried astrological and cosmic meaning. Oresme not only used the clock as a metaphor of the universe created by God; he associated the order brought about by the clock to the precision and measure of the architect. In his *De commensurabilitate vel incommensurabilitate motuum celi* (1350) he wrote: "For if someone should construct a material clock would he not make all the motions and wheels as nearly commensurable as possible? How much more ought we to think about the architect who it is said, has made all things in number, weight and measure."[64]

Commensurability, precision, and exquisite geometry were applied with rigorous precision by Pierre Robin to his design of Saint-Maclou. Shouldn't these qualities be reflected equally in the execution of work by masons through the control of time? The writings of Oresme along with other natural philosophers of the fourteenth century helped to bring the habit of quantification, known as the science of *calculationes* into the realm of late medieval thought. Quantification, measurement, orderliness, and self-reliance became the economic virtues that influenced the social habits of not only the merchants and city counselors, but artisans, masons, and architects.[65]

The clock had also developed as a moral symbol from the early fourteenth century. The clock in Henry Suso's *Horlogium Sapientiae* (late 1330s) was used as a devotional aid or kind of "spiritual alarm clock" and associated with the virtue of wisdom. In Jean Froissart's *Li Orloge amoureuse* (1360–60), the mechanical workings of the clock became metaphors for virtues of courtly love with the escapement mechanism equated to the virtues of measure, temperance, moderation, and self-control. Christine de Pisan in *L'Epître d'Othea*, a treatise on manners and morals for an aristocratic adolescent, used the clock as a symbol of the virtue of Temperance.[66] But the iconography developed in the fourteenth-century Parisian court was transformed by the Rouennais city counselors in 1452 when it was accompanied by the text of Aristotle's *Ethics*, and tied to a new technology that suited the commercial interests and burgher virtues of the merchant class.

The expanded meaning of the virtue of Temperance is made clear by an inscription attached to a similar depiction of Temperance. Emile Mâle identified another French manuscript, a historical compilation made for Jacques d'Armagnac, duke of Nemours around 1470, depicting Temperance with the same technological accouterments, including the clock. It is accompanied with the text: "He who is mindful of the clock is punctual in all his acts." Mâle points out the image was not derived from any known tradition or theological teaching but was the invention of "some wit from Rouen."[67] Although the image of Temperance and the clock evolved in the Parisian court of the fourteenth century, the association with commercial virtues was forged in Rouen in the mid-fifteenth century. The popularity of this theme in Rouen is attested to by its appearance in the cathedral stained-glass windows and again in the sculpture used by the archbishop for his chateau at Gaillon (Fig. 144). This association of the cardinal virtue of Temperance with the clock puts a positive spin on the new regulations creeping into workshop contracts. Indeed, Lynn White points out that "about 1450, the novel productive systems of Europe, based on natural power, mechanization, and labor saving invention, which have been the backbone of capitalism received the sanction of religious emotion and moral sensibility."[68]

The Late Gothic Dilemma: Economy vs. Efflorescence

It is accurate to claim that increased regulation had a direct affect on architectural expression of the late gothic period, but what form did it take and how was the conflict inherent in the elevation of time to a Christian virtue resolved? To the patron, control of time was a method of controlling costs; to the artisan, investment of time was a visible display of artisanal virtue. Hence a finial, embrasure, niche, or voussoir that was lovingly crafted, finely carved, and painstakingly executed, reflected a great investment of time and was of great professional pride and value to the masons. It was also time-consuming and expensive.

The dilemma of the value of invested artisanal time and the cost of time between masons and patrons is revealed on three separate occasions in the cathedral records. The canons called the master masons before the chapter and chastised them for taking too much time to execute their work. On 4 June 1469 Guillaume Pontis was reproached for his slowness in the execution of the termination of the tour Saint-Romain. The canons asked him to renounce the superfluous ornament and the care with which the stones were being cut because they would be placed beyond view in the upper levels of the tower.[69] The same criticism was lodged against his successor Jacques Le Roux in 1492 in his completion of the accompanying tour de Beurre. In order to further justify their argument, they added that the great finesse of his carving would only leave the stone more susceptible to weathering.[70] As we have already seen, the same accusations were made against Roulland Le Roux in 1512 by the chapter for his extremely fine sculpture of the upper parts of the central portal and facade. In all three cases, these warnings seem to have gone unheeded. Indeed, each architect continued in a highly elaborate style with detailed carving, and presumably time-consuming effort. At Saint-Maclou, however, the inclination to work less carefully in the upper portions, beyond sight, may explain why some of the upper pinnacles of the transept portals appear crudely fashioned when compared to lower-level counterparts.

Perhaps this is the great dilemma of late gothic architecture. On the one hand, there is a tremendous desire to display technical skill, artisanal achievement, and mastery all under the discipline of number, proportion, and order; on the other hand, there is a desire for efficiency and economy that required restraint and moderation. The formal tension evident in late gothic architecture can be in part attributed to the control or regulation of artisanal exuberance.

Late gothic documents are littered with efforts to resolve the conflict between conservation in costs and exuberance of style. The conflict was not just between patron and mason; in large part, it was an internal cultural dilemma: the fashion and taste of the patrons—rooted in the artisanal traditions of their own industries—indicate that they preferred the elaborate and highly crafted masonry of the master masons yet their business acumen demanded that they control costs. Likewise, the building industry since the thirteenth century had been evolving in ways that assured more efficient and economic structures. Greater reliance on drawings permitted advanced planning and more elaborate methods of prefabrication, increased specialization within the workshop assigned tasks to the most proficient and skillful workers, and guild statutes regulated all aspects of work to assure quality and productivity. Prefabrication is evident in all aspects of masonry production at Saint-Maclou. It is most obvious in the uniformity of stone course heights that define the outer and inner walls of the entire structure. However, in every bay of the lower wall of the nave and choir, two stones, clearly visible from the exterior, are significantly larger than the rest (Figs. 145 and 146). In each bay, these two blocks extend into the interior, bonding the inner and outer walls and forming the basin and baldachine for the piscina of each of the interior chapels. Because of the more elaborate carving required, these blocks could be assigned to the *appareilleur*, carved at any time, and inserted when work had reached that particular spot. The planned pattern paring discussed in Chapter 2 would be much easier to carry out. Roland Sanfaçon has observed that the pragmatic quality of flamboyant architecture is revealed in the technical logic of decorative motifs, which are concentrated on specific stones assigned to the specialists for carving.[71]

However, increased efficiency in mass production at Saint-Maclou did not necessarily mean increased economy. What might be gained economically from advanced planning is certainly lost in the high cost of complex design and heavily worked stone that required tremendous labor and long hours. The dilemma of economy and efflorescence is best demonstrated by Pierre Robin's pier design. It has been argued that the use of continuous moldings was an economic decision on the part of medieval masons, eliminating the disruptive foliate capital, the changes required in profile design above and below the capital, and the variations needed from bay to bay.[72] Indeed, the streamlined design of the pervasive continuous moldings used throughout the church, the restriction of all small base designs to one of five sizes, the use of planned pattern pairing to create identical mirrored piers on the north and south—all speak to greater efficiency in design. However, it would be impossible to argue that these were bargain-rate works. Their exquisite complexity required far more labor hours to execute than a cylindrical pier with a foliate capital. In a subtle flaunting of academic display, each pier is designed around a different geometry that reflects the size of the bay that it defines. No stone of any pier (irrespective of the north/south compliment) could be mass-produced; each depended on a separate drawing. Therefore, any economy gained through internal regulation such as advanced planning and specialization was lost in the artisanal display of sophisticated design and skillful carving.

External regulation was equally unsuccessful in controlling costs. The treasurers of Saint-Maclou and the chapter of the cathedral both exercised careful control over daily activities of masons' workshops, not only with careful recordkeeping in the form of fabric accounts, recording and regulating the exact amount of time worked by each mason, but also in a scrutiny of the quality of work done by the masons. Both sets of accounts have frequent references to the wages of masons being reduced because of their mistakes.[73] The contract between the chapter and the masons at the cathedral required that the masons return for work on Saturdays in order to correct their mistakes.[74] This regulation demonstrates as much a concern for costs as for quality and seems to be applied only when internal regulation of quality does not work. Although there are no surviving statutes for masons in Rouen in the fifteenth century, statutes for local roofers describe a monetary punishment for sloppy work.[75]

Patrons continued to demand more elaborate, more visually seductive, more highly crafted work, and more costly work at the same time that they pressured the masons to work more efficiently and economically. One resolution to the problem was turning to piecework as opposed to daywork, especially in clearly defined projects. Piecework becomes more common in the late fifteenth century in Rouen but an explanation for the change is not spelled out in the local documents.[76] It is significant that by the early sixteenth century at Saint-Maclou, all work done by the masons is on a piecework, per contract basis. Etienne Cauchée is paid 102 livres 2 sous for the construction of the tower staircase. This amount includes the payment for masons and materials to complete the project. Master mason Pierre Grégoire is paid for specific piers of the tower; between 1518 and 1519, he receives 205 livres by contract in increments for the carving of the elaborate *jubé* staircase (Figs. 147 and 148).[77] The complex sculptural carving of flowers, animals, geometric patterns, and foliage were not sacrificed for timely completion. The complexity of the staircase reveals that Grégoire's reputation as a craftsman was more important to him than the time he would save carving a less spectacular work.

It is intriguing to suspect that the reason for the rejection of late gothic architectural style in the second decade of the sixteenth century was more than just the increasing popularity of newly imported Italianate designs—ushered into Rouen by Cardinal Georges d'Amboise and his architect, Roulland Le Roux. Almost surely, tastes and fashion succumbed to pressures of the incompatibility of economic and artisanal forces.

Appendix

Departmental Archives, Seine-Maritime, Rouen, G6874 Fabric Account, 1436–1437

Receipts

Cest le conte de Colin le Roux Pierre le Coq Estiennot Dufour Guillaume de la Mare Colin le Febvre et Cardinot Coquin tresoriers de leglise par[rochi]al Sainct Maclou de Rouen pour ung an [com]menchant le p[re]mier jour du juillet mill iiii^c xxxvi et finissant a iceluy jour lan revolu iiii^c xxxvii des receptes et mises faictes en d[it] office de treso[rier] po[u]r le d[it] an

Cuilli a leuvre de leglise po[u]r le tiers aux malades

	141 l.	10 s.	5 d.

Cuilly aux reliques

Sainct Maclou	34 s.		
Sainct Cler	28 s.		
Sainct Leu	7 l.	5 s.	6 d.
Notre Dame	19 s.	1 d.	
Toussaints	62 s.		
Sainct Cler	16 s.		
Notre Dame	10 s.	10 d.	
Noel	55 s.		
1er janvier	12 s.		
Tiphaigne	13 s.		
Chandeleur	28 s.		
Pasques	21 l.	22 s.	
Notre Dame	13 s.	6 d.	
Rouvessons	8 s.		
Penthecoustes	12 s.	6 d.	
la Trinite	12 s.	6 d.	
le Sacrement	30 s.		
Sainct Jehan	10 s.		
le jo[u]r q[ui] le filx Barn[ev]ille chanta messe pour ice aux reliques	8 s.	7 d.	
	28 l.	18 s.	6 d.

Corps enterrer a eglise et les noms et les surnoms 98 l. 18 s.

Corps cy terres en gr[an]t et petit chimetiere et les noms et les surnoms 16 l. 6 s. 6 d.

Du meistier du drapperie et de boule[n]guerie 20 l. 12 s. 6 d.

Neufvaines	1 l.	12 s.	1 d.
Tressorieres	10 l.		
Rentes et louages	51 l.	10 s.	2 d.
Epousailles	3 l.	11 s.	2 d.
Cuelly devant leglise	12 l.	17 s.	3 d.
P[our] la biere	19 l.	11 s.	3 d.
Courtines chandeliers	14 l.	16 s.	6 d.

Plots pierre mortiez tombe et vieulx boit

25 l. 16 s. 6 d.

Regniement de Dieu 16 s. 8 d.

Dons a leglise veues et lays

Le ii^e jour de fevrier pour unes matines trouvees a leglise de Sainct Maclou de vendues a Robin Barlcheler clerc de la dite paroisse 12 s.

Le 1er jour de mars de Jehan Boissel pour maistre Jehan Boissel cure de Sainct Maclou de Rouen pour icelluy 4 l.

Le xxix^e jour de avril des freres de Sainct Leu baillie aux tressoriers de la dicte eglise pour laidier a paier une chambre ou les gens font leur neufvaines de mess Sainct Leu pour iceux

100 s.

113 l. 6 s. 3 d.

Sommes trouvees aux troncs de leglise 17 l. 15 s. 6 d.

578 l. 5 s. 7 d.

Expenses

Machons

7/1/1436	A Pierre Cossart pour trois jour et demi le jour 3 s. 9 d. et le demi jour 2 s. 3 d. pour icelluy 13 s. 6 d.
9/23	A Jehan le Large pour quatre jour le jour 3 s. 7 d. pour icelluy 18 s. 4 d.
1/2/1437	A Oudin de Mantes pour chinq jour le jour 5 s. pour icelluy 25 s.
1/2	A Alain le Boulenguier pour ching jour le jour 3 s. 9 d. 18 s. 9 d.
1/2	A Oudin de Mantes preste sur son annee commensant a la Chandeleur 1437 dont il doit a nous la somme de xv livres et la maison de la rue du Sa[inc]t P[ier]re sa demeure et doit son frere jouir avec luy pour prest a luy fait 100 s.

4/21   A Tassin du Porqueroult et Jehan Moreau pour avoir appareille 50 buiste pour chascun 12 d. pour iceux   50 s.

4/28   A maistre Symon le Noir machon pour 5 journee de sepmaine le jour 4 s. 2 d. pour ice   20 s. 5 d.

5/12   A Frisot le Maistre machon pour 4 jours et demi le jour 4 s. 2 d. et le demi jour 2 s. 6 d. pour ice   19 s. 2 d.

5/12   Le dit jour a maistre Pierres Robin par compte fait a luy de ses gaignes depuys le jour de lan jusques au xix^e jour de may et pour le p[ar]chemin ou leglise est gestee toute complecte et po[ur] le d[it] temps luy fu paie si c[om]me il app[er]t par sa quittanche   43 l. 10 s.

5/12   Le d[it] jo[ur] a Tassin du Porqueroult et a Jehan Moreau machons pour avoir appareille 70 buistes po[ur] chascun bui[s]te 12 d. pour iceux   70 s.

5/12   Le dit jour a Jehan Duval machon pour avoir appareille 32 buistes dont il fait 13 pour 12 et doit avoir pour chascun buit 12 d. pour iceluy   29 s. 6 d.

7/11   A Oudin de Mantes machon par [com]pte fait a luy de largent q[u]y il a eu par plusses fait sur la lon qui est fait a maison luy est qui dessus luy et son filx po[ur] ung an [com]me[n]chant le p[re]mier jour de mar iiij^c xxxvi par le pris et so[mm]e 65 T. avecques la maison de la rue   65 T.

Du fait lan devan est sur compt Il a richer 26 l. dont est a rabatre 100 s. qui sont [com]ptez au devant du jour duy et sy [comm]e il app[er]t par cest pappier esc[rip]t de la main de Mauchon et pour iceluy   21 l.

Caulx et Sablon

1437   A Mahiet le Houpeur pour 30 muye de caulx qui il doibt livrer dedens pasques 1437 ch[asc]un muy 35 s. sur ce a eu   8 l.T.

A Panche de Queret sablonier qui doibt livrer le muy de sablon 12 s. 6 d. sur ce a eu   13 l.T.

6/1   A Mahiet le Houppeur caulxnier pour 10 muys et demi de caux le muy 35 s. pour ice   18 l. 7 s. 6 d.

6/1   Le dit jour a Louis Bossencour et a Panche de Queret pour 10 muys et demi de sablon le muy 12 s. 6 d. pour ice   6 l. 11 s. 3 d.

Pierres

A Jehan de Porqueroult et son filx pour 25 tonneaulx de pier[r]e nomees buites le tonnel 12 s. 6 d. pour ice   14 l. 12 s. 6 d.

A Guillaume aux Demers et a ses compaignons p[ou]r amener la [dite] pierre p[ou]r ch[asc]un tonnel

2/10/1437   A Guillaume aux Demers et a ses compaignons p[ou]r 25 tonneaulx de buites ache[tee]s a Portgueroult et a son filx pour tonnel 18 d. pour ice   37 s. 6 d.

Les qui eulx estoient en registre en compte devant sans so[m]me sy [com]me il app[er]t p[ar] le papier icelluy pour a Raoul Trotart et a ses compaignons canees pour 54 l. tonneaulx de pierre le tonnel 12 s. 6 d. pour ice   33 l. 15 s.

Mennouvriers

8/26/1436   A Guillot Guyde pour avoir pave devant le portail de leglise pour ice   12 s. 6 d.

11/18   A Jehan Cardet pour mener les vetiennes de leglise e ordures de tailles de pierre par la [com]mandem[en]t de justice pour ice   6 s.

2/19/1437   A Jehan le Canyer Jehan Chalin Guillot Bendat Jehan Viollete Guillaume Noel Pierre de Grenouville p[ou]r aider amestre la tieulle sur legli[s]e pour ch[asc]un ung jour le jour 18 d. pour ice   9 d.

Boys carpentier late huchiers et siers dees et corbelles pelles

12/23/1436   A Jehan le Fort Jehan Gibes et Jehan le Puost pour maistre des estoiez contre la tour et pour soustenir les quatre trefs de la chappelle notre dame pour ch[ac]un trois journees le jour 3 s. pour ice   27 s.

12/23   Le dit jour a Guillaume aux Demers pour amener 4 estoies de dess[us] le cay jusqu[es] a legli[se] et fu po[ur] estoies les 4 trefs de la chapelle not[re] dame pour ice   5 s. 6 d.

12/25   A Marquet Bataille pour quatre trefs et 8 souschevrons pour refaire la nef du parmy pour ice   15 l.T.

A Jehan et Auber le Vanassoir pour la menage de dix trefs et sousschevrons pour ice   12 s.

1/13/1437   A Marquet Bataille p[ou]r ung tref pour ice   30 s.

A Jonennet du Moustier p[ou]r 12 pieces de bois pour ice   6 l. 10 s.

A Jehan le Sangnier p[ou]r 18 pieces de boys pour ice   6 l. 10 s.

A Drouet pour 5 pieces de boit pour ice
60 s.

A Robin le Jeune pour 1 piece de boit p[ou]r faire estoie pour ice   15 s.

Le d[it] jour a Guill[aum]e aux Demers et a ses [com]paignons pour amener icelluy boit devant dit po[ur] ice   25 s.

1/20   A Jehan Dupont pour 16 corbelles et pour trois pelles pour ice   1 s.

A Jaquet Demenx pour 7 claees pour ice
1 s.

A Jehan Regnault pour la fachon de deulx trous lun en laitre et lautre en la rue pour ice   7 s. 6 d.

A [ ] sieux does pour 8 bours dilande sier pour faire les moules pour ice   6 s. 8 d

A Jehan le Sesne pour 8 bours de bost di-lande pour ice

A Jehan Decessame carpent[ier] pour avoir fait la carpenterie de la nef de moustier p[ar] marche fait a luy en un et tout   22 l.

A [ ] ouvrier pour bost   50 s.

A Jehan Gompel p[ou]r 8 gros solivaux et p[ou]r lamenager   27 s.

A Colin le Roux p[ou]r 1 archon de so-liveaux et pour lamenager

2/17   A Martin le Daaim carpentier pour une journee p[ou]r maistre des solliveaux a une des essoppet pour ice   2 s. 6 d.

2/17   A Marquet Bataille pour un carteron et demy de crevons pour ch[ac]une piece 3 s. 9 d.   7 l. 6 s. 3 d.

A Sevestre le Gaignieur pour trois pieces de boit p[ou]r faire fillieres pour leglise pour ice   20 s.

A Jouen de Moustier pour quatre pieces de merrien pour legli[se] pour ice   30 s.

A Guill[au]m[e] Combault p[ou]r une piece de boit a faire filliere p[ou]r ice
17 s. 6 d.

A Jehan Guenier pour deulx pieces de merrien pour ice   35 s.

A Robin le Jeune p[ou]r une piece de mer-rien pour ice   35 s.

A Guill[aum]e Lafemant p[ou]r 30 tienons p[ou]r ch[asc]un crevon 3 s. p[ou]r ice
100 s.

A Michel Duboulay banetier p[ou]r la menage de ycellui merrien et crevons pour ice   10 s.

A Jehan le Jeune pour une piece de mer-rien pour le portail pour ice   15 s.

A Colin sieur de oes pour le portail de leglise p[ou]r ice   2 s. 6 d.

A Colin le Roux p[ou]r ung carteron de sollivieux p[ou]r ice   75 s.

2/17/1437   A Colin Huee pour 80 pieces de goutier la p[iec]e 12 d. pour ice   4 l. T.

3/10   A Jehan Bisset et a son campaignon sieurt does pour avoir sie deulx grosses pieces de boit p[ou]r ice   6 s.

A bois huchier pour une journee et de ses deulx vallet pour rapaillier les clostures de ceur de leglise pour ice   4 s. 6 d.

Item pour 3 saigles et pour faire deux font a deulx buistes saigles pour ice   4 s.

A Jehan le Jeune pour 10 solliveaux et trois crevons pour ch[ac]une piece 2 s. 6 d. pour ice   32 s. 6 d.

A Martin le Daim carpentier et Jehan Morisset carpentier pour une journee pour faire une lucarne sur la voute de Sainct Cler pour ch[ac]un 2 s. 6 d. pour ice   5 s.

A Jehan de Soysons carpentier pour s bessoingne tant pour la nef que pour autres chosez pour ice   100 s.

A icelui pour la fachon du portail de devant leglise pour ice   4 l. T.

A icellui pour avoir rapp[er]eille le pup-pitre et maistre chinq piecez de bost p[ou]r maistre le luminaire N[otr]e Dame de p[ou]r avoir rapp[er]eille puppit[re] devant Saint Leu p[ou]r ice   4 l.

4/29   A Jehan de Soisons et a Colin Machon car-pentiers pour avoir rapp[er]eille les trestes pour a menistier a pasque et pour maistre trois pieces de boys en on tref de coste de-vers Saint Leu p[ou]r maistre sierges pour ice   4 s. 6 d.

5/6   A Jehan le Hericher pour avoir fait le plamchie de aes du pippitre et p[ou]r ung huys au d[it] pippitre et p[ou]r ung huys a la maisonnete dempres le portail et pour unes fenestres de unes au maries dedens le tressor et pour une fenestres sur la voultre sur la chappelle de mess[ire] Saint Cler et pour les lanchetes des verrieres du pignon de eglise et pour plus[sieurs] autres chos[es] p[ou]r ice   67 s. 6 d.

5/14   Pour 4 pelles pour ice   20 s.

Item a icellui jour p[ou]r 4 sechles pour ice
5 s.

P[ar] a Jehan le Sesne pour 20 bors boit di-
lande pour ch[ac]un bors

A Rogier hucher pour la fachon de cinq
moules pour ch[ac]un moule 13 s. 2 d.
                    70 s. 10 d.

5/21   A Colin le Mongnier pour avoir sye 12
bors dilande p[ou]r faire les moules pour
ice   10 s.

5/21   A Guill[au]me aux Demers pour mene
chinq piez de merrien et trois tombes a la
grant estre pour ice   4 s. 2 d.

5/21   A Robier huchier p[ou]r la fachon de
deulx moules pour avoir colle deulx piecez
de bors dylande p[ou]r ice   32 s. 9 d.

6/4   A Guill[aum]e Poulain amener de tieule
pour 53 pies de goutier pour chacun pie
15 d. pour ice   67 s. 6 d.

A icellui pour 34 pies de goutier le pie
12 d. p[ou]r ice   34 s.

A icelluy pour 300 de lomgue late 6 s. le
cens pour ice   18 s.

6/23   A Jehan Damel pour avoir amene et hoste
devant leglise 6 benelleez dordure pour ice
                    2 s. 6 d.

Sereuriers et autre chaulx

8/26/1436   A Laurent du Mesnil sereurier pour avoir
rappareillie un lamppe qui est devant le
croucifix et p[ou]r ung pouliot de boit
pour ice   2 s. 6 d.

10/16   A Jehan Taillefer pour 13 livres de sondeme
la livre 18 d. pour ice   19 s. 6 d.

4/27/1437   A Laurent du Mesnil p[ou]r avoir ferre le
tronc du petit chimetier et faire une
sereure a deux clefs et pour 2 petit gond et
p[ou]r avoir mis appoint toute la ferrele du
pignon de leglise pour mettre les verrieres
pour ice   17 s. 6 d.

4/27   A Colin Lore feron pour une cayure de fer
p[ou]r maistre le crucifix pour ice   6 s.

5/6   A Laurent de Mesnil p[ou]r avoir fait et
rapplique les fers locquetes et les vergues de
verrieres du pignon du portail de lestage de
dessoubz ou est listoire de la nativite et
pour les cramppons atenir des tuyaulx des
goutieres et pour 6 grant [com]maistre les
boisses dent les pilles de bois et pour
pluss[ieurs] autres choses et p[ou]r ice 15 l.

Platre platriers huille pappors et aultre chosses

A Symonet Prenel pour une mine de platre
pour la messon dempres la clef pour ice
                   3 s. 4 d.

Le dit jour a Estiennot Dufour p[ou]r ung
carteron de tieulle p[ou]r la d[ite] maison
pour ice   20 d.

A Jehan Rogier couvieur de tieulle pour
ung jour pour couvier et emploier la platre
pour la dite maison pour iceux   2 s. 6 d.

A Colin Haulest pour deulx jours et demi
de sa paine p[ou]r platrer le pignon de
leglise de devant et le pignon du portail et
le lermier de dessoulx la goustiere pour ice
le jour 3 s. 4 d. pour demy 20 d. 8 s. 4 d.

6/2   Raoullin Labbe mareschal pour la forgivre
de 9 marteaulx et pour lachevement de
deux marteaux pour ice   10 s.

5/6/1437   Le dit jour a Bondonyne Cailler plombier
pour geste 1872 livres de plomb tant pour
goutierers qui tuyaulx que 38 l. de sondeme et pour meners et remener a la viconte pour ice   14 l. 15 s.

5/14   A Jouement Ponchel ferronnier pour avoir
refait et rapplique toutez les verriers du
pignon de le dit eglise   60 s.

5/21   Pour ung boissel de platre pour en duyre la
paray de la chamb[re] de Saint Leu au grant
porche p[ou]r ice   22 d.

A icelluy Ponchel pour 400 tieulle mis sur
la chappelle Saint Cler et on autre lieu pour
le moustier et pour la parie de sez valet
avec 4 festeniez pour   35 s.

Departmental Archives, Seine-Maritime, Rouen, G6876 Fabric Account, 1443–1446

Cy enssyent les nons et les sournons des tressoriers re-
ceulx en lan 1443 le 16 jour de septembre Pierres Le
Gay Henry Le Houppeur Jacquet La Hoteron Cardin
Fessart Thomas Fugart et Jehan Conlombel tous tressoriers de leglise de Saint Maclou de Rouen depuis le
jour dess[us] dit jusques en lan 1446 de largent cuilly
an bachin par les pariossiers cy come il a este acoustume et ordonne aux bonne festes et aux dimenches et
les nons et les sournons de ceulx qui ont cuilly et
combien ilz ont cuilly

Receipts

Pour letiers aux malades

Austre recepte fait par iceulx tressoriers

Reliques
    11/3/1443   Toussaints   60 s.
    11/10   Sainct Cler   5 s. 5 d.

11/17	Sainct Maclou	17 s.	7 d.
12/7	Notre Dame	20 s.	
12/22	Jour de la Ducasse de Saint Maclou	7 s.	6 d.
12/29	Noel	72 s.	
1/1/1444	premiere jour de janivier	20 s.	
1/6	de Lathiphayne	10 s.	
2/11	Candelieur	20 s.	
2/23	cuilly aux reliq[ues]	4 s.	6 d.
2/25	An[non]ciation Notre Dame	16 s.	9 d.
4/5	Pasque	50 s.	
4/12	Relique dernier jour de pasques	20 l. 5 s.	
4/10		70 s.	
5/10	pour le representation des passions de Notre Dame pour la paye fait	55 s.	
5/24	Rouesonis	10 s.	4 d.
6	reliques du premier jour de may	10 s.	
6/7	Pentecouste	7 s.	4 d.
6/7	reliques	11 s.	4 d.
6/7	Saint Jehan	10 s.	
6/7	Saint Maclou	36 s.	
7/19	Reliques Saint Cler	23 s.	10 d.
8/17	Reliques Notre Dame	16 s.	
9/6	Saint Leu	4 l. 10 s.	
	jour de la Nadain	15 s.	
11/1	Toussaints	57 s.	6 d.
	—	31 s.	10 d.
11/4	Saint Cler	10 s.	
11/15	Saint Maclou	32 s.	6 d.
12/13	Reliques Notre Dame	15 s.	6 d.
9/5/1445	Reliques le jour Saint Leu	4 l. 15 s.	6 d.

Corps entrez a leglise

De conssant an ung angloye enterre devant Saint Leu
    paie par messire roy   23 s.   9 d.
. . . devant Saint Cler   20 s.
. . . du moustier   60 s.
. . . la chappelle fait pour Saint Jude   30 s.
. . . devant lez fonts   40 s.
Corps enterres en petit chimetiere
Le mestier de drapperie et boulemguerie
Neupvaynes de Saint Leu et Saint Cler
Rentes et Louages de maissons
Espoussailles de ceulx qui sen vont hors de la p[arr]oisse
Cuilly devant leglise et de dens la chappelle Saint Marc
Bieres reppresentation
Courtines candeliers
Pierres blot mortiez tombez tieulleaux et vieux boit
Reguiement de dieu
Bons vestemens
Bons veuestais
Autre recepte dons tressorieres

Expenses

Misses faite par Pierre Le Gay Henry Le Houppeur
    Jaquet Le Hoteron Cardin Fessart Thomas Fugart

tressoriers de la dite eglise de Saint-Maclou de Rouen
depuit 16 jour de september 1443 jusques . . .

Pour pierres achetees

9/30/1443	A maistre Jeson par la main de maistre Symon le Noir pour ung carteron de carrel	10 l.
	A Guillaume aux Demers pour la menage dudit carrel	6 s.
3/22/1444	Pour 48 et demi tonneaulx et demi de pierre priste en place cha[cu]n tonnel 22 s. 6 d.	54 l. 11 s. 3 d.
	Item pour avoir amener les dit 48 tonneaulx et demi de Vernon jusques en cest ville pour cha[cu]n tonnel 15 s.	36 l. 7 s. 6 d.
	Item pour descharger du bastel et pour amener jusques a leglise pour cha[cu]n tonnel 2 s. 6 d. vallent dit 48 tonneaux et demi	6 l. 15 d.
6/21	Item pour 12 quateriez de pierre de 2 piez et apport de le de 13 a 14 pousses de hault et quateronnes 6 toise de lont dont cha[scu]n toise couste 30 s. pour lavoir miste sur le quay qui vallent	9 l.
7/26	Pour 4 toysies et pie de demi de lont de pierre et 2 piec 2 pousses de le et de 13 a 13 pousses de est a 30 toy vallent	6 l. 7 s. 6 d.
8/23	Pour 4 toise de pierre du Val des Leux et pie et demi et 12 quateron	6 l.
1/24/1445	Pour carreux de pierre 10 l. tonneaux paie au carrier nome Hallot priste a Vernon et l par le dit Hallot	41 l. 3 d.
7/9	Pour 7 toises de pierre du Val des Leux a 25 s. la toys vallent	8 l. 15 s.
	Pour 62 tonneaux de pierre de Vernon a 22 s. 6 d. le tonnel paie au carrier nome Hallot	68 l. 15 s.
3/6/1446	Pour chinq tonnaulx de pierre a 22 s. 6 d. pour tonnel priste a Vernon vallent	56 l. 6 s.
7/3	A Jehan Lelou et Estienne Byel pour 69 par pains de pierre du Val des Leux quateron 21 toise et 5 s. la toyse vallent en paie du dessus nomes	5 l. 7 s. 6 d.
7/10	Pour 16 toyse et demi de pierre tendres pour le mur	4 l. 2 s. 6 d.
8/28	Pour 18 tonneaux de pierre rendue devant le quay de ceste ville amise ce 27 s. 6 d. le tonnel vallent	24 l. 15 s.

Machons

| | A Prevost pour asseoir la pierre de la pistine pour sa sepmaine   30 s. |
| |
	A Friset le Mester p[ou]r sa sep[maine] avoir este a V[er]non au quarreau et ramener la pierre a ses despense 10 l. 9 s.
4/4	A meistre Symon pour la sepm[ain] de son vailet et qui cha[cu]n a prendre 10 s. pour sep[maine] 10 s.
4/11	A Guillaume le Prevost qui vent a Vernon par mastre Symon 22 s. 6 d. pour sepmain 22 s. 6 d.
7/18	A Nouel tailleur dymages pour faire 2 aglos a ung pillier au mestre ymage dessus et la chay 45 s.
9/19	A Guillaume le Prevost pour sa sep[main] dont il avoir failly ung j[our]nee 18 s. 6 d.
10/24	Prevost pour ass[urer] 3 journee 15 s.
5/22	A mestre Symon pour son vailet et qui cha[cu]n aprendre pour sep[main] 15 s.
7/24	A Guill[aume] le Prevost pour sa sep[maine] et fu rebatu pour le samadi quil fu dehors 3 s. paie 19 s. 6 d.
9/11	A Guillaume le Prevost pour sa sep[maine] rebatue ung jour qui il a este dehors 18 s.

Cauages de carestes et de beneaulx

1/6/1444	A Jehan de la Mare pour quatre benelleez dordure la benelle 5 d. vallent 20 d.
3/29	Pour descharge du bastel et amener de dessus le quay jusque a leglise 48 tonneaux et demi pour cha[cu]n tonnel 3 s. 4 d. vault pour ce la som[m]e 7 l. 17 s. 7 d.
6/27	Pour voiturer de 6 toyse de pie[rr]e et 16 carraulx par a Guill[aume] aux Demers 18 s.
8/2	Guill[aume] aux Dermers et ses [com]paignons pour voiture de 4 toises de pierre et pie et 12 q[uar]eaulx 10 s. 6 d.
2/7/1445	A Pierre le Souvier p[ou]r avoir amener de Vernon 40 tonneaux de pierre par marche fait a luy le fert de son bastel 21 l.
	A Guill[aume] aux Demers pour avoir amener 40 tonneaulx de pierre des dessus leglise a leglise pour tonnel 2 s. vallent 4 l.
7/11	A George pour avoir amener 62 tonneaulx de pierre de [Ver]non 6 s. pour tonnel paie 18 l. 8 s. 6 d. presier les dit 62 tonneaux 4 s. 6 d.

	Pour amener les 62 tonneaux de pierre de dess[us] le q[ua]y jusque au cymet[ie]re paie pour tonnel a Guill[aume] aux Demers 6 l. 2 s. 6 d.
9/5	Pour la voiturer de 6 toyses de pierre du Val des Leux p[ou]r amener de dess[us] le q[ua]y au cymeti[er]e a Guillaume aux Demers 9 s.
11/29	Pour voiture de amener 11 quateron et demi rosel pour couvrier les murs 2 s. 6 d.
9/4/1446	P[ou]r portage de 6 piech de soliveaulx et l aultre piech de boys 2 s. 3 d.
	Pour portage du ung soliviel jusqua aux sieurs de ays 5 d.
	Pour amener 8 sollivaulx de dessus leglise jusques au cymetiere le 25 d. 9 d.
	P[ou]r aportage ung curion de quay jusque au cymetiere 3 d.

Caux et Sablon

	A P[arra]in le Dur pour deulx sommees de caux le sac 6 s. vallent 12 s.
	A Jehan Colat pour deulx benelleez de sablon la benellee 2 s. 6 d. vallent 5 s.
8/20	Maistre Symon p[ou]r 2 benelleez de sablon que il avoir paiees 4 s. 6 d.
9/4	A maistre Symon pour 2 sommees de caulx dont cy estes devens a leglise paie 6 s. 3 d.
9/25	A maistre Symon le 25 de september p[ou]r som[mee]s de caulx et pour benelleez de sablon 6 s. 3 d.

Mennouvriers

	Aux Clercs pour leur 8 decouvrer les ymages 3 s.
	A une hom[m]e pour 2 journees pour vuidier le oraon dempres les machons et mestre a leglise 5 s.
	A Perrin Marchant pour 6 journees a scier les machons et la chapelle a Sainct Katrine 3 s. pour jour 18 s.
	Pour ung carpe[n]tier mestre ungne estre a la chapelle Saint Louys 3 s.

Bois carpentiers et autre chosses

| 10/10/1443 | A Guillaume Drouyne sieur daes pour trois aes comprens 6 tier de sie p[ou]r faire les moules aux machons pour ice   5 s. |
| 10/20 | A Guyot [ ] huchier pour avoir fait les moulez p[ou]r maistre Symon pour la machonerie pour avoir rabote et collez et ice   10 s. |

1/26/1444   A Dronyn Martin et a ses [com]paignons
             pour quatre carpentiers qui ont mis 6 sol-
             liveulx autour dessus fonts du cueur
                                                    13 s. 6 d.

4/10   P[ou]r mestre le merrien de la table a re-
             cever le jour de pasque paie au carpentier
                                                    2 s. 3 d.

             A Guiot huchier pour avoir fait l potente a
             la cloque   18 d.

5/17   Pour la moitie de 18 crevons dont Gre-
             nouille paie la moitie et construct 50 s.
             pour ice   25 s.

             Pour le huchier qui fist la cloture de em-
             pres le gra[n]t austel pour sa paine
                                                    10 francs

8/16   Pour ung pelle aux machons et deux
             estuilles   10 d.

4/4/1445   A Jehan Regnault pour avoir rapareille le
             letrin de leglise   3 s.

7/11   Pour asseoir le engin Grenouville en la
             chapelle Saint Katrin a quatre carpentiers
             2 jours et demi   40 s.

4/3/1446   Pour tanlaste rapareille de la chapelle de
             louest   4 s. 6 d.

4/12   Pour l tanlaste p[ou] le huys de la loge du
             cymetier gra[n]t et pour le reffaire 2 s. 3 d.

9/4   A Drouyn Martin et a la moistie et a Jehan
             Perron p[ou]r cha[cu]n quatre journee val-
             lent 9 journees affaires le dessus sur la porte
             du vicaire   42 s.

             A Robert Ponguant pour 5 grant sol-
             liveaulx   19 s. 6 d.

             Aux sciers de ayes pour scier az 5 piech de
             boys et ungne austre grad et estoit pour la
             porte du [pres]bytaire   7 s. 8 d.

Sereuriers

12/29/1443   A Colin Jouyn pour 18 marteaulx avoir re-
             forgiez   10 s.

1/8/1444   A Jehan Carmel dit Mauchelle pour une
             pannielle et une cron et pour une clef aux
             coffre aux livrez et remestre appoint la dit
             sereure du[dit] coffre et p[ou]r la penture
             de la petite cloquete p[ou]r les orguez et
             pour maistre appoint la grand boite du
             tressoz et pour une clef et une chasse pour
             la maison dempress le sest unes pour tout
             ice   6 s.

4/13   A Colin Jouyn p[ou]r 29 forguer et de
             marteaulx et p[ou]r une barrel de fer a mis-
             tre a la pistine   18 s.

11/29/1445   A Raullez labbe pour 2 l. de plot affaire su-
             douer au pilliers des chappelles   13 d.

10/2   Aux machons pour ensour le verre
                                                    20 s. 3 d.

Platre platriers tuilles pappiers

             A Louiset de Banent pour le pappier jour-
             nal de chincq mains et pour trois autres
             pappiers tout pour leglise   25 s.

             Item pour une corbelle pour les machons
                                                    9 d.

             A Jehan Camart platrier pour deulx torchez
             pesantez six l. la livre   4 s. 6 d. 27 s.

             Item pour deulx vergues de bois   9 d.

             A Friset le Meistre p[ou]r lauloge pour le
             terme Saint Michel 1443   10 s.

             A Colin Heribel pour une carte de platre
                                                    9 d.

             A Colin Heribel pour deulx boisseaulx de
             platre   18 d.

11/13/1443   A Richard Mordenet p[ou]r trois cent de
             rosel de cent 9 d.   27 s.

11/17   A Friset le Meistre et a Jehan le Prevost
             pour avoir hoste etaimez piecez qui es-
             toient a porte de vicaire   18 d.

11/24   A Jehan Turgnois couvrieur de rosel p[ou]r
             la chappell[e] devant le cueur et sur les
             loges recouvert pour tout entage pour ce
             faire ice   40 s.

12/29   A maistre Symon machon pour trois term
             cest assavoir le terme et pasque Saint Jehan
             Saint Michel 1443 pour y donnez
                                                    6 l. 15 s.

1/8/1444   A Jehan Hutte pour 18 livres de soudenre
             pour les goutierez de leglise la livre 15 d.
                                                    17 s.

             A Friset le Mestre pour avoir atremper la
             loge pour le terme de nouel   6 l.

             Item baillie a Rogier Lefort pour une
             deybte que lon a donne a leglise pour
             pourfaire la cause et pour la sacrement a
             commynoistre   5 s.

1/12   A Jehan Pres platrier pour chinq boisseaulx
             de platre et pour lay mestre emue pour la
             maison demprez les estunes pour ice   5 s.

             A Jehan Camart chirier pour deulx livres
             de chire pour trois siergez pour la bist de
             Estinnot Dufour la livre   4 s. 6 d. et

             pour la fachon et liveryson des deux buiz
                                                    10 s.

A Symon Martin carpentier pour trois piecz de boist de charpente de 6 prez
20 s.

1/26 A Richard le Jeune pour 7 piechez de sol-liveaulx la perches 5 s. vallent pour les vouste du cueur   35 s.

Item au dit Richard pour d[eu]x crevons pour ice   6 s.

Item p[ou]r amener le dit bois pour ice
20 d.

2/2 A Symonet et a Jeh[an] Sauoul pour vidier les goustierez p[ou]r nef qui ystoit   9 d.

2/9 A Guill[au]me pour 3 fait y estoit p[ou]r clore le petit porte du chimetiere   3 s.

2/23 Pour les caubomees aux machons par cellui val et fessant Estinnot Dufour et Grenou-ville   28 s. 11 d.

4/5 Pour avoir repare la croix des reliques et fait ung reliquayre neuf et repair la relique ou est la caynolle Saint Sanson et encore 2 autres reliquaires pour ce paie a Allain or-fevre   14 s.

A Michault Trouve le jour dessus dit pour avoir dore 2 an[ge]los et le bras Saint Maclou et repaire les reliques   45 s.6 d.

A Nouvel tailleur de ymages pour avoir fait des mains de levesque et reparer autres mains   3 s.

A Jeh[an] le Prevost machon qui estoit mallade de sa chute de la chappelle N[ot]re Dame donne 6 bret[on] vallent   4 s. 6 d.

Item pour avoir apair leglise pour les pro-cessions de Notre Dame qui vindrent ce jour a la dite eglise   18 d.

A meistre Symon pour sa pension de ce qu il prent p[ou]r an sur leglise p[ou]r le terme de nouvel 1443 et pasques 1444   4 l. 10 s.

Pour ung boissel et de[mi] de plastre p[ou]r asseoir la cloture de par le mestre austel
4 s. 9 d.

Item pour corbelle de platre pour asseoir la pierre de la pistine achelles

Pour les brachez de corde pour louer les pierres pesa[nt] 10 livres   8 s. 6 d.

Pour despense avec les macho[ns] et le huchier pour asseoir les pierres de la pistine et et la huche au closture dempress le mestre autel p[ou]r q[ue] ilz ne pri[n]ss[ent] point leur heures pour haster la besongne
3 s. 2 d.

8/2 Pour reffaire le grant chalice   71 s. 10 d.

12/13 A maistre Symon pour le terme Saint Jehan a dessus pour sa pension reste le terme Saint Michel   45 s.

12/27 A Friset le Meistre pour le terme de nouvel de lauloge   10 s.

1/30/1445 Pour reffaire les pendant du pies du grant austel   2 s. 3 d.

5/30 Pour le terme de pasques 1445 pour lau-loge paie a Frisot   10 s.

A mestre Symon pour les termes Saint Michel et nouvel 1444 et reste le terme de pasques 1445 qui luy et dur ce jour pour avoir terme   4 l. 10 s.

A Baudet aulogier pour avoir fait 1 rue alouloge a monter le contre poys et ra-pareille lauloge   34 s. 6 d.

A Symonet p[ou]r avoir descouvert les cha-pelles de leglise commande par mestre Symon   18 d.

Pour deulx fardaulx despries p[ou]r mestre au devant de la chapelle et pour la loge du plafond en ceste de leglise et la rue   3 s.

Pour lauloge p[ou]r le terme Saint Jehan 1445 a Frisot le Meistre   9 s.

A maistre Symon pour ses gages pour le terme de pasques 1445 et le terme Saint Je-han en suivant p[ou]r sa demy annee
4 l. 10 s.

9/12 Pour aportan le huys de bors la rue Mar-tainville pour 1445 passer la pierre parmy leglise

A meistre Symon pour le terme de nouvel 1445 pour sa demi annee le 10 de annee
4 l. 10 s.

4/10/1446 A Robinnet pour lauloge pour le terme de pasques   4 l. 46 s.

8/28 Pour les machons qui tailleure la pierre p[ou]r le mur p[ou]r leur despense et deus aux fossiers pour 1 pelle   13 s. 6 d.

9/25 Pour reffaire le degre de la maison dempres la clef pour 2 boisseaull de plastre mestre cymetiere   2 s. 3 d.

Au filx pour avoir couvert sur le mur du presbytaire et sur leglise 2 jours et demi
12 s. 9 d.

10/2 A ung couvrier de tieulle pour couver au-tour le pillier de la chapelle Saint Louys pour et asseoir sur tour pour chacun 3 journee de demi   29 s.

10/2 A Robinnet pour lauloge pour le terme Saint Michel 1446   10 s.

Departmental Archives, Seine-Maritime, Rouen, G6878 Fabric Account, 1476–1479

Cy ensuit les comptes des tressoriers de leglise de Saint Maclou de Rouen cest assavoir Estienne Ruby Richart Mallebonte Rogier Le Fevre Guill[aum]e Le Roy Michel Trouve de toutes les receptes et les mises faites par yceulx pour la fabrique de la d[ite] eglise d[ep]uiz le dimenche 22 jour septembre 1476 jusque au premier jour de novembre 1479 la faiste de jour de la toussains

Receipts

Plas de loeuvre et du tiers des mallades cueilly aux dimanches et bonnes festees par les parroissiens com[m]e il acoustume les nons et surnons de ceux qui ont cuielly

Du plat N[otre] Dame cuilly par les parroissiens ordonne le revenu a leuvre de leglise . . .

Autre recepte pour le plat a la mere dieu . . .

Du plat volant cueilly sur sepm[aine] avant leglise avecq[ues] le 15 d. pour la chapelle de ceulx qui font le pain benoist

Des dons ordinaires tous les dimanches . . .

. . . les presentations vestemens chandelliers coustumes

. . . des bierres

. . . corps enterres de dens leglise

. . . des fosse faictes a leglise

(e.g., de sire Pierre Tuvache procureur du Roy pour la fosse de sa femme mise deva[n]t le cruchefix a leglise   10 l.   12 d.)

. . . corps enterres de dens leglise

. . . corps enterres au petit chemetier

. . . reliq[ues]

1476	Saint Wulfram	9 s.	2 d.
	Toussaints	63 s.	1 d.
	Saint Maclou	43 s.	4 d.
	N[otr]e Dame	15 s.	8 d.
	Noel	74 s.	6 d.
	Pasques	15 l. 19 s.	
1477	Pasques	21 l. 12 s.	3 d.

. . . des maistres du mestier de drapperie dont cha[cu]n qui se passent maistre doibv[en]t a leglise 20 sous et les fils de maistre 10 sous

. . . le fieffes et rentes appartenantes a leglise

(e.g.) . . . recu lostel des Flagons   4 l. 10 s. 9 d.

. . . les choppes daupres le portail Saint Cler
                                                    60 s.

. . . les echoppes de derriere la chapell Saint Cler
                                                    10 s.

. . . echoppes daupres du portail Saint Cler
                                                    40 s.

. . . echoppes de la grant estre   22 s. 6 d.

. . . des laitz faiz a leglise

. . . des espousees qui vont demeurer hors de la p[ar]oisse des veuves, renoyemens de dieu

. . . des tronc de leglise et du tronc Sainte Marguerite

. . . des vieulx merriens pierre platriaux tieulliaux viel verre bloc mortier [huges langet] et plussieur extenrilles de leglise

(e.g.)   le dit 19 jour de Maistre Amboisse pour ung ton de pierre prins a laistre pour Ambroise faire ung beneficier pour ice   20s.

de Richard Mallebote pour trois carreaux de pierre print a laistre   10 s.

pour deux cens de parpens print a laistre
                                                            12 s.

Le dit 6 jour novembre recu de Pierre Maloche carpentier p[ou]r les nois vergus du grant aistre
                                                            20 s.

Expenses

Cy ensuit les mises faicte par lceulx tressoriers cy dessus de nommes tant en pierre menouvriers en touites chosses necessures pour la dite leglise depuis le dimenche 22 jour de septembre 1476 jusques au jour de toussaines 1479

pour la pierre achestee pour leuvre de leglise

10/10/1476	Paye a Guill[aum]e Hallot carrieux pour la parpaye de 33 tonnel de pierre qui luy estoit deu du tempt de Jehan le Roy tressorier du devant yceulx tressoriers de la somme de	12 l.
10/26	Paye a Guill[aum]e Hallot carrieux pour 33 tonnel de pierre la somme de	30 l. 5 s.
12/29	Paye au Coq carrier de Vern[on] p[ou]r 20 tonnel de pierre a 17 s. 6 d. pour tonnel dont a este rabatu dessus 60 s. que le dit Coq debvoit a Jehan le Roy paie iceulx tressoriers la somme de	14 l. 10 s.
2/2/1477	Paye a Guill[aum]e Hallot et son fils pour 33 tonnel de pierre la somme	30 l.
4/6	Paye au carreux de Val des Leux pour 6 toizes et demy de parpen somme	32 s. 6 d.
5/25	Paye par Michel Trouve pour 33 tonneaux de pierre de Vernon	30 l.
	Dudit jour paye a Estinne du Mare carreux de Val des Leux pour 19 toises de demye de parpens a 5 s. 6 d. la toise vallent	104 s. 6 d.
	Plus paye a lui p[ou]r une carreux de carrel	25 s.
6/1	Paye a Aland le Fort carreux de Val des Leux pour 5 toises de parpens et demy rent de carel	70 s.

6/21 Paye a Jehan le Coq carreux de Vernon pour 50 tonnel de pierre rabatu qui denbvoit a Jehan la Roy 60 s. et rabatu pour 6 tonnea   34 l. 12 s. 6 d.

7/8 Paye Aland le Fort pour 23 toise de parpens et pour ung carteron de carrel   7 l. 11 s. 6 d.

10/5 Paye au carreux de Val des Leux pour 11 toise et demy de parpen   69 s. 9 d.

12/6 Paye a Hallot pour une bastelle de pierre pour 46 tonnelle et demi   46 l. 10 s.

4/12/1477 Paye a Estienne de Maret et a Pierre Damnergne carreux du Val des Leux pour 23 toizes de parpens a 5 s. 6 d. pour toises vallent   8 l. 5 s.

5/27 Paie a Estiennot de Maret pour 30 toises de parpens a 5 s. 6 d. la toise   8 l. 5 s.

6/21 Paye a Estiennot du Maret pour 1 toize de parpens a 5 s. 6 d. la toise vallent   8 l. 10 s. 6 d.

7/26 A Estiennot du Mares pour 38 toise de parpens a 5 s. 6 d.   10 l. 9 s.

9/6 Au filz de Halot pour 60 tonnel de pi[err]e a 20 s. le tonnel dont nous luy a baille la revenue de ble de farciaulx qui doit recueillis jusque a la toussaint lan 1479 vallent la somme   60 l.

3/21/1478 A Hallot pour 50 tonnel de pierre a 20 s. le tonnel   50 l.

7/28 Aux carreux de Vernon pour une bastelle de pierre de 48 tonnel qui couste a ung nomme Hallot   41 l.

11/27 Paie pour 54 tonnel de pierre de Vernon a 20 s. le ton a Hallot   54 l.

Autres mises faictes paye par icelux tressoriers aux machons qui ont besongne depuis le dymanche 22 jour de septembre 1476 jusque au jour de toussains 1479

12/22/1476 Paye a Maistre Ambroise et pour son vallet pour une sepmaine   30 s.

A Jehan le Prevost sa sepm[aine]   17 s. 6 d.

A Fresot le Maistre sa sepm[aine] 17 s. 6 d.

A Jehan la Canne s sepm[aine]   17 s. 6 d.

A Ollivier le Rebours sa sepm[aine]   17 s. 6 d.

A Guillaume Ouyn sa sepm[aine] 17 s. 6 d.

A Gillet Luce sa sepm[aine]   17 s. 6 d.

A Jehan Quillet sa sepm[aine]   15 s.

Somme de ces presentes pour la sepm[aine] des huit machons valle[n]t 7 l. 10 s. sur re-

batu a Ollivier pour le demy heure 12 d. de la faulte p[ou]r ice   7 l. 9 s.

9/29/1477 Aux susdits huit machons pour la sepm[aine] rebatu pour une journee a Maistre Ambroise 5 s. pour ice   7 l. 5 s.

10/ Pour une sepm[aine] entierre aux dit machons   7 l. 10 s.

1476 Dudit jour paye aux dit machons po[ur] avoir besongne dedens leglise austre heure   5 s. 6 d.

6/8/ . . . paie aux mach[ons] pour septm[aine] rabatu les faultes de vallet Ambroise   4 l. 10 s. 9 d.

1/4/1477 Paie aux machons dessus dit quatre sepm[aine] deux rabatu 8 s. 6 d. pour les faultes   10 l. 9 s.

11/23 Paie pour une septm[aine rabatu les fautes comprint une sepm[aine] de Ollivier qui estoit revenu des lost

3/29/1477 Paie aux machons pour demy sepmain pour les festes de Pasques rebatus pour ice   67 s. 6 d.

4/26 Item plus paye aux dit machons pour ceste sepmaine de jubilate   6 l. 15 s.

5/24 Paie aux machons pour une sepmaine notre compte Frizot qui estoit malade pour ice   117 s. 6 d.

Dudit jour fut paie a Friset que pour les manneaux quel avoir fait a son hostel par mur pour ice   10 s.

6/14 Paie aux machons pour deux sepmaine que les estoient dues rabatu a Ambroise 12 s. 6 d. pour une journee et pour une trellie que il avoir achestee rabatu a Jehan Le Prevost pour 4 journee de 15 s.

6/21 Paie a Ambroise pour une sepmaine sans son vallet 25 s. Aux 5 autres machons pour deux sepmaines que les estoient deus pour ice   8 l. 10 s.

6/28 Paie a Amboise pour deux sepmaines a luy deux pour ice   65 s.

Paie aux autres 5 machons pour une sepmaine rabatu les faultes   4 l. 7 s. 6 d.

2/6/1479 Item paie aux dit machons pour ung moye a eux deux commandement par justice a les paie   4 l. 10 s.

10/14/1476 Paye au vicaire de la Ronde a cause de la rente de la grant aistre pour le terme Saint Michel 1476   50 s.

10/27 Payer a Messire Jehan le Bon pour les messes de N[otr]e Dame dittez par les tressoriers p[ou]r le terme Saint Michel 4 l.

11/24 Paye aux Augustins a cause de la messe dites par les nonnes pour la rente qui dems lenglaiz avoir lesses a leglise pour le terme Saint Michel 1476 5 s.

1/12/1477 Paye a Messire Jehan le Bon pour la messe N[otr]e Dame pour le terme de Nouel 1476 4 l.

Dudit jour paye pour le pain de lobit fait pour Colin le Roux 13 d.

4/14 Paye pour lobit de Maistre Jehan Prevot 2 s. 3 d.

11/5/1478 Paye a Messire Jehan Harel pour le terme de Saint Michel pour rente due a la Ronde pour le grant chemistier 50 s.

12/22/1478 Paye a Messire Jehan le Carpentier pretre sur deux prossesionaires quil a escript pour la parroisse baille euvre quil en doivt avoir 20 s.

4/13/1479 Paie a Jehan Gaultier pour avoir remis appoint les orgues 20 s. avecq[ue] ce unes vielles orgues que estoient au Tresor 20 s.

5/25 Paie par Michel Trouve pour avoir refait une verrier a la chapelle Saint Jehan et une aux Estiennes paie par luy dudit jour pour une aultres verrier audit Estiennes et pour une bondine 20 s.

Dudit jour paie pour avoir refait 3 estolles neufves et 5 vielles a Fagart 20 s.

7/20 Paie pour unes roes pour le chariot amener les pierre 15 s.

8/17 Baille aux tressoriers Notre Dame pour paie une perche de la fachon de toillet 46 s. 9 d.

Paie aux manouviers platiers carpentiers tonneurs et lautre aides

9/29/1476 De vallet de bras des machons pour 3 journees a 2 s. 1 d. pour jour pour ce 6 s. 3 d.

4/27/1477 Paie pour 4 journee de charpentier et de son vallet a besongnes a la nef 25 s.

5/28 Paie a Pacques Malide carpentier pour 12 jour luy et son vallet a besongne a la nef de leglise 36 s. 10 d.

8/10 Paye a ung carpentier pour 8 jour a besongnes a la nef de leglise 30 s.

Dudit jour pour avoir recouvert a la nef de leglise pour 4 jour et demy 16 s 10 d. pour le vallet de bras du couvier 5 s. 2 d.

8/17 Paie a Goudnot pour 8 journee avoir besongne a leglise 30 s. 3 d.

Dudit jour pour 8 journee a Gorget Le Roux et pour son filx avoir couvrier a leglise 43 s.

9/7 Paie aux manouviers pour avoir ferrer la tour 50 s.

1/18/1478 Paye a Colin le Mare pour avoir refait le palis des estimes de charpenterie 7 s. 6 d.

Dudit jour pour ung menouvrier pour avoir deffait du mortier pour 3 journees 5 s. 6 d.

1/25/1479 Paie a Jehan Hurpin dit Casteillie p[ou]r besongner faicte aux estinnes en plusiers partis de fer euvre rabatu du fer baille de leglise et rabatu pour le tiers de Guill[aum]e le Segne paie audit Casteillie 30 s.

Dudit jour paie a Teste Noir pour paint et plastre mis aux estnnes pour ledit palis 6 s. 6 d.

. . . paie au huchier pour avoir reppaver huis des estinnes 5 s.

Aux menouvriers platers couviers et huchiers

4/25/1477 Paye a Charles le Chenals huchier p[ou]r avoir refait deux huis aux estinnes 4 s.

12/20 Paie pour deux journee et demy dun me[nouv]rier pour avoir recouvert a leglise 4 s. 7 d.

12/27 A Goudart p[ou]r 5 jo[ur]nees avoir couvert a leglise 16 s. 6 d.

9/10/1478 Paie Goudart tant pour 11 l. de teuille que pour la menage que pour late clou la journee de luy et de son filz Martin a le seriur pour avoir recouvert a la nef de leglise 27 s. 6 d.

Mise faite par icelluy Michel Trouve de plussieurs parties pour lorloge

11/7/1476 A Tassrae charpentier pour boys et paine tout senvuy compris 15 s. sur quoi Cardement Malle luy a donne par dessus son marche que il aeu la somme de 17 l. 2 s. 6 d.

Dudit jour paye a Hurpin couvier par marche fait a couvrier lui pour couverir lorloge et recouvert la rue dardoise et pour avoir a bastir loriol de devant le signot 13 l. 5 s.

Dudit jour paie au plo[m]mier p[ou]r avoir ouvre 200 livre plom p[ou]r couvrier lorloge 42 s. 6 d.

Dudit jour paie a lorlogier pour avoir mis les mouvem[en]ts de lorloge a point par marche fait   6 l.

Dudit jour paye p[ou]r boys pour faire le pipitre oc sont les mouvements et p[ou]r la paine des carpentiers   40 s.

Dudit jour paye pour la journee de deux huchiers pour clore deais et dessous les engins   5 s. 6 d.

Dudit jour paie a Rogier Le Fevre pour aes de chaine a clore sous les engines   20 s.

Payes lorganist et le souffleurs pour avoir joue a leglise

Pour les acherements des marteaux pour les machons de eglise

Pour platre platriaux tuylle neufve rosel tuylhaux

10/6/1476   P[ou]r ung carteron de rosel paie a Jehan Jouen   22 d.

6/21/1477   Paie pour 4 benelees de bloc pour leglise   2 s. 9 d.

9/7   Paie pour une benelee dargille a Nouel charetier   20 d.

11/23   Paye a Pissant pour 12 livres de tuylle   32 s. 6 d.

             Dudit jour paie a Prenel pour 59 boisseaux de plastre pour leglise surre qui on luy penlt de novembre   27 s. 6 d.

1/4/1478   Paie pour rosel a estomper les huis des allees dehault le rue   3 s. 8 d.

2/22   Paye a Pissant p[ou]r tuylle employee a la rue du Sarg   16 s.

7/14   Paie p[ou]r trois boisseaulx de chim[en]t pour servir aux dalle de la nef de leglise   3 s.

8/16   Paie a Teste Noir pour avoir repaire aux estenet une nombre de cheminee   3 s. 4 d.

9/6   Paie pour 6 bois[seau]x de plastre employee aux estenets pour la porte de leglise   2 s.

Austre mise faictes

10/13/1476   Baille a Maistre Ambroise pour aller a Vernon pour avoir de pierre   2 s. 9 d.

3/15/1477   Dudit jour paie pour despense faicte par les machons en refaissant le mur a la grant aistre de messire Colin Deschamps en jour de feste   18 d.

3/29/1478   Paie le vin aux machons pour deffourr le verre p[ou]r leure accoustumer   10 s.

4/26/1478   Paie pour clou deux scilles deux estueille de bois   16 d.

8/2   Paie pour despence faicte par les machons en refaissant le murs de la grant estre   2 s. 1 d.

8/16   Paie p[ou]r avoir soude aux estennets une goustierre   3 s. 8 d.

             Dudit jour paie p[ou]r avoir cure le pint de Sainte Marguerette   22 d.

9/6   Paie p[ou]r despense pour les charrels qui ont amene la pierre a laistre   15 d.

11/8   Paie p[ou]r ung galon de vin pour le fonde de la cloche   4 s.

11/29   Paie pour despense faicte p[ar] le machons qui misent les parpaing a la loge   13 d.

2/28/1479   Paie par Olliver Blondel pour deux couvertures mis aux estinnes par la porte de leglise   3 s. 8 d.

3/14   Pour despence en faissant le marche a tasseur pour faire la carpenterie de lorloge   2 s. 9 d.

3/14   Paie pour avoir mis ung four neuf a la chaudierre des estinnes pour la partion de leglise   70 s.

             Dudit paye a celuy qui apporte le platre mis en euvre pour la porte de leglise   2 s. 6 d.

Pour les charriages de merrien portaiges de tuylle bloc

11/16/1476   Paye a Nouel charestier p[ou]r avoir hoste le ordure de la petite estre   7 s. 3 d.

5/17/1477   Paie pour avoir acharer du bois pour faire lestablie par Jehan le Roy   8 s. 3 d.

6/8   P[ou]r avoir amener 3 pieches de merr[ie]n   15 d.

6/21   P[ou]r avoir amene quatre benelees de bloc   2 s. 9 d.

8/3   Pour avoir mener 4 solliveaux   6 d.

8/10   Pour avoir amener 6 chevr[on]s et pour avoir amener lengin a lever   9 d.

10/5   P[ou]r avoir apportte de la tuille   18 d.

             P[ou]r avoir amener ung de rosel a legl[ise]   10 d.

2/29/1478   Dudit jour paie a Jeh[an] Jouen p[ou]r ung cent de rosel pour estoupper les huis dehault de cueur   3 s. 8 d.

Des mer[ri]en boys acheste p[ou]r leglise

11/10/1476   A Richart Dubosc pour ung lieutrin a faire le prone du dimenche   40 s.

5/4/1477   Paye a Jeh[an] de Rouen pour deux longue pieches de boys pour fair le traistes de la nef de leglise pour machons paie   45 s.

Dudit jour paie de Jeh[an] Rouen pour 8 pieches de bois mis a la [dite] nef de leglise
60 s.

5/18   A Geuffroy Malide pour 12 soliveau et une longe pieche de boys et pour 4 potz pour le tout
70 s.

5/25   A Jehan Teubert pour une pieche de bois pour la [dite] nef
12 s. 6 d.

5/25   A Geuffroy Malide pour une pieche de boys pour la [dite] nef
12 s. 6 d.

8/17   Paye a Bidaust pour 6 chevrons 4 solliveaux
16 s. 8 d.

Dudit jour paye a Duvant pour 75 pies de goutierre
45 s.

4/26/1478   A Jehan de Moustier 13 bloys   15 s.

Fut paye aux machons de legl[ise] par contraicte faicte en coure deglise dargent qui leur estoit deu que il nestoit pas paies dont fut paye par Estienne Ruby la some
4 l. 10 s.

Item fut paie aux [dit] machon de leglise par Michel Trouve contrai[ct] en cour delgise la some de
4 l. 10 s.

Item fut par iceluy Michel Trouve aceulx qu estoiet des le grant a onze le comptes de par monsieur lofficial et pour les escriptures de la court
30 s.

Item paie a Estienne Cauchee macon pour avoir fait en parfait une vis de pierre cy la tour de la dite eglise pour paine de macons faicte et maconniers la somme
102 l. 2 s.

Item plus le 28 jour de juillet 1515 a este paie par ledit Dufour a cinq macons pour faire a meistre les quatre vis de la dit tour a quatre solz pour jour icelle sept
4 l.

Item paie a Maistre Pierre Gregoire macon pour avoir du bois a faire des moules
4 s. 6 d.

Item paie a ung huchier quy a faire les dits moules aux macons
15 s.

Item paie aux maistres macons de la ville pour mouverer la tour pour la visite cest assin a Maistre Roulland le Roux, Pierre Gregore avec deux aultres maistres macons
7 s. 8 d.

Item paie a Guill[aum]e Gauddet 12 chevrons 12 clous ung qinzaine et pour cinq autres pieces de bois
4 l. 1 s.

Item plus paie pour le portage des dites claies et bois avec le siage de huis desdites pieces pour ice   5 s. 4 d.

Item paie pour quatre journees dung charpentier pour avoir fait la roe amontez les pieces
13 s. 6 d.

Pour deux quinzaines et deux pieces crochines 13 sous pour le siage audit bois
17 d.

Paie a la Ronllande pour quatres cunlacles a faire les establies des glone
4 s.

Item paie pour six solliveaulx de 12 pies de long pour faire les establies desdits macons compris la portage
19 s.

Item paie a Dumesnil et a son compaignon macons pour une journee quilz ont besongne audit galleries dehault de ladit eglise pour faire dedens les rans et pour avoir recymete les joindz des dalles
35 s.

Item paie en icelle septmaine pour ung muy de chaulx et ung muy de sablon
25 s.

Item ce dit jour paie ausdits macons pour avoir taille a leur tache 52 marche pour fournir lesquelles quatre vis de ladite tour par marche fait a ceulx pour la somme
6 l. 5 s.

Item paie a Jaquet le Prevost carrieux demeurant au Val des Leux pour 52 marches a 3 s. chacune marche
7 l. 13 s.

Item paie a Ancel Ramachant pour le chariage de 10 tonneaux de pierre de Vernon pris sur les cays ce Rouen
20 s.

Item plus paie pour deschargage dicelle pierre du bateau au basteliers qui amener ladit pierre
5 s.

Item plus paie audit Ancel Ramachant pour 36 tonneaulx de pierre a charter jusques a la petite estre   72 s.

Item paie audit pour 34 tonneaux de pierre a chartee de la grant estre de Saint Maclou jusque a la petit estre a 20 d. pour ch[acu]n tonnel
61 s. 8 d.

Item pour a Chiment du Moustir plastriers audit jour 20 juillet pour avoir couvert sur les allee de coste des chappelles pour chinq journees
20 s.

Item paie pour le plaitre quel a fallu avoir p[ou]r besongner aux verrieres
6 s.

Aultres mis faictes . . . pour acheve lune des tourelles de la tour vers le presbytere

Le [ ]eme jour de mars 1515 avant pasques paie pour la septmaine de neuf macons
6 l. 16 s.

Item paie ce dit jour a Ancel Ramachart pour amener charne de dessus le quay a la petit estre de la tour et aussi quatre tonneaux de pierre de demy a 2 sous pour chacun tonnel
9 s.

Plus paie ausdit macons pour leur boullie et pour le charbon
17 s.

Item paie a Frouland forgeur de marteaulx et macon pour ung terme eschus a la penthecouste 1516 ainsi quil appert par sa quittance
37 s. 6 d.

Item paie le dernier jour de may 1516 pour la dernier tourelle vis laure a Estienne Cauchee et a ses compaignons pour leur sepm[aine] 7 l. 19 s.

Item pour paie la septm[aine] ensuit pour 12 macons la chapelle Sainct Pierre Pol et leur aide paie ces journees 9 l. 10 s.

A deux charpentiers pour aider a faire et deffaire lesquels etablies 9 s.

Item en icelle septmaine pour ledit Olliver Bretend et une autre menouvrier pour aider a refaire par bas la maison a monsieur le cure vers la petite estre 12 s.

A Guill[aume] Papillon pour 24 huiandes pour la facon 16 s.

Item paie pour quatre ayes a faire lesquels huimandes 8 s.

Item plus paie pour quatre boites de lathes a ardoise pour ice 3 s. 4 d.

A Guill[aume] Furel charpentier a ung jour avec ung manouvrier pour ung jour et demy 15 s. 9 d.

A la Roulland pour quatre chevrons 10 s.

Paie deux autres chevrons a faire les establies aux macons 4 s. 6 d.

Pour la portage des [dites] chevrons 12 d.

Item plus paie corde et ficelle tant pour lesquels establies que pour la lampe de leglise 5 s.

Item paie a Gaudier fondeur demeurant au court de la rue aux pretresses les deux chantepleurs aultre donnes quy sont devant establies 20 s.

Item plus paie six aes a faire lesquelles huiandes 12 s.

Item paie pour trois charpentier qui ont vacque une jour et demy pour faire les establies aux macons 18 s.

A Jehan Pothyn ymaginier pour huit journees pour avoir taille de bois de noyers ung propheste p[ou]r faire ung moule et patron pour les plombieres 45 s.

Item paie au Testu platrier pour cinq cent le latte a ardoise 25 s.

Item paie pour demy cent carrel audit Testu platrier pour paner en leglise devant la chaire a prescher comprins la portage 2 s. 10 d.

A Martin Desperrois pour une piece de bois de noier de laquelle a este taille ledit propheste pour lesquel plombiers 30 s.

Item paie pour trois chappeaulx de roses pour Saint Sacrement 4 s.

A ung paintre nom[me] Jehan de Lion pour avoir painct en la dit tour ung grant prophete de plomb 30 s.

Item paie a ung dignar qui escure les chandelliers dentour le cueur et quatre autres chandelliers avec la croche de cueur et cinquante deux bacynes dehault dentour ledit

cueur et nef de ladite eglise pour lentree a Pasques 1516 55 s.

Paie par Maistre Louys Orel pour chyment 2 s. 3 d.

Pluse paie par lequel Orel aux charpentiers pour les establies et pour le pillier Nicolas Jolly 16 s.

Plus paie ausquels machons pour la boullies et charbon 15 d.

Pour lesquels macons pour neuf pouchers de plaitre 4 s. 9 d.

A Pierre Lacanne estaimyer pour avoir plo[m]bine les crampons du pipitre de leglise et pour avoir plombine le pillier a Nicolas Jolly 4 s.

Pour avoir faict escripte en grosse lettres et notter sur parchemyn le Passion de mardy en la septmaine sainte 28 s.

Pour 6 leviers pour les macons p[ou]r lever leurs pierres 3 s.

Pour avoir du bois a faire les trestes pour la table ou les gens sont reuonyes a Pasques lesquellz trestes ou este deffaiz pour la Pasques 1516 6 s. 6 d.

A dit Maistre Loys Orel pour clou pour le portage du plomb

Paie pour le plomb de messire de N[otr]e Dame envoie peser par les plombiniers tant pour la vicomte que pour la portage et raportage 7 s. 8 d.

Pour avoir recue le plomb de messiere de Notre Dame pour 2192 l. de plomb et pour avoir aporte le pois de la vicomte a le peser 10 s.

Pour avoir donne a boire aux bronettiers qui ont mis le plomb au pois 3 s.

Paie a Lignard Flesche paitre pour avoir fait ung pourtrait pour le sacaire et custode du corpus domini lequel avoir fait contraindre Colin Ausoult 15 s.

A Jehan le Tellier qui a la charge de arrimer lorloge de leglise pour trois annees 18 l.

A Guill[aume] le Maistre qui a la charge de arrimer le kadren pour deux ans trois termes 5 l. 10 s.

Aultres mises de macons des deux pilliers dentres les quatres tourelles

Paie a Maistre Pierre Gregoire pour deux pilliers dentre lesquel tourelles par marche fait a luy ainsi quil appert par sa quittance 44 l.

A ce comprins quatre livres tournoi quy luy ont este donnees pour sa paine davoir trace les pierres aux compaignons de deux tourelles

Item paie a deux macons pour agreez en ladit tour tant a la lanterne qui ailliers a chacun 8 jours et deux jour et demy pour ung manouvrier 70 s. 3 d.

Pour deux macons quy ont besongne a chacun quatre journee et demy sur la voute de la lanterne 36 s.

Paie au serviteur du fossier pour prendre garde sur lesq
    macons   2 s.

A deux macons pour avoir parfait les degres de quatre
    tourelles de la lanterne   40 s.

A Ancel Ramachart pour le charriage de sept tonneaulx
    et demy de pierre aportes de des[sus] le quay a 3 s.
    pour ch[acu]n tonnel de descharge   22 s. 6 d.

Plus paie audit Ramachart pour avoir acharie une pierre
    printe a Notre Dame   4 s.

Paie aux [] de Notre Dame pour ladit pierre comprins le
    charge fait par eulx jusque a Notre Dame   50 s. 2 d.

A deux charpentiers pour avoir fait les establies des petitz
    pilliers dentre lesquelles tourelles chacun ung jour
                                          8 s.

A ung macon pour avoir assis des marches a ung pillier a
    une des quatre dix   3 s. 6 d.

A deux charpentier quy ont dessendu le bois de la tour
    aussi au fossier et a son compaignon   26 s.

Paie en corde pour les dites establies   2 s. 6 d.

A ung benelier pour avoir oste les orions de la petite estre
                                         22 s.

Paie a la femme Michault Laubs pour une piece de bois a
    parfaire les barrieres des entrees de cymetiere   9 s.

A deux charpentiers qui ont faut lesquelles barrieres et
    clostures dudit petit estre   24 s.

Paie a Loys Papillon huchier pour la chaire de Saint
    Maclou   11 s. 3 d.

Item paie a Maistre Pierre Gregoire pour avoir fait refaire
    la muraille et passage de la petite estre du coste de la
    barriere au trois macons sont bargue trois journees a
    cha[cu]n ung jour   12 s.

Paie a Pierre Huillart pour avoir paint des fleurs de lis de
    noir sur le plomb de la t[ou]r le 4 may 1517   30 s.

Paie pour ung huys pour clorre la lanterne   9 s.

Item paie a ung couvieur qui a laste aud enpartie de la
    dite tour pour deux journee et demy   10 s.

A ung charpentier nomme Berthrenle merrier luy trois
    pour avoir faite une lucarne sur lhuis de la lantern
                                   17 s. 6 d.

A ung couvrier pour avoir parlasse en ladit tour pour trois
    jours   12 s.

A ung huchier pour avoir fait une chaise neufre apres cher
    pour monsieur le cure   6 l. 10 s.

A Michel le Serf serrurier par les maings de mon frere Je-
    han Dufour a quy luy ont baille largent pour avoir fait
    la ferraille des barrieres tant de la grante estre que de
    petit estre   40 s.

Item paie a ung dignart pour avoir escure les pilliers den-
    tour le cueur et croix comme en a de coustume tous
    les ans pour ce pour lan a Pasques   55 s.

Pour ung pouchon de vin pour lesquels Pasques 1517
    comprins le charrage   6 l. 2 s. 3 d.

Pour erbes a sens en leglise a la feste Notre Dame   22 d.

Item paie a Jacques de Dessus la Mare pour sa maison qui
    a este abattue a lentree du Roy en Claquerel la somme
    de 50 livre tournois sans autres 50 tournois augmente
    livres que a paie Jehan Dufour conseille aud dessus la
    Mare pour ce paie par ledit Dufour son frere tressorier
                                      50 l.

Item paie au fossier pour une eschelle pour servir en
    leglise   3 s. 4 d.

Item paie pour le sacrement pour le corpus domini trois
    chappeaulx de roses   5 s.

Item paie a mon frere Jehan Dufour laisne conseilles sur la
    somme de cinquante livre tournois quil a preste a
    leglise pour aidder a fournir la somme de cent livres
    pour bailler a Jacque de Dessus la Mare sur ce quy luy
    peult estre debv a cause de la denanture de sa maison
    assise en la rue Claquerel quy a este battue a lentre de
    Roy la somme de 20 livres tournois est luy debu doive
    de reste trente livres tournois   20 l.

Departmental Archives, Seine-Maritime, Rouen, G6879 Fabric Account, 1514–1517

Compte du tresor et fabrique de leglise et parroisse de
    Mons Sainct Maclou a Rouen fait par Jehan Dufour le
    jeune filz de deffunct Pierre Dufour Jehan Dufour
    le jeune quarternier et Maistre Louys Orel tresoriers
    de ladite eglise commench[an]t a la Toussaintz lan de
    grace mil ve et quatorze et finissant semblable jour de
    Toussaincts mil ve dix et sept

Receipts

Ensuit la recepte faite par ledit Jehan Dufour le

Jeune . . . de loeuvre	411 l.	19 s. 9 d.
. . . reliques	364 l.	6 s. 9 d.
. . . le plat vollant	11 l.	5 s. 2 d.
. . . vierge mairie	734 l.	5 s.
. . . malades	6 l.	11 s. 8 d.
. . . devocions	141 l.	16 s. 8 d.
. . . laiz faitz	15 l.	81 s. 5 d.
. . . fosses	174 l.	14 s. 4 d.
(e.g.), des gens inhu[me]s dedens la dite eglise		
. . . hausses	27 l.	1 s. 8 d.
(e.g.), droit de drapperie		
. . . de demere des lettres donnees qui estoient debues de messires de lhostel de la ville de Rouen	254 l.	6 s.
. . . devocions pour le plomb	149 l.	2 s. 9 d.

. . . rentes et revenues des maisons aparte-
nantes a la d[ite] eglise
. . . louages de maisons

Expenses

Cy ensuit les misse faictes de ce p[rese]nt compte A este
preste par Jehan et Anthoine diz Dufour freres le 13
jour de juing 1513 la somme de deux cent livres
tournoi

Item apie par ledit Jehan Dufour tresorier a Jehan le
Preux plombinier la somme de deux cent sept livres
six sous six deniers ainsi quil appert par trois quitances
signees par ledit le Preux pour ladite somme

207 l. 6 s. 6 d.

Item plus paie audit Guill[aum]e Comte sur ce qui luy
peult estre debu pour la dite eglise et conpte la quittance la somme trente livres

Item paie par ladit Jehan Dufour tresorier a Symonet le
Cousterier carrier de Verno[n] pour pierre quil a
livree a ladite egli[se] la somme   158 l.

Item paie a Martin Le Bourc serrurier pour la croix de fer
de lesquille Sainct Maclou quil a faicte toute neufve
pesant 756 livres de fer a 2 solz t[ournois] chacune
livre   73 l. 17 s. 6 d.

Item paie au paintre qui a dore ledit cocquet pour ce et
pour paint   5 l.

Item paie a Barante pour avoir dore ung archet de plomb
pour scavoir comb[ie]n lesquels pilliers pourroient
couster a dorer   2 s. 6 d.

Item emplus paies auditz Noel Barante pour avoir dore et
blanchy de blanc de plomb a huille ladite croix de fer
et la ditz pomme de lacon pour or et paint douvier
ainsi quil appert par sa quittance la somme   8 l.

Item paie audit Noel Barante pour acheter six cent de fin
or pour dorer les dauphins daup[re]z ladite croix

9 l. 18 s.

Item paie a Pierre Huillart sur les huit pilliers dentour
lesquille de la dite eglise pour avoir de lor

15 l. 12 s. 6 d.

Item paie a Pierre Champaigne et a Yvon de Clerc ser-
ruriers pour avoir monter en hault a lesquille de la
dicte tour jusques a la croix pour voir et visiter la dicte
croix qui trembloit   20 s.

Item paie ledit Jehan Dufour a Maistre Martin Desperrois
charpentier compte trois quittance signees de sa main

50 l.

Notes

Introduction

1. Bartolomeo Facio, *Liber de viris illustribus*, 1454–55, as cited by G. Faggin, *Complete Paintings of the Van Eycks*, 9.

2. Chanoine L. Prévost, *Histoire de la paroisse et des curés de Saint-Maclou*, 25–30.

3. Charles Ouin-Lacroix, *Histoire de l'église de la paroisse de Saint-Maclou*, 98–99. The privilege of the holy oil was granted in 1514 by Cardinal Georges d'Amboise after the fire that destroyed the spire of the cathedral crossing. The oil, along with other holy relics, reliquaries, and vestments from the cathedral were temporarily stored at Saint-Maclou. Arthur Fillon was rewarded by the archbishop for his generous gifts and solicitations for the reconstruction of the cathedral spire by granting the parish church the possession of the oil and the right of its distribution to other parishes.

4. Philippe Deschamps, "Les Entrées Royales à Rouen."

5. François Farin, *Histoire de la ville de Rouen*, 124.

6. New studies include Linda Seidel, *Jan van Eyck's Arnolfini Portrait*; Craig Harbison, *Jan van Eyck: The Play of Realism*, and *The Mirror of the Artist*; Edwin Hall, *The Arnolfini Betrothal*. See Chapter 6, note 34.

7. The secondary sources on Saint-Maclou frequently mentioned in this study are the following: François Farin, *Histoire de la ville de Rouen*; Charles Ouin-Lacroix, *Histoire de l'église et de la paroisse de Saint-Maclou de Rouen*; Charles de Robillard de Beaurepaire, "Notice sur les architects de Saint-Maclou"; Julien Loth, *Une visite à l'église Saint-Maclou*; René Herval, *Saint-Maclou de Rouen*; Alfred Léon Jouen, "Eglise de Saint-Maclou"; Jean Taralon, "L'Eglise de Saint-Maclou caractères"; Elizabeth Chirol, "Saint-Maclou de Rouen"; Chanoine L. Prévost, *Histoire de la paroisse et des curés de Saint-Maclou*; Catherine Bodin-Cerné, "Saint-Maclou de Rouen."

Chapter 1. History of Construction Through Written Sources

1. A full French transcription of the church fabric accounts appears in the Appendix. The Latin and French transcriptions of other types of documents are found in the footnotes.

2. The Troyes building accounts have been published by Stephen Murray, *Building Troyes Cathedral*; the Gaillon accounts were published by A. Deville, *Comptes de dépenses*. Extensive building records exist for other late gothic monuments, including Prague Cathedral: see Joseph Neuwirth, *Die Wochenrechnungen und der Betrieb des Prager Dombaues*; on Xanten, see S. Beissel, *Die Baufuhrung der Mittelalters*.

3. The *petit cartulaire* is a small folio of ninety-five parchment sheets, collated and certified by the Rouen notaries, Robert Le Vigneron and Jehan Gouel.

4. The *Grand Chartrier* or register of charters is a fully illuminated manuscript on 489 folios of vellum. The register was compiled at three different times. The first part, folios 1 through 399, includes material pertinent to the construction of the church.

5. The principal primary sources pertinent to the construction of Saint-Maclou are cataloged in the G series of the departmental archives (running from G 6869 to G 8847) and are summarized in the *Inventaires sommaires des archives départementales antérieures à 1790*, vols. I–IV, Paris, 1868–87, and vols. V–VII, Rouen, 1892–1912, assembled by Charles de Robellard de Beaurepaire for the department of Seine-Inférieure (now Seine-Maritime). What fabric accounts for the period of construction survived were transferred to the archives by Beaurepaire in the late nineteenth century; the majority, however, had been lost sometime before. Until that time they were housed in the choir treasury of Saint-Maclou, located above the chapel of the curate. The documents relative to construction fall into four cate-

gories: (1) cartularies (G 6872 or the *petit cartulaire* and G 6873 or the *Grand Chartrier*); (2) fabric accounts (G 6874 to G 6885); (3) register of the deliberations of the fabric beginning in 1582 but containing information relative to restoration; and (4) miscellaneous loose documents, most of which are found in duplicate transcription in the cartularies.

6. Hughes d'Orgues, from a wealthy Burgundian family, was elected as the seventy-fifth archbishop of Rouen in 1431 after a two-year vacancy. In the same year he attended the Council of Basel along with the curate of Saint-Maclou, Jean Mercier. Both Hughes and Mercier died in 1436. F. Pommeraye, *Histoire des archevêques de Rouen*, 553.

7. Rouen, Archives Seine Maritime, G6872 (*Petit cartulaire*), fols. 54–55 and G7040 (loose parchment). Published in French translation by Paul Le Cacheux, *Rouen au temps de Jeanne d'Arc pendant l'occupation anglaise, 1419–1449*, 246–47. Dated 16 September 1432, and conferred by Robin Le Vigneron, notary, on 3 September 1436:

> Hugo miseratione divina Rothomagenis archiepiscopus universis et singulis Christi fidelibus salutem in domino prosperam et felicem. Sicut mater in bonis filiorum jocundatur ita nos in operibus virtuosis subditorum nostrorum catholice viventium, maxime que spiritualia videntur et ad vitam ducunt eternam, merito congaudemus. Exhibita siquidem nobis nuper pro parte dilectorum nostrorum thesaurariorum et parrochianorum ecclesie parrochialis Sancti Macuti Rothomagensis peticio continebat ipsam parrochialem ecclesiam Sancti Macute Rothomagensis inter ceteras parrochiales ecclesias nobis subditas notabiliorem reputatam casa fortuito et vetustatis in maximam ruinam versam et a paucis diebus citra ad terram pro media parte dejectam, adeo quod pro quarta parrochianorum et aliorum ibidem affluentium parte suscipienda non sufficiebat nec sufficit porcio residua, reedificacione repparacionibusque non modicis atque sumptuosis indigere; que quidem sine piis Christi fidelium elemosinis et donis caritativis fieri non possunt. Nos igitur cupientes et desiderantes domino populum nobis commissum reddere acceptabilem et bonorum morum et operum sectatorem, fideles ipsos ad complacendum et quasi quibusdam allectivis indulgentiarum nuctrimentis videlicet et remissionibus incitamur ut inde reddantur divine gracie

aptiores et ut ipsi Christi fideles ad eamdem eo libencius confluant et ad ejus reedificacionem et repparacionem manus suas adjutrices porrigont quo ex hoc ibidem uberius dono celestis gracie conspexerint se reffectos. Omnibus vere penitentibus et confessis qui in Nativitatis, Resurectionis, Ascensionis et Penthecostes ac Eucaristie domini nostri Jesu Christi, necnon Assumpcionis, Nativitatis, Concepcionis et Annunciationis gloriose virginis Marie, Omniumque Sanctorum nativitatis Sancti Johannis Baptiste apostolorumque Petri et Pauli festivitatibus ac eciam in dicti gloriosisimi confessoris Sancti Macuti duorum festorum annalium solennitatibus ac in primis verperis singularum festivitatum et solennitatum predictarum singulisque aliis diebus pie et devote dictam ecclesiam visitaverint et ad reedificacionem et reparacionem ejusdem manus suas porrexerint adjutrices de omnipotentis Dei misericordia ac glorisose virginis Marie apostolorumque Petri et Pauli et beatissimorum Romani et Hugonis, ecclesie Rothomagensis archiepiscoporum piis meritis et intercessionibus confisi, pro singulis festivitatibus et solennitatibus predictis quadraginta, vesperis autem triginta et singulis aliis diebus viginte dies de injunctis sibe penitentiis misericorditer relaxamus. Datum sub mago sigillo curie nostre Rothomagensis anno domini millesimo ccccl xxijo die decim sexta mensis septembris.

8. Rouen, Archives Seine-Maritime, G6873 (*Grand Chartrier*), fol. 373.

9. Rouen, Archives Seine-Maritime, G6874 (Fabric Account for 1436–37) See Appendix.

10. For a discussion of drawings and design, see Chapters 2, 3, and 6.

11. This is based on the evidence discussed in Chapter 5. In 1412, Pierre Robin was paid 72 sous for a drawing of the facade gable of the chapel of Saint-Yves in Paris. Thus, the considerable sum 43 livres 10 sous suggests that the payment was for more than a daily wage and a single drawing.

12. Rouen, Archives Seine-Maritime, G6872 (*Petit cartulaire*), fol. 29ff. 19 October 1434: "faire dire chanter et celebrer en la dite eglise Saint Maclou tous les jours de lan une messe en la chapelle Notre Dame nouvellement encommencee a faire pour les ames des donneurs leurs peres et meres parents amis et bienfacteurs trepasses." This mass was to be said daily and sustained with rev-

enues from the gift of a house on the rue du pont Honfray, three rents on a house on the rue de la Foullerie, and seven livres of rent on a house in the parish of Saint Paul.

13. Rouen, Archives Seine-Maritime, G6872 (*Petit cartulaire*), verso of cover. The poem was first published by Charles Beaurepaire, "Notices sur les architectes de Saint-Maclou," *Nouveau recueil des notes historiques et archéologiques*, II, 1888, 296–297. Beaurepaire transcribed the Latin date, now partially effaced, "Actum anno Domino millesimo quadringentesimo tricesemo sexto in mense maii de XXIII." Julien Loth (*Saint-Maclou de Rouen*, 13–14) mistakenly records the date as 23 May 1446.

> A celle fin qu'on ait memore
> d'aucuns biens faiz et benefices
> que on a fait et fait encore
> pour croistre l'euvre et edifices
> d'un lieu ou les divins services
> sont faiz et diz devotement.
> C'est de l'eglise proprement
> de Saint Maclou qui commencée
> est puis nagueres en pencée
> ont eu les Tresoriers presens
> qui pour eulx est un très grant sens—
> de faire escrire en telle guise
> Aucuns prouffiz de leur église
> qu'on peult nommer chartres par nom
> à celle fin qu'on si avise
> Dorenavant et par raison
> car plusieurs lettres ce scet on
> sont empirées par mal garder.
> Qui ne men croit voit regarder.
> Beneiz soient ceulx en Paradis
> qui le temps passé, com je dis,
> ont donné de leurs biens au lieu
> et posées soient au milieu
> les amês de ceulx à venir
> qui pour ledit lieu maintenir
> et pour aidier à le parfaire
> en auront aucun souvenir
> comme de leur omosnc y faire.

14. Elizabeth Chirol ("Saint-Maclou de Rouen," 2–3) suggested that the present church was begun only after 1436.

15. Jean Taralon provides a good description of the damage sustained by Saint-Maclou in 1944 and the subsequent restoration in "L'Eglise de Saint-Maclou, caractères."

16. Rouen, Archives Seine-Maritime, G6874. See the Appendix.

17. Raymond Quenedey, *L'habitation rouennaise*, 204–9. Quenedey provides translations of the medieval carpentry terms into modern French. The *souschevrons* (*sousquevrons*) refer to the principal rafters separated by the *chevrons* (*crevons*) or upper rafters by the *fillière* or *panne*. The *solive* (*soliveau, solivel, sollivier*) are the joists that rest on the tie beams or *entraits*, referred to in the medieval texts as *trefs*.

18. Rouen, Archives Seine-Maritime, G6872 (*Petit cartulaire*), fol. 28, and G7062 (loose parchment). Dated 22 March 1428: "A tous ceulx que ces lectres verront orront Pierre du Bus garde du seel de obligatione de sa buonte de Rouen salue savoir faisons que par devant Pierre Charite tabellion sise en la dite viconte fu presents Jehanne deguerpie de feu Jehan Capperon demeurante en la parroisse Saint Maclou de Rouen laquelle meue de devotion de sa bonne vonlonte sane mille contrain te recognut et confessa avoir donne quarre transporte et par ces presentes donne quarre transporte et delaisse afin dheritage a tous jour pour elle et pour ses hoirs pour dieu et en omosne au tresor et fabrique de la dite eglise Saint Maclou et pour laugmentation de loeuvre dicelle sest assavoir tout."

19. For a discussion of Pierre Robin, see Chapter 5.

20. For a discussion of the craft of masonry in the parish of Saint-Maclou, see Chapter 6.

21. 67 livres far exceeds the yearly pension of other Rouennais master masons. The amount is difficult to read in the fabric accounts and may be a mistranscription or reflect an error in entry.

22. For a full discussion of the individual master masons of Saint-Maclou, see Chapter 5.

23. Frédéric Godefroy, *Dictionnaire de l'ancienne langue française*, I, 397. Jean Marie Perouse de Montelos, *Principes d'analyses scientifiques en architecture*, I, 62.

24. Léon Mirot, "Paiements et quittances," 267, dated 21 June 1408: "Quittance de Jean de Portqueroult, carrier, du Val-des-Leux, à Guilllaume le Comte, gouverner et payeur des ouvrages du Pont-de-Seine à Rouen, de 13 l. 6 s. tournois pour vente de 241 carreaux employée aux talus de la chaussée de Pont-de-Seine à Rouen," MS fr. 26036 no. 4045.

25. The use of inferior and inexpensive stone for foundations may have been standard practice. Stephen Murray states that inexpensive local chalk was used for the foundations of Troyes Cathedral,

causing unmeasurable difficulties (Building Troyes Cathedral, 9–10).

26. The term *bors d'illand* is used several times in the accounts of Saint-Maclou. O. Thorel ("Le 'Bors d'illand' à la cathédrale d'Amiens," 53–79) shows that the term refers to oak cut on the quarter rather than in planks. This wood was more expensive but was less likely to warp. As a result, *bors d'illand* was used for special projects that required an even grain and plane surface. A Rouen Cathedral account (Rouen, Archives, Seine-Martime, G2510) of 1465–66 records the purchase of six hundred pieces of *bors d'illand* from Fredig Franzon (*hollandais* and merchant of wood) to be used for the choir stalls. These characteristics also make it suitable for templates. Quenedey points out that this type of wood had to be imported due to the deforestation of land around Rouen by the end of the fourteenth century (*L'habitation rouennaise*, 119).

27. Rouen, Archives Seine-Maritime, G6876 (Fabric Account for 1443–46), For complete transcription, see the Appendix.

28. Rouen, Archives Seine-Maritime, G6876. Dated 24 November 1443: "A Jehan Turgnois couvrieur de rosel pour la chappelle devant le cueur et sur les loges recouvert pour tout entage pour ce faire ice . . . 40 sous."

29. Rouen, Archives Seine-Maritime, G6876: "A Jehan le Prevost machon qui estoit mallade de sa chute de la chappelle Notre Dame donne 6 breton vallent 4 sous 6 denier."

30. Rouen, Archives Seine-Maritime, G6876: "Pour ung carpentier mestre ungne estre a la chapelle Saint Louys 3 sous."

31. Rouen, Archives Seine-Maritime, G6876. 11 July 1445: "Pour Asseoir le engin Grenouville en la chapelle Saint Katrin a quatre carpentiers 2 jours et demi, 40 sous."

32. Rouen, Archives Seine-Maritime, G2087 (Cathedral Chapter Register) and G7070.

33. E. De LaQuérière, *Saint-Laurent, ancienne église paroissiale de Rouen*, Rouen, Boissel, 1866, 12.

34. Rouen, Archives Seine-Maritime, G7040 (loose parchment) and G6873 (*Grand Chartrier*). Published in French translation by Charles Ouin-Lacroix, *Histoire de l'église de la paroisse de Saint-Maclou de Rouen*, 223–27.

35. A full discussion of patronage and building revenues is found in Chapter 4.

36. Rouen, Archives Seine-Maritime, G7040 (loose parchment) and G6873 (*Grand Chartrier*). Dated 6 February 1447 and notarized 29 July 1448:

Henricus dei gratia francorum et anglie rex ad perpetuam rei memoriam regi regum per quem vivimus regnum et regnamus gratum speramus impendere obsequium si pro ipsius reverentia suorum vota fidelium favore prosequimur gracioso et ad ea que dominum cultus comerunt augmentum et locorum sacrorum ampliacionem atque decoramentum gratium manum liberaliter extendamus Notum igitur facimus universis presentibus pariter et futuris humilem supplicacionem pro parte dilectorum nostrorum parrochianorum parrochialis ecclesie sancte maclonii in civitate nostra rothomagensis nobis porrectam nos cum favore intellexisse continentem ex ipsi supplicantes mediante adinutoris aliarum devotarum personarum que ad hoc manus suas preestenderunt adiutrices ecclesiam illam que ex vetustate diu caduca et ruinosa extiterat evelli fecerunt et maiorem atque pulcriorem quam antae fuerat omnino de novo maximus suis sumptibus reedificari faciunt et jam per multos annos inceperunt pro quibus operibus perficiendis necnon pro amplicacionem cimiterii eiusdem ecclesie ipsi supplicantes ad vtilitatem illius acquisiuerunt fundum unum eidem ecclesie ex una parte contiquum quantitatis quatuor perchatarum cum dimidia terre vel circiter super quo stat domus una cum intersignis vulgariter dicto les flagons ab alia parte adheret domini maginderam ecclesie rothmagensis et ab alia parte uno publio ante ecclesiam illam se extendenti cunent tamen ipse supplicantes qui officiarii nostre fundum illum eos diu possidere non permiterent nisi de gracia nostra speciali per admortisacionis munus deremendum promideretur oportuno illud cum humilitate ad vtilitatem dicte ecclesie instanter imploramus huic est quod nos ob Reverentiam dei omnipotentis saluatoris nostri eiusque gloriose genetricis virginis marie et dicti sancti maclonii ut ordinum suffragiorum aliorum que priorum operum in eadem ecclesiam fiendorum participes effici mereamus. Predictis supplicantibus nomini sepeinte parrochialis ecclesie sancti maclonii et ad vtilitatem euisdem in perpetuum degracia nostri speciali certa sciencia et auctoritate regia.

37. Rouen, Archives Seine-Maritime, G7040 (loose parchment) and G6873 (Grand Chartrier). Dated 6 May 1452:

Overmus miseratione divina tantum Sancti Martini in montibus sacrosancte romane ecclesie presbyter cardinalis de Estoutevilla Wigariter nuncupatiis in regno francie singulisque Galliarum provinciis apostolice sedis legatus universis christi fidelibus praesentates litteras inspecturis salutem in dominum sempiternam ecclesiarum fabrins manus porrigere adjutrices principium et neaturum reputantes frequenter christi fideles ad impendendum eis auxilium nostris litteris exhortamur et ut ad ideo forcius animentur quo se speraverint animarum commodum adipisei pro hiis temporalibus nonnumquam eis spiritualia munera videlicet remissiones et indulgencias elargimur cupientes igitur ut parrochialis ecclesia Sancti Macuti Rothomagensis perficiatur reparetur et augmentetur ac congruis frequentetur honoribus et ut ipsi christe fideles eo libentius devotionis causa ad eamdem confluant ac ad perfectionem reparacionem et augmentationem structurarum ediffiiciorum librorum et aliorum ornamentorum eiusdem manus promptius porrigant adiutrices quo se senserint celestis dono gracie uberius reffectos de omnipotentis dei nomina ac Beatorum petri et pauli apostolorum eius et qua fungimur in hac parte autoritate confisi omnibus et singuliis vere penitentibus et confessis qui in Beate Marie Virginis conceptionis et assumptionis et sanctorum Macuti Egidii et Lupi et Clari necnon diebus dominicis videlicet in qua cantatur letare Jerusalem et in Ramis Palmarum et die veneris sancta festivitatibus et diebus dictam ecclesiam devote visitaverint annuatim ac ad perfectionem reparationem et augmentacionem structurarum ediffiicorum calicum librorum et ornamentorum eiusdem manus porrexerint adiutrices videlicet in Sancti Macuti et sanctorum Egidii et Lupi pro quolibet unum annum et singulis aliis festivitatibus et diebus supradictis centum dies de injunctis eis penitentiis misericorditer in domino relaxamus presentibus perpetuis temporibus duraturis in quorum omnium et singulorum fidem et testimonium premissorum presentes litteras per secretarium meum infrascriptum subscribi si-gillique nostre oblongi fecimus appensione communire datum rothomagsi anno incarnationis domini millisimo quadrigentesimo quinquagesimo secundo die sexta mensis maii pontificatus sanctissimus in christo patris et domini nostri domini Nicolai divina providencia pape.

38. Rouen, Archives Seine-Maritime, G 7071 (loose parchment and paper). Herval (p. 45) published a list of the names of the *dizainiers* and the *centeniers*. Their subscription gifts range from two sous to larger amounts. Laurent Leduc, for example, donated one hundred sous.

39. Etienne Dufour is listed as a *centenier* and Bodin-Cerné suggests that he died in 1448. A *centenier* was a parish representative appointed by the city government and responsible for monitoring the nonresidents of the parish. See Philip Benedict, *Rouen during the Wars of Religion*, 37. Catherine Bodin-Cerné, "*Saint Maclou de Rouen*," 57.

40. F. Perrot, "Le Vitrail à Rouen," Rouen, 1972, 27.

41. Beaurepaire, "Notice sur les architectes des Saint-Maclou," II, 300. Beaurepaire does not cite his source. Dated 8 August 1453: "en consideration de lexcellent notable et somptueulx edifice de grace Dieu merveilleusement commence et designantement en chapelles faictes fondemens et ustres edifices en lhoneur de Dieu et dudit patron glorieux bien advance."

42. Recorded by François Farin, *Histoire de Rouen*, 1668, 158. Tomb inscription was originally located in Chapel of Sainte-Clothilde (SIIAII), destroyed in 1944: "Ci repose Maître André Pajot, pour le salut de l'ame, duquel Maître Jean Pajot, Chanoine en l'Eglise de Rouen, et Pierre Pajot son frère, Beneficier en ladite Eglise, enfans dudit André, decede l'an 1460 ont fondé."

According to Beaurepaire ("Notices sur les architectes de Saint-Maclou," 300), Pierre Pajot, canon of Rouen and curate of Saint-Laurent-en-Caux, left 10 livres to Saint-Maclou in remembrance of his father and sister. Pajot's nephew, Pierre Coutier, a royal physician and citizen of Aix-en-Province, was buried in Saint-Maclou. On 23 February 1461 Coutier gave a property in Neuville-sous-Farceaux to the church.

43. Ci-devant git Jean de Grenouville,
Homme prudent, Marchand, né d'Etteville,
Empres . . . en cette Paroisse,

Vint demourer du tems de sa jeunesse
De ses deniers, et par sa grand franchise
A fait faire le plus de cette Eglise,
Qui trépassa en l'an mil quatre cents
Soixante et six en Aout fina son tems
Dont il étoit le quatorzième jour,
Sa femme aussi fille Estienne du Four
Et ses enfans gisent tous sous la lame,
Qui trépassa la bonne preude femme
L'an quatre cens mille et soixante-quatre,
Au mois de Mars, il n'en faut rien rabattre,
Il en étoit le jour vingt et cinquième,
Prions à Dieu pour achever la Poesme,
Que leurs ames, après le jugement,
L'à sus en gloire conduise sauvement.

44. Published by Beaurepaire, "Notes sur les architectes de Rouen," 74. Beaurepaire does not cite the archive number: "Mardi, xiiiie du mois de janvier, presente a Jol. Chauvin, maistre macho de s. maclo, lequel espousa, le dit jour la fille de comte, xv s."

45. Rouen, Archives Seine-Maritime, G7047 (loose parchment) and G6873 (*Grand Chartrier*). Dated 27 May 1458, address given by Guillaume Gombaut, Vicomte of Rouen: "a lentour et au circuit et espace de la dite eglise au lieu et en la place au estoit lancien et viel mur sur rue faisant closture et separation entre le cemetiere joignant a leglise et la voirie apres toise fait par maistre Richard Dusbustz, Estinne Le Maire, Martin Le Bourgois, Colin Duval, Jehan Le Prevost, Robin Riviere, Jehan Pontis, Jehan Chauvin, ouvriers jures des metiers et maconnerie et de charpenterie a Rouen depuis et a lenviron de lostel des Flagons jusques au vieux muret estant au cimetiere a lendroit de la chapelle Saint Katherine."

46. Ibid. ". . . comptet et appartient de entretenir garder et maintenir la voire du Roi en son ancien point et estat sans ce que aucunes personnes de quelque estat ou condicion qu ilz soient puissent aucunement entre prendre commencer ou innover aucuns ediffices sur icelle voire."

47. Epitaph recorded by Farin, *Histoire de la ville de Rouen*, 158, in the chapel of Saint Esprit. Still visible in the chapel dedicated to Saint Anthony of Padua (SIIWII): "Ci-devant git honorable et prudente personne Messire Jean de la Cayne, en son vivant curé de Saint Antoine-de-la-Forêt, qui a été Vicaire de cette Eglise, et qui trépassa lan 1465, le 23 octobre."

48. Rouen, Archives Seine-Maritime, G6877, (Fabric Account for 1465–70). The receipts for this period were 3,188 livres 3 sous 7 denier.

49. Rouen, Archives Seine-Maritime, G3694.

50. Rouen, Archives Seine-Maritime, G6873 (*Grand Chartrier*). It was this type of tax that gave rise to *encorblement* and *avant-soliers* in the construction of timber houses in the fifteenth century. These were construction methods that could increase the square footage of a house without increasing taxes by extending the second floor over the street. Quenedey, *L'Habitation rouennaise* 86–88.

51. Rouen, Archives Seine-Maritime, G6876 (Fabric Accounts for 1476–79).

52. Rouen, Archives Seine-Maritime, G2503 (Chapter Deliberations of the Rouen Cathedral): "Collation avec les maitres de maconnerie de Rouen c'est assavoir Le Cignere, Ambroise de Saint Maclou et Jehan Le Ville pour savoir si le tour Saint Romain pourroit porter et soustenir ungestage de machonnerie de hauteur . . . 25 sous 6 denier."

53. Rouen, Archives Seine-Maritime, G7654, (Fabric Account for the parish church of Saint-Vincent, Rouen for 1468–72). These accounts were published in part by Charles Beaurepaire, "Notice sur Saint-Vincent," see also Abbé Edmond Renaud, *Eglise Saint-Vincent*; and Anne Savoie, "Saint Vincent de Rouen."

54. See Chapter 3.

55. Rouen, Archives Seine-Maritime, G6873 (Grand Chartrier), fol. 114: "et en autres icelle veufve a donne et amosne au dict tresor tous les deniers qu'il es conviendra pour lachapt du voirre necessaire estre mis à l'OO du grant portail du celle eglise sainct maclou et six petis fourmeementz de voirre qui sont en dessoubz dudict OO et aussi pour ce que icelle veufve promist faire faire et payer à ses despens le pavement et allé de endroict la chapelle Sainct Symon Sainct Jude."

56. Beaurepaire, "Notice sur les architectes," 301. Jacques Le Roux was the mason at this time.

57. Rouen, Archives Seine-Maritime, G6879, (Fabric Accounts for 1514–17). See the Appendix.

58. Rouen, Archives Seine-Maritime, Tabellionage de Rouen 3035. Published by Beaurepaire, "Notes sur les architectes," III, 1903, 64.

59. Rouen, Archives Seine-Maritime, G2523 (cathedral deliberations). Published by Charles Beaurepaire, "Notice sur le grand portail de la cathédrale de Rouen," 142.

60. Rouen, Archives Seine-Maritime, G6873 (*Grand Chartrier*), fols. 371–72.

61. Rouen, Archives Seine-Maritime, G6873 (*Grand Chartrier*): "Ecclesiam illam que ex vetustate dui caduca et ruinose extiterat evelle fecerunt, et majorem et pulcriorem quam amico fuerot omnino de novo, maximis suis sumptibus reedificoni facuent et jam per multos annos inceperunt." "There remains to complete a lantern begun in stone with a spire which the parishoners intend to construct of wood." Published by Beaurepaire, "Notice sur les architectes," 294.

62. Rouen, Archives Seine-Maritime, G6879, G6880, and G6881. (Fabric Accounts for 1514–17, 1517–20, and 1520–23 respectively). See the Appendix for G6879.

63. Rouen, Archives Seine-Maritime, G6843.

64. Rouen, Archives Seine-Maritime, G6879.

65. Rouen, Archives Seine-Maritime, G6880. Payments are made of 23 November 1518 for 30 livres, 10 January 1519 for 20 livres, 19 February 1519 for 20 livres, 2 April 1519 for 30 livres, 14 May 1519 for 30 livres, 5 July 1519 for 20 livres, and 11 September 1519 for 55 livres.

66. Ibid., and Rouen, Archives Seine-Maritime, G6881. This organ buffet was replaced twenty-five years later. In 1541, a contract was made between the treasurers and Master Jean Goujon for two marble columns to support the new organ in the nave of the church above the central portal (Rouen Archives Seine-Maritime, G6884, Fabric Accounts for 1538–42). It was at that time that the choir *jubé* was destroyed and the *jubé* staircase of Pierre Grégoire was moved to the western entrance where it stands today supporting the organ loft. The enormous cost of the organ buffet and staircase of the original choir *jubé* were partially paid for by another parish subscription "pour ayder a faire les orgues" (Rouen, Archives Seine-Maritime, G6880). This list dated November 1518 includes the names of the curate, Arthur Fillon, as well as the Dufours, and Nicolas de la Chesnay. In the first year, 121 livres 9 sous 6 denier were collected.

67. Cauchée first appears as a *valet* (*varlet*) for Roulland Le Roux working at the cathedral between 1508 and 1509 (Rouen, Seine-Maritime, G2524). In 1513 he is cutting voussoirs for the central portal.

68. This tower was destroyed in storms of the eighteenth century and replaced in the nineteenth century by the present stone spire. The original form of the lantern can be reconstructed from the model of Saint-Maclou in the Musée des Beaux Arts in Rouen and from the illustration of the church in the *Livres des Fontaines* of 1525 (Figs. 3, 5a and 5b).

69. The cathedral chapter chose the wooden spire designed by Martin Desperrois over a stone spire designed by the cathedral master mason Roulland Le Roux. This decision may have been partially based on economic or structural factors, but in any case, Desperrois' spire was never constructed. Marcel Aubert, "La cathédrale de Rouen," 21–22.

70. Once again the treasurers relied on a parish subscription to raise the money for the lead to cover the spire. In the fabric account it is listed under "Devocions pour le plomb," Rouen, Seine-Maritime, G6979.

71. Rouen Archives Seine-Maritime, G6881 (Fabric Account of 1520–23): "Dons fait à l'offrande de Sainct Maclou pour les quatre chappes de damas rouge dont monsr maistre Artus Fillon, curé de la dicte parroisse, a donné son offrende le jour de la Dédicace de la dicte église, qui fait le xxve de juing 1521."

Chapter 2. The High Gothic Canon

1. An exception to this rule are small-scale chapels such as the Sainte-Chapelle of Paris (as well as Vincennes, Riom, and probably Bourges).

2. The statutes of the stonecutters of Strasbourg of 1459, some of the most detailed for the period, indicate that continuity of work between master masons was of great concern for patrons. Regulations were included in the statutes to ensure control over design on the part of the patrons at periods when there was a change in master. Article 10 stipulates that "si un maître a accepté la construction d'un ouvrage et qu'il en a établi le dessin tel que l'oeuvre doit étre exécuté, il ne doit pas modifier ce tracé primitif. Mais il doit exécuter l'ouvrage selon le plan qu'il aura présenté aux seigneurs, villes ou pays afin que l'oeuvre ne soit pas diminuée ou dépréciée." Statutes were published by Dieter Kimpel, "Les méthodes de production des cathédrales."

3. A discussion of the contemporary architecture in Rouen and Paris is taken up in Chapters 4 and 5.

4. Erwin Panofsky, *Gothic Architecture and Scholasticism*, and Michel Bouttier, "La Reconstruction de l'abbatiale de Saint-Denis au XIIIe siècle."

5. A discussion of the iconography of the architecture from the perspective of the patrons is found in Chapter 4.

6. Saint-Urbain and Saint-Maclou are both twice as long as they are wide and their transepts are centrally placed between the nave and the choir. The width to length dimensions of Saint-Urbain are approximately 25.3 m × 51.6 m (to outside walls) and at Saint-Maclou the dimensions are 26.1 m × 52.2 m (to outside walls). The dimensions for Saint-Urbain, Troyes, were provided by Michael T. Davis. More extensive surveys of the plans of Saint-Ouen, Rouen, and Saint-Urbain, Troyes, were undertaken in 1992 by Davis and Neagley and will offer more precise data concerning the design and relationships of these three buildings.

7. Panofsky, *Gothic Architecture and Scholasticism*, 59.

8. The term "classic" was also used by Rolland Sanfaçon to describe French thirteenth-century architecture ("Le rôle des techniques, 111).

9. See Chapter 5 for a discussion of the regional development of the fillet base, plinth, and molding.

10. The fillet plinth, base, and molding is used, for example, in Roulland Le Roux's embrasures of the central portal of Rouen Cathedral and by Martin Chambiges in this facade designs of Troyes and Beauvais Cathedrals.

11. The use of graded components was an essential characteristic of Rayonnant architecture as pointed out by Christopher Wilson, *The Gothic Cathedral*, 122.

12. For corpus on late gothic base profiles see Richard Morris, "The Development of Later Gothic Mouldings in England, c. 1250–1400, part I and part II," Morris includes a few examples of French monuments but no exhaustive study of Flamboyant base profiles exists.

13. Panofsky, *Gothic Architecture and Scholasticism*, 50–51.

14. This observation did not escape John Ruskin, writing in 1880. See Chapter 6.

15. This idea was first suggested to me by Stephen Murray during a graduate seminar at Indiana University. The notion of gothic as an expression of medieval modernism that tended to subvert the "classicist" vocabulary of columns, capitals, and bases of "historicist" architecture of Romanesque is argued by Marvin Tractenberg, "Gothic/'Italian' Gothic: Toward a Redefinition."

16. Continuous moldings appear in the nave of Saint-Urbain, Troyes, and in the nave triforium of Auxerre Cathedral. In both cases, the question of aesthetics may be secondary to considerations of economics. See Michael T. Davis, "On the Threshold of Flamboyant."

17. Caroline Bruzelius ("The Construction of Notre-Dame in Paris") has already pointed this out for the choir of Notre-Dame.

18. Optical illusion is best seen in the contemporary work of Jan van Eyck whose paintings such as the Ghent altarpiece of 1432 combine images of painted sculpture and metalwork with architecture and landscape to create a variety of levels of reality for the viewer. The conscious manipulation of viewer perception in sculpture is discussed by A. Neumeyer, "The Meaning of the Balcony Scene at the Church of Muehlhausen in Thuringia."

19. For Saint-Vivien, Rouen, see the brief article by Daniel Lavallée, "Notes sur l'église Saint-Vivien de Rouen."

20. Individual expression within the rigid confines of workshop tradition and regulation can be linked to changing criteria for the establishment of professional identity as discussed in Chapter 6.

21. Bouttier, "La reconstruction de l'abbatiale de Saint-Denis."

22. Although intentional variety in tracery pattern is not common in French architecture until the second half of the fourteenth century, some exceptions do exist. The clerestory windows in the choir of Le Mans Cathedral, constructed between 1217 and 1254, displayed a north/south paired diversity.

23. I owe the descriptive term "tulip tracery" to Leslie Cavell, a former graduate student at the University of Michigan.

24. The sculpture reliefs in the spandrals of the axial chapel of Lisieux, constructed in 1432, also demonstrate the change from figurative forms to geometry. These linear exercises of stars, circles, pentagons, and polygons decorate an area in the dado that was once occupied by foliage, angels, or animals.

25. E. Viollet-le-Duc, *Dictionnaire raisonné de l'architecture française du XIe au XVIe siècle*, III, s.v. "clef," 272–76.

26. In 1280 the archbishop of Rouen, Guillaume de Flavacourt gave to the chapter dean, Philippe d'Ambleville, a portion of the archiepiscopal manor bordering on the north side of the church "ad faciendam et construendam portam seu introitum ex

parte septentrionali" in exchange for two houses of lesser value. The attribution to Jean Davi is based on a cathedral chronicle of two years earlier that cites "Johanne Davi magistro operis tunc temporis." See A. Deville, *Revue des architectes de la cathédrale du Rouen*, 17–18.

27. Viollet-de-Duc, *Dictionnaire raisonné*, VII, s.v. "portes," 432–53.

28. The dimensions for the cathedral are taken from A. M. Carment-Lanfry, *La Cathédrale Notre-Dame de Rouen*, 65. The width of Saint-Maclou is taken from pier axis to pier axis.

29. James Snyder, *Medieval Art*, 401.

30. Maurice Allinne, "La façade occidentale de la cathédrale de Rouen," and Georges Lanfry, *La façade occidentale de la cathédrale*. The facade-screen appliqué conceived to dress up the cathedral to receive the heart of Charles V was a response similar to the refurbishing of the choir of Gloucester Cathedral to house the body of King Edward II.

31. C. Beaurepaire, "Note sur le grand portail de la cathédrale de Rouen."

32. This was suggested by Daniel Lavallée in the catalogue, *La Renaissance à Rouen*, an exhibition held at the Musée des Beaux-Arts de Rouen, 28 November 1980–28 February 1981, 35.

33. A. Chauvel, "L'Eglise Saint-Maclou de Rouen, Destruction et Consolidation," 164: "C'est un édifice construit à la limite des lois de l'équilibre. Les porte-à-faux y sont nombreux. Les piles ont la section minimum nécessaire à la stabilité."

34. Letter by Laquet, inspection report of 28 October 1944. Monuments historiques dossier, archives no. 1400, 4, 1941–45: "L'opération est difficile non seulement en raison des dommages causé par les bombardements mais aussi en raison de la manière défectueuse dont est construite la tour manière qui défie tout principe de statique et de construction." The damage to the crossing piers had been further aggravated by the placement of a stone spire on the crossing tower in the nineteenth century. The medieval piers were design to support only a wooden spire.

35. The exterior walls of the chapels average .442 m and the interior walls dividing the chapels at floor level are .930 m.

36. Michael T. Davis, "On the Threshold of Flamboyant, 874. According to Davis, the nave pier dimension of pier C is 2.66 m (north-south) × 2.54 m (east-west) with a bay span of 8.4 m. Thus, the ratio of pier diameter to bay span is 1:3.2.

37. Patrice Colmet Daage, *La Cathédrale de Coutances*. Jules Fossey, *Monographie de la cathédrale d'Evreux*.

38. A. Jouen, *La cathédrale de Rouen*.

39. A. Masson, "Le bouchement des piliers de la croisée à Saint-Ouen de Rouen in 1441."

40. Lucien Prieur, "L'Eglise Saint-Germain d'Argentan."

41. A. Masson, *L'Abbaye de Saint-Ouen de Rouen*.

42. This might be compared to the vaults thickness of 30 cm recorded by Marcel Aubert for the cathedral of Rouen ("La cathédrale de Rouen"). The vault of the axial chapel of Notre Dame at Caudebec-en-Caux is of the same thickness as the chapel of Sainte-Clotilde at Saint-Maclou. It was constructed by Guillaume Le Tellier who was directly influenced by the work at Saint-Maclou. Henri Julien, "Clé de voûte de la chapelle de la vierge à Caudebec-en-Caux."

43. The cross section drawing by Vincent of the nave shows five courses in *tas-de-charge* and the west wall of the north transept. These stones extend to the outer wall of the transept. The extensive use of *tas-de-charge* in the choir high vaults became problematic during the restorations after World War II. Chauvel, referring to the north side of the choir, reported that "les maçonneries en tas de charge des compartiments subsistaient seules dans le vide, provoquant une surcharge et surtout une traction sur le mur nord du choeur." After the vaults fell in 1944, these large stones had to be taken down in order to secure the safety of the workers. Chauvel, "L'Eglise Saint-Maclou de Rouen," 166.

44. Iron rods were visible in the damaged flying buttress struts on the south side of the nave before they were restored in the late 1970s.

45. Inconsistencies in the execution of a monument have always been used by the art historian as primary evidence for unraveling the building history. For example, Michel Bouttier uses changes in the design of window tracery to identify and attribute works in mid- thirteenth-century Paris to various masters. Stephen Murray ("The Choir of the Church of Saint-Pierre, Cathedral of Beauvais") convincingly identified changes in underlying geometric schemes of the choir plan of Beauvais Cathedral to illustrate a significant change in masters with different visions, and Michael Davis ("On the Threshold of Flamboyant") has demonstrated that changes in base and molding profiles in the nave of Saint-Urbain reflect shifts in the funding at

the collegiate church. Hans Reinhardt (*La Cathé-drale de Reims*) discusses changes in capital types at Reims Cathedral to illustrate chronology of construction that can be attributed to the four master masons identified in the labyrinth.

46. Stephen Murray has demonstrated that an error in the pitch of the buttress slope presented severe structural problems at Troyes Cathedral, "Master Jehançon Garnache and the Construction of the Vaults and Flyers of the Nave of Troyes Cathedral."

Chapter 3. "le parchemin ou leglise"

1. An expanded discussion of the plan design of Saint-Maclou appears in my article "Elegant Simplicity: The Late Gothic Plan Design of Saint-Maclou in Rouen."

2. Larger axial chapels were added to the Norman cathedrals of Rouen (1302), Coutances (c. 1371–86), Lisieux (c. 1432), Evreux (second half of the fifteenth century), and the abbey of La Trinité at Fecamp (begun 1489 and designed by the Rouennais master mason, Jacques Le Roux).

3. The Porch of the Marmousets, begun in the late fourteenth century by Jean de Bayeux, attached to the south transept of the royal abbey of Saint-Ouen, bears some resemblance to the porch of the Saint-Chapelle in Paris with its boxy massing, double stories, framing buttresses, rose windows set back above the second story, and tympanum depicting the Coronation of the Virgin above the portal at the lower level. The function of the upper room of the porch of the abbey has never been identified but it may have served as a chamber for the visiting duke of Normandy or French king. The porch for the cathedral is linked to its function for the "viri galilae," discussed in Chapter 2.

4. The mean averages of the bay dimensions from west to east are 5.154 m (from the inner wall), 5.417 m, 5,857 m, 6.744 m (transept), 5.857 m, and 5.050 m (Fig. 80).

5. For the Saint-Gall plan, see Walter Horn and Ernst Born, *The Plan of St Gall*. For Cistercian planning, see H. Hahn, *Die frühe Kirchenbaukunst der Zisterzienser*, 236–38. Villard de Honnecourt's drawing of an ideal Cistercian church demonstrates the importance of the transept square in determining other bay dimensions. See H. Hahnloser, ed., *Villard de Honnecourt, Kritische Gesamtausgabe des Bauhuttenbuchs ms. fr. 19093 der Pariser Nationalbibliothek.*

6. S. Murray and J. Addiss, "Plan and Space at Amiens Cathedral." Murray establishes the transept square and adjacent bays as the primary design unit. Caroline Bruzelius points out the symbolic significance of the transept square and aisles at Saint-Denis as it relates to central planned royal mausoleum, *The Thirteenth-Century Church at St-Denis*, 33–42.

7. The width of the central vessel of the hemicycle as read from the center of the piers is 7.574 m. This does not seem to be related to the macromodule square. As François Bucher points out, the great flexibility provided by progressive squaring allowed for a significant number of arbitrary decisions. F. Bucher, "Medieval Architectural Design Methods, 800–1560," 40. The actual dimension of the central vessel, 7.547 m is a slight contraction of the ideal dimension (7.652 m) suggested by the macromodule square.

8. Caroline Bruzelius, "Cistercian High Gothic," 48, states that the radiating chapels were designed around squares of 4.50 m. Michael Davis, "The Choir of the Abbey of Altenberg," 134, points out that squares of 4.80 m were used for the chapels at Altenberg.

9. See R. Krautheimer, "Introduction to an 'Iconography of Mediaeval Architecture.'" Both Suger and Gervais refer to measurements taken from the old church. Michael Davis, "The Choir of the Abbey of Altenberg," 132, suggests that the length and width of the new chevet of Altenberg were derived from the length of the twelfth-century transept.

10. The following is not an attempt to identify conclusively the specific sequence of steps that were actually used at Saint-Maclou but to prove that the abstract geometric relationships established by the plan could easily be translated to simple procedure at the site with only the knowledge of how to construct a right angle and how to set a point through the intersection of arcs. The procedure is quite flexible and the plan could have been set out according to numerous variations of the following procedure. According to illustration 78b point C is established at right angles to line AB and two squares, 0ADC and 0BHC were set out. Using points 0, A, and C, arcs were swung to intersect with the diagonal of square 0ADC and the placement of all the piers and walls was determined. The intersection of 0A with diagonal 0D located point E, the intersection of C0 with diagonal AC located point G, and the intersec-

tion of A0 with diagonal AC located point F. Thus, 0A = 0C = 0E and A0 = AD = AF and C0 = CD = CG.

11. The width of the central vessel or AE was established from the transept. A right angle was constructed at the center point of AE or $0'$ to locate C at the same distance as $0'A$ and $0'E$ (Fig. 81b). The center point (cp) of lines AC and CE were found and $0'B$ and $0'D$ were marked off on radials passing from $0'$ through these centerpoints at the same distance from $0'$ as $0'A$, $0'C$, and $0'E$. As the length of $0'A'$ was known from the transept, then $0'B'$, $0'C'$, and $0'D'$ were marked off along the same radials. B2 is established by the intersection of arcs swung from $C'0'$ and $A'0'$. A2, C2, D2, and E2, are marked off at the same distance along the radials from $0'$ and $0'B2$.

12. Using the centerpoint 03 as the design center, half the distance of the diagonal B2C2 establishes F and G by intersection arcs B203 and 03B2 to create F and C203 to create G (Fig. 82b). The depth of the chapel to the outside wall is equal to the width of the chapel opening $B'C'$ that was established from $0'$ and therefore the chapel is designed around a square.

13. 02A is established and 02B is marked off at the same distance along the axis from the transept (Fig. 83b). The centerpoint (cp) of diagonal AB is found and the point E is marked off where arc A02 intersects with the diagonal AB. The distance from 02 to A', D', C', E', and B' is taken from the transept (it is equal to the side of the transept macromodule, or 18.474 m). This distance is marked off along these radials, the procedure is repeated on the south side, and then the point on the north (D') is connected to the corresponding point on the south (F'), forming the plane for the northern porch buttresses. The placement of the buttresses along these plane lines is determined by the position of the interior arcade piers and chapel-opening piers whose east-west axes are continued to the exterior.

14. Paul Frankl, *Gothic Architecture*, 201. Daniel Lavallée also suggests that the design evolved in the late fifteenth century at the time of its construction, *La Renaissance à Rouen*, exhibition held at the Musée des Beaux Arts de Rouen, 28 November 1980–28 February 1981, 35.

15. N. Prak discovered the king's foot at Amiens, "Measurement of Amiens Cathedral." John James identified the Roman foot of .295 m at the Sainte-

Chapelle in Paris (*The Template Makers of the Paris Basin*, 70–76), and David Walsh proved the Roman foot was used in the plans of the Cistercian abbeys of Bordesley, Fountains, and Kirkstall ("Measurement and Proportion at Bordesley Abbey," 113). William Steinke demonstrated that the Roman foot was used in the nave of Notre-Dame in Caudebec-en-Caux in the early fifteenth century, while the king's foot of .324 was used in the choir of fifty years later ("The Flamboyant Gothic Church of Caudebec-en-Caux, 74–82).

16. See the Appendix.

17. Raymond Quenedey, "Métrologie rouennaise. Instruments et mesures de longueur."

18. The difference between the king's foot of .325 m and the Rouen foot of .324 m established by Quenedey is negligible.

19. Cord Meckseper, "Über die Fünfeckkonstruktion bei Villard de Honnecourt und im späteren Mittelalter."

Chapter 4. The Mercantile Patrons

1. The records of donations of rents, properties and foundations that constitute the primary form of extraordinary revenues used for the construction of the church and recorded in the cartularies (G6872 and G6873) have been published in part by Julien Loth, *Saint-Maclou de Rouen; René Herval, Saint-Maclou de Rouen*; and Catherine Bodin-Cerné, "Saint-Maclou de Rouen."

2. See Chapter 1.

3. Saint-Maclou was begun before the death of the duke of Bedford in 1435. His reputation as a builder distinguished him from the other English who held positions on the continent. Rouen was his primary residence and he could not have failed to notice the importance or significance of the parish church being constructed directly to the east of the cathedral. An anonymous Parisian wrote in 1436: "The English ruled Paris for a very long time, but I do honestly think that never any one of them had any corn or oats sown as much as a fireplace built in a house—except the Regent, the Duke of Bedford. He was always building, wherever he was, his nature was quite un-English, for he never wanted to make war on anybody, whereas the English, essentially, are always wanting to make war on their neighbors without cause." A Tuetey, ed., *Journal d'un Bourgeois de Paris, 1405–1449*, 320.

4. These figures are taken from a manuscript in the Departmental Archives of Seine-Maritime by François Basset, "La vie municipale à Rouen au XVe siècle, 1447–1471," document F466. Basset cites the accounts of the Archives de le Bibliothéque municipale de Rouen, comptes xxi, sr. 447–48.

5. Philip Benedict, *Rouen during the Wars of Religion*. Benedict cites the records of individuals taxed more than 10 livres in 1565 for the construction of the consular jurisdiction, A.D.S.M., C 216., 28. The juxtaposition of wealthy and artisan houses in the parish of Saint-Maclou is indicated by Raymond Quenedey, *L'habitation rouennaise*.

6. M. Guitard, "La draperie à Rouen des origines aux réformes de Colbert."

7. Charles Ouin-Lacroix, *Histoire des anciennes corporations,* 92. He published the 1424 statutes of the cloth corporation.

8. Michel Mollat, *Le commerce maritime, normand* 275–77.

9. The second most populous segment of society living in the parish were the masons. The implications of their presence on the architecture of Saint-Maclou will be explored in Chapter 6.

10. Mollat, *Le commerce maritime,* Chap. 14, passim. Other Rouennais families whose strength and prestige increased in this manner included the Le Seigneur, Le Gras, Le Pelletier, and the Caradas.

11. Mollat, *Le commerce maritime,* 484.

12. Loth, *Saint-Maclon de Rouen,* 120.

13. See Note 70.

14. Bodin-Cerné, "Saint-Maclou de Rouen," 25 (Rouen, Archives Seine-Maritime, G8843)

15. Ibid., 25 (Rouen, Archives Seine Maritime, G6873)

16. Mollat, *Le commerce maritime,* 284 (Rouen, Archives Seine-Maritime, G58).

17. Loth, *Saint-Maclou de Rouen,* 121.

18. Appendix Fabric Account for 1445.

19. Appendix Fabric Account for 1514–17.

20. Epitaph dated 27 June 1514, in the Chapel of Saint Claude and Saint Léonard was recorded by François Farin, *Histoire de la ville de Rouen,* 1668. It is no longer visible.

> En l'an mil cinq cens quatorzième,
> De Juin le jour vingt et septième,
> Pour Jean du Four fils non ainé
> De noble Pierrre le puiné.
> Les Notaires de Cour d'Eglise
> Pour terre que de lui ont prise

> Convindrent par lettres passez
> Le lendemain des Trépassez,
> Faire dire en cette Chapelle
> Que Saint Leonard on apelle
> Une Messe et de profundis,
> Priez Dieu qu'en son Paradis
> Il veuille mettre tous les ames
> Des Sieurs du Four et leurs femmes.

21. This contract from the *Grand chartrier* was published by C. Beaurepaire, "Contract de Fondation à l'église Saint-Maclou", *Bulletin de la Commission des Antiquités de Seine-Inférieure,* XII, 1900–1902, 409–412.

22. See Bodin-Cerné, "Saint-Maclou de Rouen"; Loth, *Saint-Maclou de Rouen*; and Herval, *Saint-Maclou de Rouen*.

23. Nadine-Josette Chaline, *Histoire des diocèses de France,* ed. Palanque and Plongeron, vol. 5: *Le Diocèse de Rouen-Le Havre,* 46.

24. The source of receipts listed in the accounts of 1443–47 are not always identified, are sometimes undated, or are illegible. Therefore, it is impossible to determine precisely the receipts for individual categories or totals.

25. It is curious that the same property, the Hôtel des Flagons, was mentioned in the foundation contract of 1441 by Pierre Dufour.

26. See Chapter 6 for a discussion of materials and prices.

27. See Chapter 6 for the implications of the change in method of payment on architectural style.

28. Rouen, Archives Seine-Maritime, G6879.

29. Mollat, *Le commerce maritime,* 62.

30. Ibid., 529–30.

31. Ibid., 331.

32. This same lack of correspondence between general economic prosperity and building activity was pointed out by David B. Miller, "Monumental Building."

33. A. Chéruel, *Histoire de Rouen pendant l'époque communale 1150–1182.* Alain Sadourny, "Des Débuts de la guerre de Cent Ans à la Harelle," in *Histoire de Rouen,* ed. M. Mollat, 99–122.

34. R. Vale, *Charles VII,* defines an *aide* as an indirect tax on consumables and a *gabelle* as a tax on a compulsory purchase of salt (243–44).

35. The standard sources for the political history of Rouen in the first half of the fifteenth century are Adolphe Chéruel, *Histoire de Rouen sous la domination anglaise*; and Paul Le Cacheux, *Rouen au temps de Jeanne d'Arc.* Both contain appendixes with ex-

tensive documentation. More recent study of local history is found in Michel Mollat, ed., *Histoire de Rouen*, Toulouse, 1979.

36. Thomas Johnes, Esq., trans., *The Chronicles of Enguerrand de Monstrelet*.

37. Guillaume de Montreuil, *Chronique de Cousinol, Chronique de la Pucelle, La Chronique de Normandie de Pierre Cochon*, 435. Cochon writes, "Et fu la ville si affamée qu'il convenoit mengier les chevax, chienz, chas, ras, a bonne saveur. Ca il avait en la ville trop de peuple de hors de la ville qui estoit venue à reclaim qui y furent enfremés."

A contemporary English poem describes similar conditons:

> Then to die they did begin,
> All that rich city within
> They died so fast on everyday
> That men could not all them in the earth lay.
> Even if a child should other wise be dead
> The mother wouyld not give it bread
> Everyone tried himself to live
> As long as he could last
> Love and kindness both were past.

From John Page, "The Siege of Rouen," in *The Historical Collections of a Citizen of London*, ed. J. Gairdner, 59.

38. Chéruel, *Histoire de Rouen sous la domination anglaise*, 39. Henry V placed himself at the porte Hilaire in the convent of the Chartreux, Notre-Dame de la Rose. His brother, duke of Clarence, took over the partially destroyed church of Saint-Gervais near the porte Cauchoise; Count Marechal camped near the porte Rouvreuil; the duke of Exeter at the porte Beauvoisine; Harrington, later replaced by Warwick, at the porte Martainville; and Huntington on the left bank facing the porte Mathilde.

39. The full amount of the ransom was never paid. As late as 1430 Henry VI reduced the sum to 24,000 saluts d'or, half to be paid immediately, a quarter by Easter, and the remaining sum by Saint Michaels, 1431. This amount was borrowed from individual citizens. Le Cacheux, *Rouen au temps de Jeanne d'Arc*, 185.

40. Michel Mollat writes, "La dépression commerciale n'a pas sévi tout le temps de l'occupation anglaise. Pendant dix à douze ans, le commerce a connu peut-être ses meilleures années du siècle," *Le commerce maritime*, 25.

41. M. Mollat, "Une expansion différée par la guerre, 1382–1475," in *Histoire de Rouen*, ed. M. Mollat, 135.

42. Vale, *Charles VII* 31. Vale points out that the disinheritance of the dauphin was not based on doubts of his legitimacy as suggested by E. Perroy, *The Hundred Years' War*, 257, but by his involvement with the assassination of the duke of Burgundy in 1417. This is significant because in 1429 Charles VII reasserts his claim to the throne in the coronation at Reims, and in 1435, Chancellor Rolin sought a legal flaw in the treaty of Troyes by claiming a king could not pass sovereignty to his son-in-law over his legitimate son.

43. Henry V died in 1422; upon the death of Charles VI in the same year, Henry VI refers to himself King of France and England.

44. This was in compliance with the Treaty of Troyes, which stipulated that *tailles* (the chief tax in France based on income and levied on commoners) and subsidies be imposed only in accordance with existing laws and customs of the country. B. J. H. Rowe, "The Estates of Normandy under the Duke of Bedford, 1422–1435," 553. Instead of viewing the calling of the Estates as a compliance with the treaty and a recognition of Normandy's right to govern itself, Charles Beaurepaire questions Bedford's motives, suggesting that the Estates only gave the appearance on popular support for his heavy taxation policy. Cf. Charles de Robillard de Beaurepaire, *Les états de Normandie sous la domination anglaise*.

45. Perroy, *The Hundred Years' War*, 257.

46. This value was proportionate to the real value of the uncoined metal. Joseph Stevenson, *Letters and Papers*, I, xl. The currency in this period fluctuated from 9 livres tournois as the equivalent of a marc d'argent in Rouen in March 1419 to 26 livres tournois in May 1421. The equivalent of an ecu d'or given by the merchants for this period ranged from 2 livres 10 sous in March 1416 to 12 livres in November 1421, to a leveling off in 1423 of 1 livre 10 sous. Mollat, *Le commerce maritime*, 28.

47. Mollat, *Le commerce maritime*, 26. He chose the Rouennais measure for grain, the Argue measure for wood, the Parisian measure for cloth and the Troyan marc as a measure for the weight of a livre.

48. Mollat, *Le commerce maritime*, 44. During the period of occupation, commercial trade in Rouen was limited to the territory including Paris, Dieppe, England, Ireland, Scotland, the Low Countries, and to the south including Brittany, Poitou, Saintonge, Guyene Biscaye, and Portugal. The main items of

export were herring, onions, hemp cloth, salt, iron, wool-carding instruments, and playing cards.

49. E. Chirol, "Saint-Maclou de Rouen," 3.

50. Le Cacheux, *Rouen au temps de Jeanne d'Arc*, lxxxii.

51. Alexander Héron, ed., *Deux chroniques de Rouen*, 85.

52. Bedford was buried in the cathedral of Rouen at the left of the altar near the foot of the sepulcher of Henri Le Jeune or Count Martel and under the reliquary of Saint Sevier, bishop of Avranches. The tomb was destroyed by the canons of the cathedral in 1732. Bedford's wife, Anne, sister of the duke of Burgundy, had died in 1431 cutting the last tie between England and Burgundy.

53. Stevenson, *Letters and Papers*, II, xxvii.

54. Ibid., xxvii.

55. Perroy, *The Hundred Years' War*, 250.

56. Stevenson, II, xxix.

57. Rowe, "The Estates of Normandy," 561.

58. Mollat, *Le commerce maritime*, 580.

59. Ibid., 62.

60. Beaurepaire, *Bulletin de la commission des antiquaires de la Seine-Inférieure*, XIII, 1903–5, 94–95. From the Tabellionage of Rouen dated 15 December 1420, "en la couleur et semblable painture du cueur de l'église S. Ouen de Rouen."

61. See Chapter 5 for an expanded discussion of the work and documentation in Rouen of Jenson Salvart and Alexandre de Berneval.

62. Roland Sanfaçon, *L'architecture flamboyante en France*, 75.

63. Thomas Campbell, in his discussion of ceremony and drama in fifteenth-century Rouen, attributes the surge in public presentation in Rouen between 1440 and 1470 to "the national fervor for civic spectable during the fifteenth century." ("Cathedral Chapter and Town Council," 106). The iconographic potency of visible and public retrospection was heightened by changing attitudes toward consumption, increased spending, and luxuries. Joel Kaye claims that the dislocation brought about by the war acted to reshape the relationship between wealth and display of social status ("The Impact of Money," 253).

64. Kenneth Fowler, "Introduction: War and Change in Late Medieval France and England," *The Hundred Years' War*, ed. Fowler, 20–23.

65. Ibid., 21.

66. B. J. H. Rowe, "Henry VI's Claim to France."

67. See P. S. Lewis, "War Propaganda and Historiography in Fifteenth-Century France and England"; Elizabeth Danbury, "English and French Artistic Propaganda during the period of the Hundred Years War: Some Evidence from Royal Charters," in *Power, Culture and Religion in France, c. 1350–1550*, ed. C. Allmand, 73–97; and Catherine Reynolds, "'*Les Angloys, de leur droicte nature, veullent touzjours guerreer*': Evidence for Painting in Paris and Normandy, c. 1420–1450," in *Power, Culture and Religion in France, c. 1350–1550*, ed. C. Allmand, 37–55.

68. Le Cacheux, *Rouen au temps de Jeanne d'Arc*, ciii.

69. Le Cacheux, *Rouen au temps de Jeanne d'Arcs*, 27, publishes document G1202 (Rouen, Archives Seine-Maritime), dated 21 July 1421.

70. Scholars are not in agreement when this actually took place. Mollat, *Le commerce maritime*, 284, states that Pierre Dufour received the letters from Charles VII. Herval, *Saint-Maclou de Rouen*, 31, writes that the Dufour were ennobled by Louis XI and Henri de Frondeville, *Les Conseilleurs du Parlement*, II, 327–33, points out that these letters were not registered by the *chambre des comptes* or *cour des aides*, and the descendents of Pierre Dufour did not secure them until 1582.

71. Albert Mirot and Bernard Mahieu, "Cérémonies officielles à Notre-Dame au XVe siècle."

72. E. Chirol, "Saint-Maclou de Rouen," 3.

73. Germain Lefèvre-Pontalis, "La guerre des partisans." See also Chapter 5.

74. Documents relevant to Pierre Robin are discussed in Chapter 5.

75. Perroy, *The Hundred Years' War*, 292, describes the nobility in "extreme poverishment" by 1450.

76. Philippe Contamine, "The French Nobility and the War," in *The Hundred Years' War*, ed. Kenneth Fowler, 134–162.

77. Chéruel, *Histoire de Rouen pendant l'époque communale*, 76. Chéruel lists the distribution of confiscated noble properties in Rouen. The duke of Exeter was given the Hôtel d'Harcourt, the *comté* of Harcourt, the fiefs of Quatre-Mares and Routout and the seigneuries and château of Lilleborne. The chevalier, Louis Robertsort, was given the hotel and seigneurie of Granville; Robert Balthroy was given the hotel of Jean de Lesmes; Gautier de Beauchamp, the hotel of Jean Auber; and John de Gray, the comté of Tancarville and hotel facing Saint-

Martin-sur-Renelle. In a few cases, the citizens of Rouen participated in the demise of the local nobility. Guy le Bouteillier, captain of Rouen before the siege, received from the English the fiefs of Plessis, of Conches, and Bois Guillaume. The cathedral canon, Nicolas de Venderes, obtained the house of the grand vicaire, Robert Delivet who was taken hostage to England.

78. Contamine, "French Nobility," 143. There was an inherent conflict between being a nobleman and making money through commerce, considered to be a derogative activity not appropriate for nobility. The act of Louis XI provided a way around these mutually incompatable catagories. A fine or *taille* was to be paid if the possessers of fiefs engaged in anything "derogating nobility."

79. Jonathan Dewald, *The Formation of the Provincial Nobility*, 13.

80. Contamine, "French Nobility," 143.

81. P. S. Lewis, *The Recovery of France in the Fifteenth Century*, 12.

82. The *Livre des Fontaines* was commissioned by Jacques Le Lieur in 1525 and given to the counsellors of the city to commemorate the installation of seven new fountains in the city. A facsimile of this manuscript in the Bibliothèque municipale de Rouen was published by T. de Jolimont, *Les principaux édifices de la ville de Rouen en 1525*.

Chapter 5. Pierre Robin

1. Charles Ouin-Lacroix, *Histoire de l'église*, 10. Charles de Robillard de Beaurepaire, "Notice sur les architectes de Saint-Maclou," 110. Adolph Lance, *Dictionnaire des architectes français*, 246.

2. Charles Bauchal, *Nouveau dictionnaire biographique*, 508, lists five Robins active between 1378 and 1450. A Robin is master of the works at Samur in 1378 and in the same year Robin le Machon is working on the prisons of the château of Arques with Jehan Davout. In 1400 Pierre Robin is listed as master of the works of Paris but is replaced by Pierre de Hellebucerne in March 1411. Bauchal identifies the Pierre Robin designated in the account of the provost of Paris 1429–31 as "Maître Pierre Robin, sergent d'armes et maçon general du roi notre sire," as being the son of the previously mentioned master of the works at Paris. Another Robin, Guillaume, is listed as master of the works

for King René Anjou working as Saint Maurice at Angers in 1451.

3. Stephen Murray, *Building Troyes Cathedral*, 160.

4. The best review of documents related to Pierre Robin in Paris are found in Isabell Taveau, *L'architecture civile et religieuse à Paris sous la régne de Charles VI*," 349–51. The following document citations are taken from her dissertation. For Saint-Yves, Taveau cites Arch. Nat. LL 963 B, fol. 76, "Pour le parchemin et pourtraiture du portail de l'église que Pierre Robin avoit fait, LXXII S."

5. René Couffon, "La chapelle Saint-Yves à Paris," *Bulletin monumental*, 358–59. Couffon does not mention Robin but lists Jean Manicet as master mason and Jean James, Geoffroy Sevestre, and Simon Le Noir as stonecutters.

6. Taveau "L'Architecture civile," cites Bibl. Nat. Nouv. Acq. fr. 7932, fol. 296.

7. Taveau, "L'Architecture civile," cites B. Prost, *Archives historiques, artistiques et littéraires*. T.I., 1889/90, 212–16. A detailed description of the ceremony is provided by Ralph E. Giesey, *The Royal Funeral Ceremony in Renaissance France*. See also, Albert Mirot and Bernard Mahieu, "Cérémonies officielles à Notre-Dame au XVe siècle."

8. Taveau, "L'Architecture civile," cites Y. Grandeau, "La mort et les obséques de Charles VI," *Bulletin Philologique et historique du Comité des travaux historiques et scientifiques* (1970), 150–86.

9. Taveau, "L'Architecture civile," cites Prost, *Archives historiques*, 216.

10. Taveau, "L'Architecture civile," cites Arch. Nat. KK 1009, fol. 24.

11. Henri Stein, *Les architects des cathédrales gothiques*, 22.

12. See Note 1.

13. Recent dissertation work by a number of young scholars including Abbey McGehee of the University of California at Berkeley and Mayra Rodriguez of the University of Michigan at Ann Arbor promises to correct lacunae.

14. For a discussion of the late gothic parts of these monuments, see my "The Parish Church of Saint-Maclou and Late Gothic Architecture in Rouen," Also, M. Dumoulin and G. Outardel, *Les églises de France*; Abbé Lebeuf, *Histoire de la ville et de tout le diocèse de Paris*; and Amédée Benoit, *Les édifices religieux de Paris*.

15. Couffon, *Bulletin monumental* 240–41. Also, R. Couffon, "La confrérie de Saint-Yves à Paris et

sa chapelle"; Aubin-Louis Millin, *Antiquités nationales; ou, Recueil de monuments*, IV, chap. 37, "Chapelle de Saint-Yves," 1–21; and Yolande Zephirin, "Saint-Yves et sa chapelle parisienne de la rue St. Jacques."

16. Engraving of Du Chemin de Carpentier, 1751, from A.-L. Millin, *Antiquités nationales*, BN. Est. Va 260 h. I would like to thank Michael T. Davis for bringing this engraving to my attention.

17. Engraving from Manisson-Millet, *Géométrie pratique*, 1702, Musée Carnavalet, Topo PC 100 I.

18. Michael T. Davis has suggested that Saint-Jean-en-Grève is a reduced version of Notre Dame ("Towards a New Architecture, 1320–1350," paper given at the 1988 Meeting of the Society of Architectural Historians).

19. Viollet-le-Duc points out that the original choir design of Notre Dame did not include a transept, *Dictionnaire raisonné de l'architecture française*, IX, 222. His statement was confirmed by Caroline Bruzelius, "The Construction of Notre Dame in Paris," 543.

20. This extant drawing of the plan of Notre-Dame (sheet 21 verso in the *Oeuvre Notre-Dame*, Strasbourg) does not include the transept but proves that a complete plan drawing may have existed. For Notre-Dame plan drawing see O. Kletzl, "Ein Werkriss des Frauenhauses von Strassburg"; and more recently, R. Recht, ed. *Les Bâtisseurs des Cathédrales Gothique*, 417–18.

21. A detailed description of the decoration, structure, and meaning of the choir changes of the cathedral of Notre Dame during the reign of Philip the Fair was provided by Michael T. Davis, "Splendor and Peril: The Cathedral of Paris, 1290–1350," forthcoming.

22. Bauchal, *Nouveau dictionnaire*, 532. Geoffroy Sevestre was paid 240 livres on 25 January 1417 for his work on the chapel of Vendôme at Chartres.

23. A summary of the documentation for Jean Aux Tabours is found in my "Flamboyant Architecture of Saint-Maclou, Rouen, and the Development of a Style."

24. Documents and chronology for Vernon are discussed in 386–92. See also, Docteur Couton, "L'église Notre-Dame de Vernon"; E. Deville, "Registres des comptes de la collegiate de Vernon (1432–1439)"; T. Michel, "L'Eglise de Notre-Dame de Vernon."

25. At Saint-Maclou the arcade bases rise to 1.67 m and at Vernon, the nave arcade bases rise to 1.31 m.

26. Ernst Kitzinger, "On the Interpretation of Stylistic Changes in Late Antique Art", in *The Art of Byzantium and the Medieval West: Selected Studies by Ernst Kitzinger*, ed. W. Eugene Kleinbauer, 32–41.

27. This type of "triforium grille", identified by P. Heliot as uniquely Norman, had its origins at Sées Cathedral (upper parts of the choir date after 1270) ("Triforiums et coursières dans les églises gothiques de Bretagne et de Normandie").

28. Neagley, "Flamboyant Architecture," 392–94. See also, J. Richard-Rivoire, "La reconstruction de Notre-Dame des Andely à l'époque flamboyante"; Louis Regnier, "Document du XIVe siècle relatif à l'achèvement de l'église Notre-Dame d'Andely"; and J. Vallery-Radot, "Remarques sur le style des église des Andelys."

29. H. Colvin, *The History of the King's Works*, I The Middle Ages, 457–463.

30. A summary of the documentation associated with Alexandre de Berneval and Jenson Salvart is provided by Charles de Robillard de Beaurepaire, "Notes sur les architectes de Rouen," *Bulletin de la Société des Amis des Monuments rouennais* (1902), 67–93.

31. The royal palace, completely demolished by the eighteenth century, was built on land provided for in the terms of the capitulation in 1419 and acquired for 2,630 livres tournois. Unlike the policy which Henry V followed at Calais, there was no attempt to employ only English workmen in Rouen. H. M. Colvin, *The History of the King's Works*, I, The Middle Ages, 461.

32. G. Lefèvre-Pontalis, "La guerre des partisans dans la haute Normandie."

33. The profound change in flamboyant architecture in 1430 was first noted by George Huard, *L'art en Normandie*. The term *proto-flamboyant* was applied by William Steinke in "The Flamboyant Gothic Church of Caudebece-en-Caux: A Neglected Masterpiece of French Medieval Architecture," 5, to designate flamboyant architecture before 1430. However, Steinke associated this earlier phase with the sporadic appearance of English curvilinear Decorated architecture. In Rouen, both English Decorated and English Perpendicular architecture played a role in defining style between 1380 and 1430. In addition, a great range of other influences and experimentation characterized the transitional gothic of the transepts and porch of Saint-Ouen and the west facade of the cathedral.

34. Beaurepaire, "Notes sur les architectes (1902), 67. Beaurepaire summarized the documentation of Salvart's lengthy career. He points out that the name Jenson Salvart, which appears in the documentation in various spellings (Jesson Sallvatt, Jehan Son Salvart, Jehan Son), is not of Rouennais origin.

35. G. Lebévre-Pontalis, "La guerre de partisans, 14.

36. *Ordonneur* appears to be a classification distinct from master mason or master of the works. It suggests a purely supervisory role.

37. For a full transcription of the Tancarville accounts, see Achille Deville, *Histoire du Chateau de Tancarville*.

38. Ibid. The link between the master carpenter and master mason seems to be made through Salvart's ability to supply drawings. "A lui pour ung voiage qu'il fit de Rouen à Tancarville, par le commandement de Monrs, le mardi ixe jour dudit moiz de decembre, mon dit sr estant au dit lieu, euquel voiage icelui maistre Jenson fist faire et meitre par ordonnance les devises de plusieurs ouvrages que mon dit se avoit ordonées, tant machonnerie que charpenterie."

39. Rouen, Archives Seine-Maritime, Tabellionage de Rouen 16, fol. 158v.: "ung marchie fait par Jehan Salvart et Martin de Roux doive touche ( ) des tressoriers de Saint-Maclou par la prie de iiic euc dor paie la aymt ensuit."

40. Beaurepaire, "Notes sur les architectes (1902), 73.

41. A. L. Frothingham, "Discovery of an Original Church Model by a Gothic Architect."

42. Franz Bischoff, "Les Maquettes d'Architecture," in *Les Bâtisseurs de cathédrales gothiques*, ed. R. Recht, 287–95; *La Renaissance à Rouen*, exh. cat., Musée des Beaux-Arts, 28 Novembre 1980–28 February 1981, 35; Charles de Robillard de Beaurepaire, "Modèle en carton de l'église Saint-Maclou," 335–37; A. Frothingham, "La Modèle de l'église Saint-Maclou de Rouen", 211–224; A. Frothingham, "Discovery of an Original Church Model by a Gothic Architect"; Paul Le Cacheux, "Le Modèle de l'église Saint-Maclou de Rouen"; Jean Lafond, "La prétendue maquette de l'église Saint-Maclou de Rouen."

43. The most detailed account of the facade work is described by Maurice Allinne, "La façade occidentale de la cathédrale de Rouen," 73–97, and George Lanfry, *La façade occidentale de la cathé-*

drale de Rouen. The late twelfth-century facade must have appeared exceedingly old-fashioned to the canons and the antithesis to the typical facade of a high gothic catheral with twin towers and vertical integration. Both Lanfry and Allinne accept J.-B. Foucher's reconstruction of the original late twelfth-century facade (see Lanfry, *La facade occidentale*, 8) showing a pyramidal massing of turrets, lancet windows, and triangular gables clearly separated from the three portals below by a blind lancet dado forming a strong horizontal element. The twelfth-century tour Saint Romain stood to the north of the facade, and the Butter Tower, begun in 1467 stood to the south. Perier is first mentioned in documentation when he gives his lecture to the chapter of the cathedral in 1462 upon his appointment as master mason. Delisle in *Lettres et mandements du roi Charles VI*, as cited by Beaurepaire, "Notes sur les architectes" (1901), 86, points out that he was chosen by Charles V as sculptor and that in 1368 Perier worked with the Flemish sculptor, Hennequin de Liége, on a reliquary of marble and alabaster to receive the heart of King Charles V, duke of Normandy. The cathedral fabric account (Rouen, G2463) records a payment to Perier in 1382–83 of 10 florin francs for twelve sculptures of stone to be placed on the portal of Saint Romain. The motive to transform the facade through the use of paneled screens was possibly supplied by the decision of Charles V to have his heart buried in Rouen. A similar transformation occurred at the abbey of Gloucester after 1329 by encasing the Romanesque choir and transepts in Perpendicular paneling to provide an appropriate setting for the burial of Edward II. See John Harvey, *The Perpendicular Style, 1330–1485*, 51.

44. Camille Enlart, *Rouen* (Villes d'Art célèbres).

45. Ci gist maistre Alixandre de Berneval, maistre des ouevres de machonnerie du roy mostre sire au bailliage de Rouen et de cest église, qui trespassa l'an grace mil cccc xl, le ve jour de janvier, priez pour l'ame de luy.

46. Beaurepaire publishes documents relevant to the career of Alexandre de Berneval, "Notes sur les architectes," 2 (1902), 85. Two documents in the archives at Fécamp are also published by Beaurepaire in "Travaux des architectes," 85–87.

47. This contract between the prior of Fécamp and Alexandre de Berneval of 12 October 1420 is published by Beaurepaire (ibid., 85). The contract states he was to be paid 200 livres tournois and was

to include the sculptures of seven bishops, archbishops, dukes, and pilgrims before a church. It was to be made of stone from Saint Leu de Serens. Beaurepaire mentions that the sculpture was executed in Rouen by an unknown sculptor under the direction of Berneval.

48. Beaurepaire, "Notes sur les architectes" (1902), 87. Documentation of Berneval's numerous activities in this capacity are published by Paul Le Cacheux, *Rouen au temps Jeanne d'Arc*, 174–78, 288–90, 42–43, 132–46. See also G. Lefèvre-Pontalis, "La guerre de partisans," 5–54.

49. André Masson, "Le bouchement des piliers de la croisée à Saint-Ouen de Rouen en 1441."

50. Beaurepaire, "Notes sur les architectes" (1903), 73. In his capacity as master mason for the city, Simon arbitrates a dispute at the Hôtel de la Tuile in 1438, in 1441 is a member of an expertise called to examine problems of the buckling tower at Saint-Ouen, and in 1452 is engaged in work at the chateau of Rouen. Jules Quicherat, "Documents inédits sur la construction de Saint-Ouen de Rouen", 468.

51. See the Appendix. The week-by-week records between September 1443 and All Saints' Day 1446 indicate that Simon was paid 5 sous per day in addition to a yearly pension of 6 livres 15 sous. He generally worked one day per week although his valet, who was paid 5 sous per week, was employed full-time except during the cold months of December, January, and February 1443 and 1444 and January 1445.

52. The fabric accounts for the parish church of Saint-Vincent in Rouen are published in part by Charles de Robillard de Beaurepaire, "Notice sur Saint-Vincent." See also Abbé Edmond Renaud, *Eglise Saint-Vincent*; and Anne Savoie, Saint Vincent de Rouen, paroisse de marchands au XVème siècle.

53. G 2503 (chapter deliberations): "collation avec les maitres de maconnerie de ouen c'est assavoir Le Cignere, Ambroise de Saint Maclou et Jehan Le Ville pour scavoir si le tour Saint Romain pourroit porter et soustenir ung estage de machonnerie de hauteur—25 sous 6 denier."

54. Rouen ASM G 7654, fabric account of the parish church of Saint-Vincent of Rouen for 1468–72. These accounts were published in part by Charles Beaurepaire, "Notice sur Saint-Vincent." See also Abbé Edmond Renaud, *Eglise Saint-Vincent*; and Anne Savoie, "Saint Vincent de Rouen, Paroisse de merchants au XVeme siècle."

Pour dépense faites avecques Gillet et Regnault diz Faucon, machons, en faisant le marchié de l'oeuvre de la machonnerie de la croisée de ladite église es presences du maitre machon de l'oeuvre Sint Maclou—34 sous 6 denier.

Pour déspense faite avecquez maistre Ambroise qui estoit venu édiffier la place au les estoies sont assisis la place au la croisée et le nouvel édiffice se fait 63 sous 9 denier et gester les moules sur les ii premier pieres qui sont asisis sur les fondements—8 sous 9 denier. (Beaurepaire, "Notice sur Saint-Vincent," 118–19)

55. Charles de Robillard de Beaurepaire, "Notice sur Saint-Vincent."

56. Paul Frankl, *Gothic Architecture*, states that the western porch of Saint-Maclou was designed by Harel.

57. Beaurepaire, "Notice sur Saint-Vincent," summarizes the documents.

58. The decision-making process in the second half of the century at the cathedral was far more democratic than in earlier periods. There was no single authority to decide how the architecture should look. Even the entire body of cathedral canons no longer held sole power of decision. Throughout Pontis's career every major project was discussed at length numerous times and "on consultait tout le monde," according to Julien Loth (*La cathédrale de Rouen*, 118). Consultations involved the chapter, various experts, bourgeoise, masons, and for any one project, alternate plans were proposed to give this extended decision-making body several choices. As a result these deliberations often took years and the master could begin according to one plan and switch to another halfway through the project. Thus the continuity at Saint-Maclou, established by the treasurers over several successive generations, is all the more unique. The conflicts between master masons and cathedral chapter are discussed in Chapter 6.

59. The financial difficulties of the chapter prior to 1467 prevented any major work from being undertaken. Before Pontis began the tour Saint-Romain termination he may have worked on the enlargement of the north transept windows. Enlargement of the nave clerestory had begun in the fourteenth century, was continued by Jenson Salvart in 1431, and probably continued by Geoffrey Richier in the 1450s. Richer held the position of master mason of the cathedral only for a brief time.

However, the early impact of the new work of Saint-Maclou may have emerged in his designs. The old and the new styles coexist in a single window of the south transept clerestory where fillet plinths, bases, and continuous moldings frame lancets composed of thin round shafts, with trumpet bases and fragile capitals.

60. For an outline of the documents concerning Pontis, see Beaurepaire, "Notes sur les architectes" (1902), 54. Construction of the tour Saint Romain was spurred on by Cardinal d'Estouteville, archbishop of Rouen, who in 1453 had given the chapter a bell that was forged in the cour d'Alban (on the north side of the nave); the bell was called Marie d'Estouteville, and weighed seven thousand pounds.

61. Julien Loth, *La cathédrale de Rouen*, 118.

62. Rouen, Archives Seine-Maritime G2423, fabric account 1507–8: "Le xxviie jour de janvier furent mandés par le commandement des messrs de chapitre maistres Jehan le Boucher et Pierres Le Galloys machons, pour veoir les traictz faictz par maistres Jacques et Roullant dictz Le Roux pour ledit portail en la salle de la Ville ou furent commis maistres Pierre Mesenge et Batencourt, chanoines, at après la cidte visitacion ordonnèrent bailler ausd. machons, pour aller boire—10 sous."

63. Beaurepaire, "Notes sur les architects" (1905), 120: "ils l'invitèrent à ne point trop rechercher le fini dans les sculptures de la partie supérieure, en lui faisant observer qu'à la hauteur ou elles seraient placées, elles n'avaient pas besoin d'etre traités avec une perfection scrupuleuse, observation qui doit nos paraître d'autant plus juste que les voussures du portail, fouillées avec un soin extreme, bien que placées à une moindre hauteur, sont encore trop loin de nos yeux pour que nous puissions apprécier ce qu'elles représentent d'habileté, de temps et de dépense."

64. A. Deville, *Revue des architectes*, 56–59.

Chapter 6. The Craftsmen

1. Don Antonio de Beatis, *Voyage du Cardinal d'Aragon en Allemagne, Hollande, Belgique, France et Italie (1517–1518)*, trans. and introd. Madeleine Harvard de la Montagne, Paris, 1913. This text is a French translation of the sixteenth-century italian manuscript.

2. Ibid., 140, "La cathédrale est grande, avec une belle façade travaillée de figures sculptées, elle a deux clochers très hauts dont l'un n'est pas encore terminé; ils sont faits d'une pierre tendre, mais qu'on a pu cependant sculpter avec beaucoup d'art."

3. John Ruskin, *Seven Lamps of Architecture*, 65.

4. Charles Ouin-LaCroix, *Histoire de l'église*: "Qui n'a contemplé avec admiration cette lanterne si svelte, ces piliers si hardis, ces voûtes si légères, ces mille arceaux qui courent et s'entrelacent dans toutes les parties de l'édifice comme les fils délicates d'un réseau de soie, cette longue galerie si finement ouvragée qui se déroule autour de ses flancs comme une ceinture ornée des plus riches dentelles?" (49–50).

5. John Ruskin, "The Nature of Gothic," from *The Stones of Venice*, 128.

6. Ibid., 129.

7. J. Huizinga, *The Waning of the Middle Ages*, (1989), 250.

8. Ibid., 248.

9. The last generation of scholars writing on late gothic architecture has focused primarily on documents and drawings. A good overview of current approaches to late gothic is found in the catalog of the Strasbourg exhibition on gothic building and technology. See Roland Recht, ed., *Les Bâtisseurs des cathédrales gothiques*, passim.

10. Roland Recht and A. Chatelet, *Automne et Renouveau, 1380–1500*, 1988, 5.

11. Michel Mollat, *Le commerce maritime*, 529–30.

12. Dieter Kimpel, "Le développement de la taille," 215–16. Lynn White cites James Crowther in his reference to the increase of burgher-class wealth whose activities centered around the production and sale of tangible goods: "The mediaeval bourgeoisie thus accomplished something that had never been done before. It made the properties of materials the chief interest of the ruling class." Lynn White, "Natural Science and Natualistic Art in the Middle Ages"; and James Crowther, *Social Relations of Science*, 239.

13. Taillepied, *Antiquités de la ville de Rouen*, Rouen, 1610, as cited by Charles Ouin-Lacroix, *Histoire des anciennes corporations*, 238.

14. Ouin-Lacroix suggests that the masons formed a company as early as 1145 when Archbishop Hugues sent a group to Chartres to help in the rebuilding of the cathedral after the fire that destroyed portions of Fulbert's church. See Ouin-Lacroix, *Histoire des anciennes corporations*, 227. An undated contract between the chapter of Rouen Cathedral and the masons appears in the cathedral

documents (Rouen, Seine-Maritime, G2094) and was published by Charles de Robillard de Beaurepaire, "Notes sur les architectes de Rouen" (1902), 92–93. Based on the paleolography, Beaurepaire suggests a date of 1445. See Note 62 for a full transcription of the contract.

15. Rouen, Archives Seine-Maritime, G6876 (fabric accounts of Saint-Maclou, 1443–46), "corps entrez a leglise la chapelle fait pour Saint Jude 30 s." and G6873 (*Grand Chartrier* of Saint-Maclou), "icelle veufve promist faire faire et payer a ses despens le pavement et alle de endroict la chapelle Sainct Symon Sainct Jude."

16. Beaurepaire, "Notes sur les architectes" (1901–5), passim. Approximately one-third of the masons discussed by Beaurepaire lived in the parish of Saint-Maclou (out of the thirty-three parishes in the city). Jean de Bayeux owned houses in the parish of Saint-Maclou including one called the Fleur de lis and one in front of the church called the Pot d'Etain, and his widow lived on the rue Damiette (1901, 92); Geoffroy Richer lived in the parish with his wife and son (1903, 49); Jacques Le Roux, master mason of Saint Maclou in 1496, lived on the rue Notre Dame in the parish (1903, 64); Pierre Le Signerre and his wife Marguerite live in the parish in 1488 along with sons Guillaume, Pierre, and Jean (1903, 71). He had a house on the rue Damiette near the rue Haute Marriage in 1478. His brother Michael Le Signerne also had a house in the parish (1903, 72); Jacques Vitecoq and son Simon lived on the rue du Figuire in 1524 (1904–6, 131); and Pierre de Lorme lived near the Clos S. Marc in 1506 and 1513 (part IV, 1904–6, 142).

17. Beaurepaire, "Notes sur les architectes" (1903), 49. (Rouen, Archives Seine-Maritime, Acts of the Tabellionage): Samedi Ve jour de Février (mil) IIIc LXXIX, v.s., Huguecte, veufve de defunct maistre Guieffroy Richier, en son vivant maistre des oeuvres de machonnerie de l'église N.-D. de Rouen, ladicte Huguecte demourant en la par. S. Maclou de la dite ville, laquelle, pour la bonne amour naturelle qu'elle avoit à Jehan Richier, fils dudit deffunct maistre Guieffroy Richier et de lad. Huguecte, de son bon bré, congnut soy estre donnée et rendue à icellui son filz avecques tous ses biens, meubles, heritages, rentes et revenues quelzconques, où qu'ilz soient situez et assis, sans riens, etc., à la charge de telles rentes, arrérages de rentes et debtes quelzconques qu'elle

pourroit debvoir pour le présent, ceste rendue faicte moyennant et parmy ce que led. Jeh. Richier, qui reésent estoit, se submist et promist quérir et trouver à sa dicte mére toute ses neccessitez de boire, mengier, couchier, lever, vestir, chausser, feu, lit, hostel, demeure, et résidence, mesmes icelle, en la fin de ses jours, fiare mectre et inhumer en l'église S. Maclou de ladi. ville, auprès de son dit deffunct mary, faire faire ses obsèques et funérailles, le tout bien et honnorablement selon l'estat de led. Huguecte et que à son cas appartient, promectant lad. Huguecte ceste présente rendue tenir etc., et lad. Jeh. Richier ce que dessus est dit faire et accomplir, obligeant l'un à l'autre beins. Présens Ygou et Guieffron Des Vignes." Rouen, Archives Seine-Maritime, G6881 (fabric account of Saint-Maclou for 1520–23). Money was given for the burial of Jacqueline de Mousey, *dame des Vitecoqs*, in the church of Saint-Maclou.

18. According to Ouin-Lacroix, the confraternity of the *drapiers/drapant* was at Saint-Godard and the confraternity of the *drapiers/detailleurs* was at Saint-Ouen; the *tisseurs de drap* had their confraternities at Saint-Vivien and Saint-Nicaise; the *foulors* at Saint-Vivien; the *lanneurs* at the cathedral; and the *merciers* at Saint-Jean (*Histoire des anciennes corporations*, 104–5). Under fabric account receipts, fees for the master *drapiers* are recorded: Rouen, Archives, Seine-Maritime G6874 (fabric account for Saint-Maclou, 1436–37), "du meistier du drapperie et de boulenguerie, 20 livres, 12 sous, 6 denier; G6876 (fabric account for Saint-Maclou, 1443–46), "le mestier de drapperie et boulenguerie"; G6878 (fabric account for Saint-Maclou, 1476–79), "des maistres du mestier de drapperie dont chacun qui se passent maistre doibvent a leglise 20 sous et les fils de maistre 10 sous"; G6879 (fabric account for Saint-Maclou, 1514–17), "droits de drapperie." From 8 July 1436 to 23 June 1437, fifteen apprentices, including eleven sons of masters and a valet, were admitted and from 16 September 1443 to 7 August 1444, twenty-five apprentices, including seventeen sons of masters, are admitted to the *draperie*.

19. Ouin La-Croix, *Histoire des anciennes corporations*, 236–37.

20. Beaurepaire, "Notes sur les architectes" (1902), 83.

21. For tables of salaries of carpenters, masons, plasterers, and roofers in the fifteenth century, see Raymond Quenedey, *L'habitation rouennaise*, 390–91.

22. Beaurepaire, "Notes sur les architectes" (1902), 74.

23. Christopher Wilson, *The Gothic Cathedral*, 190.

24. Roland Sanfaçon, *L'architecture flamboyant en France*, 14.

25. Stephen Murray, review of Sanfaçon's *L'architecture flamboyant en France*, in *Architectura. Zeitschrift für Geschichte der Architektur* (1974), 88–92. In his critique of Sanfaçon, Murray writes, "Rather than searching for the elusive concept of "individualism" in the abstract forms of Flamboyant, it might be wiser to seek the individuality or identity of master masons, as expressed in their total contribution to the building and in the details of the forms which they use" (91–92).

26. A good bibliography on studies on medieval drawing, see Peter Pause, *Gotische Architekturzeichnungen in Deutschland*, 5–17; Hans Koepf, *Die gotischen Planrisse der Wiener Sammlungen Wien*, 1969; Sergio Sanabria, "A Late Gothic Drawing of San Juan de los Reyes in Toledo at the Prado Museum in Madrid"; and Michael T. Davis, "'Troys Portaulx et Deux Grosses Tours': The Flamboyant Façade Project for the Cathedral of Clermont."

27. Robert Branner, "A Fifteenth-Century French Architectural Drawing from the Cloister" (written 1971). Branner lists the Reims palimpsest, the late Gothic facade of Clermont-Ferrand Cathedral, the "cathedra" of Rouen Cathedral and the Cloisters portal as the four extant French drawings.

28. Abbé Sauvage, "Note sur un dessin original du XVe siècle appartenant au chapitre de Rouen"; Jean Taralon, "Le Moblier et le Trésor"; E.-H. Langlois, *Stalles de la cathédrale de Rouen*. Although the wooden choir stalls still survive along with the figurative misericords, the archbishop's chair was destroyed in 1793. *Le Trésor de la Cathédrale de Rouen*, exh. cat., Musée des Antiquités de la Seine-Maritime, Rouen, 1993, 83–84.

29. Branner, "A Fifteenth-Century French Architectural Drawing," 136, associates the drawing with portals at Saint-Maclou in Rouen, Notre-Dame d'Esperance at Montbrison (after 1443), Saint-Wulfran at Abbeville (1488), and Saint-Germain at Argentan.

30. Luc Mojon, *St. Johannsen*, Bern, 1986.

31. The tomb is identified by the inscription surrounding the first figure: "CI GIST MAISTRE ALIXANDRE DE BERNEVAL, MAISTRE DES OEUVRES DE MACHONNERIE DU ROY NOSTRE SIRE AU BAILLAGE DE ROUEN ET DE CEST EGLISE, QUI TRESPASSA L'AN DE GRACE MIL CCCC XL, LE VE JOUR DE JANVIER, PRIEZ DIEU POUR L'AME DE LUY." André Masson, *L'abbaye de Saint-Ouen de Rouen*, 24. Alexandre de Berneval had traced out a rose window; on the basis of this tomb inscription, the south rose of the Abbey of Saint-Ouen has been attributed to him. His son, Colin, who succeeded his father at Saint-Ouen in 1441 appears to have drawn a plan of a tower or a chapel, perhaps a detail of the crossing tower under construction at that time.

32. This alabaster funerary plaque is a nineteenth-century copy of the original and is located in the Virgin Chapel of the choir. The inscription reads: "CI-DEVANT GIT GUILLAUME LE TELLIER, NATIF DE FONTAINE LE PIN, PRES DE FALAISE, EN SON VIVANT MAITRE MACON DE CETTER EGLISE DE CAUDEBEC, QUI PAR L'ESPACE DE TRENTE ANS ET PLUS EN A EU LA CONDUITE PENDANT LEQUEL TEMPS A ACHEVE L'OO DE COUPELLES AVEC LE HAUT DE LA NEF D'ICELLE EGLISE, PUIS A FONDE ET ELEVE TOUT LE CHOEUR ET CHAPELLES ENTOUR ICELLE, ET LEVE JUSQU'AUX PREMIERES ALLEES AVEC LA CLE PENDENTE DE CETTE PRESENTE CHAPELLE, TREPASSA LE PREMIER JOUR DE SEPTEMBRE MIL QUATRE CENT QUATRE VINGT ET QUARTRE, OU DELAISSA SEPT SOUS SIX DENIERS DE RENTE A CETTE PRESENTE EGLISE. PRIEZ DIEU POUR SON AME. AMEN." B. Pigoreau, *L'eglise de Caudebec-en-Caux*, 32.

33. Erwin Panofsky, *Early Netherlandish Painting*, 181.

34. This is an old unresolved debate. The futility of this line of thinking is suggested by Craig Harbison in the most recent study on Jan van Eyck by avoiding a discussion of the panel altogether. Baldass, De Tolnay, and Desneaux believe the panel was a preliminary study or incomplete work whereas van Puyvelde and Winkler suggest that it was a finished work. Panofsky straddles the argument, suggesting that van Eyck turned an elaborate preparation into a finished drawing. L. Baldass, *Jan van Eyck*, 59; C. de Tolnay, *Le Maître de Flémalle et les frères Van Eyck*, 32 and 67; M. Friedländer, *Altniederländische Malerie*, 1, 62; L. van Puyvelde, *L'agneau mystique*, 80; E. Panofsky, *Early Netherlandish Painting*, 185; J. Desneaux, "Underdrawings and *Pentimenti* in the Pictures of Jan van Eyck," 19; Craig Harbison, *Jan van Eyck, The Play of Realism*.

35. The original marblized frame bears the inscription "IOH[ANN] ES DE EYCK ME FECIT. 1437."

36. The literature is extensive on German drawings. Most recently they have been discussed and summarized in Roland Recht, ed., *Les Bâtisseurs des Cathédrales gothique*. For the spire elevation drawing of Strasbourg Cathedral, see 401–2; Ulm tower project drawings, 409–11; Vienna tower drawing, 412–13.

37. Sergio Sanabria, "A Late Gothic Drawing of San Juan de los Reyes." 161–73. In his discussion of the presentation drawing of Juan Guas for the transept and sanctuary of San Juan de los Reyes, c. 1479–80, Sanabria points out that the architect did not employ consistent one-point perspective but rather a splayed perspective that easily conveyed the idea of spatial enclosure. He comments that the complexity of the drawing suggests that it required "close perusal like miniatures from a book of hours" and that the drawing reflected the contributions of a full array of craftsmen, including masons, sculptors, painters, and glaziers. This further supports that the boundaries between professions were far more blurred and would permit van Eyck to demonstate his interest in architectural drawing.

38. Specific actual models for van Eyck's architecture have never been identified. See summary provided by Harbison, "Architectural Style and Sculptural Symbolism," from his *Jan van Eyck: The Play of Realism*, 151–57.

39. Joseph Leo Koerner, *The Moment of Self-Portraiture in German Renaissance Art*, xix.

40. Rouen, G2126, (Archives Seine-Maritime, Cathedral Fabric Account): "Pour enrichir et ennoblir et plus enluminer le cueur de l'église de Rouen a par plusrs foys esté conféré avecques maistre Jensson Salvart, maistre des oeuvres, et aveuc maistre Jehan Roussel, lesquielx après ce (que) ont conféré aveuc autres maistres ouvriers et bachelers et expers en machonneries, nous ont figuré pour les chinq petites fourmes du chevet d'icellui cueur en une manière trenchée en parchemin, et, pour les autres fourmes plus grandes, que sont aux deux costés en une autre manière et pour lesquelles manières avoir plus en memoire, sans en riens diminuer, icellui maistre Jansson a signe ledit parchemin de son sain manuel, et si a tranchée pour mielx estre congneue, sur le plancher de la maison de l'oeuvre, la petite fourme dessus dicte en son long et en son le justement, et si a promis par la foy de son corps reparer à ses propres cousts le dommage qui pour l'ouverture et cretenmeure de la vieille fourme sur la vieille machonnerie pourroit advenir en temps advenir sur l'obligacion de ses biens meubles et héritages, présens et avenir, en nous affermant en bonne foy que la petite fourme ne coustera oultre cent dix frans et la grande point plus de cent chinquante frans en la machonnerie; et si a promis rendre prestes et assizes en toutes machonneries trois des dites fourmes dedans la feste Monsr Saint Michiel prochain venant, se ne sourvient, que Dieu ne veulle! par cas inopiné empeschement excusable, et aussi nous paierons et livrerons les deniers raisonnablement pour paier les ouvriers tailleurs et aultres. Pour fermeté de laquelle chose nous par commun consentement avons escript ceste presente carte-partie, et sera paiés par chacun ouvrier chinq soulz pour jour ou mendre pris segon ce que sera convenu et apointié par les maistres de l'oeuvre, Ainse signé: J. Son." Beaurepaire, "Notes sur les architectes" (1902), 80.

41. Beaurepaire, "Notes sur les architectes," includes transcriptions of signatures of Roulland Le Roux (1904–5, 130) and Simon Vitecoq (1904–6, 135).

42. These documents were published by Beaurepaire, "Notes sur les architectes" (1903), 51–63.

43. Ibid.

44. Ibid. Deliberations for 5 and 12 June and 11 July 1479.

45. Ibid.

46. The conflict between both Jacques Le Roux and his nephew, Roulland Le Roux and the cathedral chapter over construction projects is discussed by Yves Bottineau-Fuchs, "Maître d'oeuvre, maître d'ouvrage," 183–94.

47. Beaurepaire, "Notes sur le grand portail de la cathédrale de Rouen," 139. He cites the cathedral chapter deliberations: "7 mai 1507, Visa papiro figurata per expertos lathomos de et super reformatione seu compositione unius novi portalicii magnifici et sumptuosi inter duas turres hujus ecclesie pro ruina ejus inter eas consistentis, cujus figuratio duntaxat existit in complantatione illius, Domini dixerunt ipsam papirum figurari et compleri in integrum pro elevacione portalicii, ut tandem ipsum portalicium, pro intentione artificum figuratum, videatur et inspiciatur, et postmodum deliberabitur de onere illius compositionis assumendo, etc. . . . et de eo etiam advertatur Rmus Do. cardinalis, sine cujus beneficio opus ipsum non poterit compleri neque etiam inchoari."

48. Ibid., 143. Beaurepaire cites a fabric account for 1507–8, G2523: "le XXVIIe jour de janvier, furent mandés par le commandement de Messrs de Chapitre maistres Jehan Le Boucher et Pierres Le Galloys, machons, pour veoir les traictz faictz par maistres Jacques et Roullant dictz Le Roux, pour ledit portail, en la salle de la Ville où furent commis maistres Pierre Mesenge et Batencourt, chanoines; et après la dicte visitaciion, ordonnèrent bailler ausd. machons, pour aller boire, x sous."

49. François Bucher, "Micro-Architecture as the "Idea" of Gothic Theory and Style."

50. Jacques Le Goff, "Merchant's Time and Churches' Time in the Middle Ages," 29.

51. Ibid., 35.

52. See Lynn White, *Medieval Technology and Social Change*, 122–123.

53. There are numerous studies on the early development of the mechanical clock. See Ernest L. Edwards, *Weight-Driven Chamber Clocks of the Middle Ages and Renaissance*; and Carlo Cipolla, *Clocks and Culture, 1300–1700*. Other early clocks include those at the cathedral of Beauvais (1324), Cluny (1340), Chartres (1359); by 1370, Charles V had installed clocks in his residences—the Royal Palace, Vincennes, and the Hotel St. Paul.

54. The Harelle of 1382 was a revolt against increased taxation by Charles VI primarily by cloth workers from the eastern parishes of the city, including Saint-Maclou. Charles VI responded by dissolving the Rouen commune that had existed in the city since the mid-twelfth century, fining the city 60,000 livres, suppressing the function of the mayor, and turning over gubernatorial powers to his bailiff. Because the bell tower had been a symbol of communal authority, it was razed and the bell "Rouve" or Raoul that called the workers to revolt was destroyed. Delsalle suggests that the installation of a municipal clock was a pretext for the reconstruction of the belfry tower. Although there have been numerous changes to the Gros Horloge since the fourteenth century, the clock is still the one built by the clockmakers Jourdain Delestre and Jehan de Félanis in 1389. Lucien René Delsalle, *Rouen et les Rouennais au temps de Jeanne d'Arc, 1400–1470*, 150–52; Henri Loriquet, *Le Beffroi de Rouen Avant la sédition de la Harelle*; and Charles de Robillard de Beaurepaire, "Recherches sur les horloges de les horlogers de la ville de Rouen."

55. Delsalle, *Rouen et les Rouennais*, 148, cites communale archives of 25 July 1390: "Les machons ouvrans au belfroy n'auront pour jour que deux heures c'est assavoir demi heure à déjeuner, 1 à disner, demi heure à ressie. En cas que ils feront le contraire, seront mis en prison, ou l'on l'en leur déduira sur leur journée."

56. Beaurepaire, "Recherches sur les horloges", 481.

57. Ibid., 482.

58. Beaurepaire, "Notes sur les architectes" (1902), 81 n. 1. "Domini [the canons] lathomis in fabrica hujus ecclesie laborantibus ad finem quod melius sciante tempus et horas laborandi et veniendi in opere, tradiderunt eisdem in mutuo horologium quoddam in hac ecclesia existens, quod fuit datum per duratum de Monteforti, tamen pro ponendo dictum horoloium in dicta fabrica et non alibi" (G2126) (Ibid., 482). The curate of Montfort gave the clock to the canons for placement in the lodge and the masons were now regulated by municipal time. "Et se il eschiet que l'orlge de la ville faille; ils yront disner en tout temps de l'an quant la grant messe sonne et reviendront quant elle est dite." Delsalle, *Rouen et las Rouennais*, 153.

59. The fabric accounts are sprinkled with references to the early clocks.

60. The documents related to the fifteenth-century clocks at Saint-Maclou are published by Beaurepaire, "Recherches sur les horloges," 493–98.

61. Beaurepaire, "Notes sur les architectes" (1902), 82. "Comparuerunt in Capitulo operarii Fabrice, qui fuerunt multum reprehensi eo quod, non debite, sed male adimplebant et faciebant dietas suas pro Fabrica hujus ecclesie, et de hoc murmurabant catholici hujus civitatis qui de hoc male contentabantur, quia negocium Fabrice provenit de puris elemosinis a Christi fidelibus, et in hiis ipse lathomi operarii multum onerabant consciencias suas, et quod precaverent pro tempore futuro, 7 janvier 1445 (v.s.)" (2130).

62. Ibid., 92–93. Beaurepaire cites an insert into a cathedral register containing obituaries, (G2094). Transcription:

Cy ensieut la manière de l'ordenance comme les machons de Notre-Dame de Rouen doivent ouvrer. Premièrement:

En tous temps de l'an doivent venir en besongne quand le sacrement de la messe

Saint-Pierre est fait et commencer quand elle est dicte.

Et doivent desjeuner en la loge quant prime sonne de volée jusques au commencement de prime en cueur.

En karesme, quand Ouynet a laissié à sonner jusques au commencement de prime en cueur comme dessus.

De Pasques jusques à Rouvoisons et du premier jour de septembre jusques à la Saint-Michiel doivent aller disner à xij heures et revenir à une heure après douze.

De Rouvoisons jusques au premier jour de septembre doivent aller disner à xij heures et revenier à une heure et demie.

De la Saint-Michiel jusques à Pasques doivent aler disner quant la grant messe est sonnée et revenir quand elle est dicte.

De Pasues jusques à la Saint-Michiel doivent prendre leur vin de nonne quant nonne Nostre-Dame va de volé jusques au premier son des vespres.

Et se il eschiet que l'orloge de la Ville faille, ilz yront disner en tout temps de l'an quant la grant messe sonne, et revendront quanD elle est dicte.

Le jeudi absolut doivent aler disner quand le preschement est commenchié et revenier quand il est fait, et s'en doivent aler après disner, quant le Mandé aux çlers est fait.

Le vendredi saint, ilz ne doivent commencer oeuvre jusques à ce que le service soit dit et que ilz aient disne et s'en iront à heure acoustumee.

Le samedi viennent au matin en besongne pour amender leurs deffaultes et s'en vont quant on sonne en l'église, et leur vaudra celle sepmaine v jours, se il n'y a feste; et se il eschiet que il y ait feste, ilz ne auront que iii jours et demi.

A la vegille de Rouvoisons, S. Jehan Baptiste, S. Pierre et S. Pol, de l'Assumpcion, de la Nativité Notre-Dame, s'en yront quant on sonne nonne à Saint-Vivian et par les paroisses, et en auront plaine journee, et ne doivent point desjeuner, fors se ilz veullent boire, ilz doivent boire sur leur pierre.

A Nouel, le jour de l'an, de la Tiphaingne, Karesme prenant, le Sacrement, S. Laurens, S. Martin, la Toussains, la Purificacion, l'Annonciacion, la Concepcion Notre-Dame, S. Mathias, S. Marc, S. Phelippe, Saint Jaque, Saint Jehan porte latin, S. Barnabé, S. Marcial, S. Jaque S. Berthelemieu, S. Mahieu, S. Lucas, S. Simon et Jude, S. Andrieu et S. Thomas, à ces xiiii festes dessus dictes s'en yront quant vespres seront sonnees, et en auront plainne journée. Le jeudi d'apr-s Pasques et la veille S. Michel, s'en yront à nonne Notre Dame de volée et en doivent avoir planne journée.

Et s'il eschiet en une sepmaine deux festes, la samedi ne vauldra que demi jour.

Item s'il eschiet en une sepmaine une feste tout seullement, le samedi vaudra plain jour.

Et ouvreront chiens toutefois que on oeuvre par la ville, et seront poiés du mouton de l'Ascencion et du vin de la Saint-Martin, ainsi que l'on a acoustumé.

Et trouvera l'en la forge aux dis machons

Et s'il eschiet que aultres ouvriers, comme carpentiers, plombiers, verriers, couvreurs, plastriers, ou aultres ouvriers, quelzconques ouvriers que ce soient, oeuvrent en la dite oeuvre, ilz ouvreront comme les devant dis machons, mais à v. vegilles dessus dictes ne auront que demi jour et ne leur vauldra le samedi que demi jour, se la sepmaine n'est entière.

Item s'il eschiet que ouvriers quelzconques, ouvriers que ce soient, oeuvrent ès maisons de l'oeuvre qui sont en la ville, ilz ourvreront et seront poiés ainsi que les ouvriers qui oeuvrent par la ville.

[Here follows the rules of ordinance under which the masons of Notre-Dame must work. First:

At all times of the year, (they) must come to work when the sacrament of the Mass of Saint Peter is said and begin work after it has been said.

And (they) must eat at the lodge when (the bells of) prime sound until the beginning of prime in the choir.

During Lent, when Ouynet has rung the bells until the beginning of prime in the choir as above.

From Easter until Rogations and from the first day of September until Saint Michaels they must go eat at 12:00 and return at 1:00.

From Rogations until the first day of September they must go eat at 12:00 and return at 1:30.

From Saint Michael's until Easter they must go eat when the bells are rung for High Mass and return when it has been said.

From Easter until Saint Michael's they must take their nones wine when (the bells of) nones of Notre-Dame sound until the first sound of vespers.

If it should happen that the clock of the city fails, they will eat at all times of the year when the great mass sounds and return when it has been said.

On Maundy Thursday they must go eat when the preaching has begun and return when it is finished, and they must go after eating when the *Mande aux Clers* (washing of the feet) has been done.

On Holy Friday they must not begin work until the service is said and when they have eaten they will go at the usual hour.

Saturday they will come in the morning to work to repair their mistakes and they will go at the sound of the bell in the church and this week will have five days if there is no feast and if it happens that there is a feast they will have three and one-half days.

One the vigil of Rogations, Saint John the Baptist, Saint Peter and Saint Paul, the Assumption, the Nativity of our Lady, they will go when the bells sound for nones at Saint Vivien and by the parishes and they will have a full day, they can not eat, although they can drink, they must drink at their stone (places).

A Christmas, New Year's Day, Ephiphany,

during Lent, the sacrament, Saint Lawrence, Saint Martin, All Saints', the Purification, the Annunciation, the Conception of our Lady, Saint Matthias, Saint Mark, Saint Philippe, Saint James the Lesser, Saint John before the Latin Gate, Saint Luke, Saint Simon and Saint Jude, Saint Andrew and Saint Thomas, on these fourteen feast days mentioned above they leave when vespers is sounded and they will work a full day. The Thursday after Easter and the vigil of Saint Michael, they will leave at nones of Notre-Dame and they must work an entire day.

If two feast days fall in one week, they must work only one half-day on Saturday.

Also, if only one feast day falls in the week, then they must work a full day on Saturday.

And they will work just as they work throughout the city and they will be paid with mutton on the Ascension and wine on Saint Martin's as they have been accustomed to.

And one will find there the forge belonging to the said masons.

If it should happen that other workers like carpenters, lead workers, glaziers, roofers, plasterers, or other workers, whatsoever kind of worker that this may be, should work in the said work as the aforesaid masons, but at the five vigils mentioned above they will only have a half-day and Saturday will only be a half-day for them if the week is not full.

Item, if it should happen that any kind of worker, whatsoever kind of worker that this may be, work on the houses of the work that are in town, they will work and be paid just as the workers who work in the town.]

63. Emile van Moé, "Les ethiques politiques et économiques d'Aristote traduits par Nicole Oresme"; A. D. Menut, "The French Version of Aristotle's *Economics* in Rouen, Bibl. Municipale, MS 927"; Marshall Clagett, "Nicole Oresme and Medieval Scientific Thought."

64. Otto Mayr, "The Rise of the Clock Metaphor," 33–37;

65. Joel Kaye, "The Impact of Money on the Development of Fourteenth-Century Scientific Thought," 251.

66. The development of the iconography of Temperance is treated by Lynn White, "The Iconography of *Temperantia* and the Virtuousness of Technology," in *Action and Conviction in Early Modern Europe: Essays in Memory of E. H. Garbison*, ed. Theodore K. Rabb and Jerrold E. Seigle, 197–219; and Mayr, "Rise of the Clock Metaphor," 33–37.

67. Emile Mâle, *Religious Art In France*, 291.

68. White, "The Iconography of Temperance," 202.

69. Beaurepaire, "Notes sur les architectes" (1903), 55.

70. Ibid., 64,

71. Roland Sanfaçon, "La rôle des techniques dans les principales mutations de l'architecture gothique": "Mais cette 'structure décorative' ou ce 'décor structurel' de l'architecture flamboyant sont exécutés de façon très pratique avant tout" (111).

72. The cost-saving argument for continuous moldings was used by Michael T. Davis, "On the 'Threshold of the Flamboyant."

73. Rouen, Saint-Maclou fabric accounts for 1479–79 (G6878): "paie aux machons pour septmaine rabat les fautes de vallet Ambroise . . . 4 livres 10 sous 9 denier."

74. See Note 62.

75. Ouin-Lacroix, Histoire des anciennes corporations, 611: "Se aucun du dit mestier est trouvé coulpable d'avoir fait faulx ouvrage . . . il sera appelé devant le bailly en présence des gardes, amendera sa faulte et paiera dix sols tournoi au roi" (611).

76. The contemporary accounts of Troyes Cathedral offer some insight as to the motivation of patrons. Jehançon Garnache, master mason of Troyes from 1485 to 1502, received daily pay for work on the flying buttresses but was paid 50 to 60 pounds per vault. Since vault construction did not provide the opportunity to linger over extravagant detail, the piecework contract was more an incentive to complete the work quickly. A similar contract for piecework for Garnache was used to complete the nave windows. On the other hand, contracts for the construction of the choir screen provide clues concerning the expense of time. On 28 October 1382, the chapter made a contract with Henry of Brussels and Henry Soudan for the construction of the choir screen. The contract outlines in detail the daily working hours and pay of the masons. "Good caution" money of 400 francs is held by the chapter to assure that they will work well and faithfully according to the approved drawing. However, by the following year, it appears that Henry along with some of his masons are occupied with work at Auxerre and that the Troyes choir screen work was not proceeding. Because of the master's lack of commitment to the Troyes project, the canons decide to issue a contract for piecework. They agree to spend 200 livres per year to finish the screen. For a complete transcription of the contracts see Stephen Murray, *Building Troyes Cathedral*, 80–81, 129–30, and 135.

77. See Chapter 1, Note 65.

Selected Bibliography

Adelman, Lorado Samuel. "The Flamboyant Style in French Gothic Architecture." Ph.D. dissertation, University of Minnesota, 1973.

Allinne, Maurice. "La façade occidentale de la cathédrale de Rouen." *Bulletin de la Société des Amis des Monuments rouennais* (1912), 73–100.

———. "Le pilier de la porte centrale de la façade occidentale de la cathédrale de Rouen." *Bulletin de la Société des Amis des Monuments rouennais* (1905), 109–22.

Allmand, C., ed. *Power, Culture, and Religion in France, c. 1350–c. 1550.* Woodbridge, Suffolk, 1989.

Aubert, Marcel. "La cathédrale de Rouen." In *Congrès archéologique de France*, Rouen, 1926, 11–101.

Baldass, Ludwig. *Jan van Eyck.* London, 1952.

Basset, François. *La vie municipale à Rouen au XVe siècle, 1447–1471.* Rouen, 1974.

Bauchal, Charles. *Nouveau dictionnaire biographique et critique des architectes français.* Paris, 1887.

Beaurepaire, Charles de Robillard de. "Contract de la Fondation de l'église Saint-Maclou." *Bulletin de la Commission des Antiquités de Seine-Inférieure* 12 (1900–1902), 409–12.

———. *L'Entrée de François Premier Roi de France, dans la ville de Rouen au mois d'août 1517.* Rouen, 1867.

———. *Les états de Normandie sous la domination anglaise.* Paris, 1859.

———. "Extrait du testament de Guillaume Auvre chanoine de Rouen et curé de Saint-Maclou de Rouen de 1478–1480." *Bulletin de la Commission des Antiquités du département de la Seine-Inférieure* 3 (1877), 151–52.

———. *Inventaires-sommaires des archives départementales antérieures à 1790.* Ser. G (Archives ecclésiastiques), vols. 1–4, Paris, 1868–1887; vols. 5–7, Rouen, 1892–1912.

———. "Modèle en carton de l'église Saint-Maclou." *Bulletin de la Commission des Antiquités du département de la Seine-Inférieure* 10 (1894–95), 335–37.

———. "Notice sur le grand portail de la cathédrale de Rouen." *Bulletin de la Commission des Antiquités du département de la Seine-Inférieure* 9 (1894–96), 124–43.

———. "Notice sur le palais de l'archevêque de Rouen." *Précis Analytique* (1890–91), 237–67.

———. "Notice sur Saint-Vincent." *Bulletin de la Commission des Antiquités de la Seine-Inférieure* 4 (1876–78), 115–27.

———. "Notice sur les architectes de Saint-Maclou." *Nouveau recueil des notes historiques et archaéologiques* 2 (1888), 290–315.

———. "Notes sur les architectes de Rouen." *Bulletin de la Société des Amis des Monuments rouennais* I (1901), 75–96; II (1902), 67–93; III (1903), 47–77; IV (1904–6), 119–53.

———. "Recherches sur les horloges de les horlogers de la ville de Rouen." *Bulletin de la Commission des Antiquités du département de la Seine-Inférieure* 8 (1890), 472–526.

———. "Travaux des architectes Alexandre de Berneval et Jacques Le Roux en l'église abbatiale de Fécamp." *Bulletin de la Commission des Antiquités du département de la Seine-Inférieure* 4 (1876–78), 82–91.

Beissel, S. *Die Baüfuhrung der Mittelalters, Studien über die Kirche des hl. Victor zu Xanten*, Freiburg, 1889.

Benedict, Philip. *Rouen during the Wars of Religion.* Cambridge, 1981.

Benoît, Amédée. *Les édifices religieux de Paris.* Paris, 1910

Bialostocki, Jan. "Late Gothic Disagreement about the Concept." *British Archaeological Association*, ser. 9, 29 (1966), 76–105.

Bodin-Cerné, Catherine. "Saint-Maclou de Rouen, L'église—la paroisse au XVe et XVIe siècles." Thesis, Mémoire du D.E.S., Faculté des Lettres de Caen, 1962.

Bottineau-Fuchs, Yves. "Maître d'oeuvre, maître d'ouvrage: Les Le Roux et le chapître cathédral de Rouen." In *Artistes, Artisans et Production Artistique au Moyen Age*, Colloque international Université de Rennes, May 1983, I; Les Hommes, Picard, 1986.

Bouttier, Michel. "La reconstruction de l'abbatiale de Saint-Denis au XIIIe siècle." *Bulletin Monumental* 145, no. 4 (1987), 357–86.

Branner, Robert. "A Fifteenth-Century French Architectural Drawing from the Cloister." *Metropolitan Museum of Art Journal* 11 (1976), 133–36.

Brodard, Paul. *Rouen et ses environs.* Paris, 1925.

Bruzelius, Caroline. "Cistercian High Gothic: The Abbey Church of Longpont and the Architecture of the Cistercians in the Early Thirteenth Century." *Analecta Cisterciensia* 35 (1979), 3–204.

———. "The Construction of Notre-Dame in Paris." *Art Bulletin* 69, no. 4 (1987), 540–69.

———. *The Thirteenth-Century Church at St.-Denis.* New Haven, 1985. Bucher, François. "Medieval Architectural Design Methods, 800–1560." *Gesta* 11 (1972), 37–51.

Bucher, François. "Micro-Architecture as the "Idea" of Gothic Theory and Style," *Gesta* 15 (1976), 71–89.

Campbell, Thomas. "Cathedral Chapter and Town Council: Cooperative Ceremony and Drama in Medieval Rouen." *Comparative Drama*, ed. C. Davidson and J. Stroupe, 27 (1993), 103–12.

Carment-Lanfry, A. M. *La Cathédrale Notre-Dame de Rouen*. Rouen, 1977.

Chaline, Nadine-Josette. *Histoire des diocèses de France*, ed. Palanque and Plongeron, v *Le Diocèse de Rouen—Le Havre*. Paris, 1976.

Chartes et privilèges accordés à plusieurs églises et abbayes de Normandie. Bibliothèque municipale de Rouen, Fonds Coquebert de Monbret, 1849.

Chauvel, Albert. "La cathédrale de Rouen: Les destructions, le sauvetage." *Les Monuments historiques de la France* 2, no. 2 (April–June 1956), 55–92.

———. "Eglise Saint-Maclou de Rouen." Rapport du 15 octobre 1955 et documents annexes. Dossier des Monuments Historiques, Paris.

———. "L'Eglise Saint-Maclou de Rouen, Destruction et Consolidation." *Les Monuments historiques de la France* 4 (1958), 163–72.

———. "Etude sur la taille des pierres au moyen âge." *Bulletin monumental* 93 (1934), 435–50.

Chéruel, Adolphe. *Histoire de Rouen pendant l'époque communale, 1150–1382*. 2 vols. Rouen, 1843–44.

———. *Histoire de Rouen sous la domination anglaise au XVe siècle*. Rouen, 1840.

Chirol, Elizabeth. "Saint-Maclou de Rouen," *Connaître Rouen*, II (Bulletin des amis des monuments rouennais), 1970, 1–15.

Chirol, Pierre. *Cathédrales et églises de Normandie*. Rouen, 1939.

———. "Le Palais de Justice." *Congrès archéologique de France* (Rouen, 1926): 178–93.

Chirol, Pierre, and René Herval. *Rouen à travers les âges*. Paris, 1941.

Cipolla, Carlo. *Clocks and Culture, 1300–1700*. New York, 1967.

Clagett, Marshall. "Nicole Oresme and Medieval Scientific Thought." *Proceedings of the American Philosophical Society*, 108 (1964), 298–309.

Cochet, Abbé Jean Baptiste. "Notice sur une pierre limite de l'abbaye de Saint-Ouen de Rouen." *Bulletin de la Société des Antiquaires de Normandie* 2 (1870–73), 273–76.

———. *Les porches des églises de la Seine-Inférieure à propos du porche de Borc-Bordel près de Buchy*. Dieppe, 1871.

———. *Répertoire archéologique du département de la Seine-Inférieure*. Paris, 1871 (reprint, Brionne, 1975).

Colvin, H. M. *The History of the King's Works*, I, *The Middle Ages*. London, 1963.

Couffon, R. "La confrérie de Saint-Yves à Paris et sa chapelle." *Mémoires de la Société des Côtes-du-Nord* (1933), 1–65.

Couffon, René. "La chappelle Saint-Yves à Paris," *Bulletin monumental* (1933), 240–41, and (1934), 358–59.

Couton, Docteur. "L'Eglise Notre-Dame de Vernon." *Bulletin de la Société des Amis des Monuments rouennais* 11 (1911–12), 89–104.

Crowther, James. *Social Relations of Science*. New York, 1941.

Daage, Patrice Colmet. *La Cathédrale de Coutances*. Paris, 1933.

Davis, Michael T. "On the Threshold of Flamboyant: The Second Campaign of Construction of Saint-Urbain, Troyes." *Speculum* 59 (October 1984): 847–84.

Davis, Michael T. "The Choir of the Abbey of Altenberg: Cistercian Simplicity and Aristocratic Iconography." In *Studies in Cistercian Art and Architecture*, ed. Meredith P. Lillich, Kalamazoo, Mich., 1984, 2:130–60.

———. "'Troys Portaulx et Deux Grosses Tours': The Flamboyant Façade Project for the Cathedral of Clermont." *Gesta* 22, no. 1 (1983), 67–84.

Dayot, Armand. *La Normandie monumentale et pittoresque*. Le Havre, 1893.

Delsalle, Lucien René. *Rouen et les Rouennais au temps de Jeanne d'Arc, 1400–1470*. Rouen, 1982.

Denifle, P. Henri. *La Guerre de cent ans et la désolation des églises, monastères et hôpitaux en France*. Paris, 1899.

Denis de Sainte-Marthe, ed. *Gallia Christiana in Provincias ecclesiasticas distributa*. Paris, 1874.

Deschamps, Philippe. "Les Entrées Royales à Rouen." In *Connaître Rouen*. III, 1970, 1–20.

Desneaux, J. "Underdrawings and *Pentimenti* in the Pictures of Jan van Eyck." *Art Bulletin* 40, no. 1 (March 1958), 13–21.

Deville, Achille. *Comptes de dépenses de la construction du château de Gaillon*. Paris, 1850.

———. *Histoire du Château de Tancarville*. Rouen, 1834.

———. *Revue des architectes de la cathédrale du Rouen jusqu'à la fin du XVIe siècle*. Rouen, 1848.

Deville, E. "Registres des comptes de la collégiale de Vernon (1432–1439)." *Bulletin historique et philologique du comité des travaux historiques et scientifique* (1910), 161–78.

Dewald, Jonathan. *The Formation of the Provincial Nobility: The Magistrates of the Parlement of Rouen, 1499–1610*. Princeton, N.J., 1980.

Doncoeur, P., and Y. Lanhers. *L'Enquête du Cardinal d'Estouteville en 1452*. Paris, 1958.

Dossier historique et généalogique de Dufour. Bibliothèque municipale de Rouen, Collection Martainville, 2897–2970, carton no. 32.

Dumoulin, M., and G. Outardel. *Les églises de France: Paris et la Seine*. Paris, 1936.

Duplessis, Dom. *Description géologique et historique de la Haute Normandie*. Rouen, 1740.

Duranville, Léon de. "Les foires à Rouen." *Précis des Travaux de l'Académie des Sciences, Belles-Lettres et Arts de Rouen* (1878–79).

Edwards, Ernest L. *Weight-Driven Chamber Clocks of the Middle Ages and Renaissance.* Altrincham, England, 1965.

Estaintot, Robert C. *Rapport sur le projet de restauration de la porte de Saint-Maclou de Rouen.* Rouen, 1875.

Enlart, Camille. *Manuels d'archéologie française,* 2 vols. Paris, 1919–20.

———. "Origine anglaise du style flamboyant." *Bulletin Monumental* (1906), 38–81, 511–25; (1910), 125–47.

———. *Rouen.* (Villes d'art célèbres), Paris, 1928.

Fallue, Léon. *Histoire politique et religieuse de l'église métropolitaine du diocèse de Rouen,* 5 vols. Rouen, 1850.

Farin, François. *Histoire de la ville de Rouen,* 3d ed., 2 vols. Rouen, 1738 (first published, 1668).

Felix, J. *Comptes rendus des échevins de Rouen, 1409–1701.* Rouen, 1890.

Floquet, M. *Histoire du privilège Saint-Romain.* 2 vols. Rouen, 1873.

Fossey, Jules. *Monographie de la cathédrale d'Evreux.* Evreux, 1898.

Foucher, J. B. *Souvenir d'un tailleur de pierre: Etude sur les usages, les moeurs, la façon de travailler des artistes de la pierre à Rouen, première moitié du XIXe siècle.* Rouen, 1899–1901.

Fouquet, Henri. *Histoire civile, politique et commerciale de Rouen,* 2 vols. Rouen, 1876.

Fowler, Kenneth, ed. *The Hundred Years' War.* London, 1971.

Frankl, Paul. *Gothic Architecture.* Baltimore, 1962.

Friedländer, M. *Alterniederländische Malerei.* Berlin, 1924.

Frondeville, Henri de. *Les Conseillers du Parlement de Normandie au seizième siècle.* Rouen, 1960.

Frothingham, A. L. "Discovery of an Original Church Model by a Gothic Architect." *Architectural Record* 22 (1907), 110–16.

———. "La Modele de l'église Saint-Maclou de Rouen." *Monuments et Memoires. Fondation Eugène Piot.* Paris, 1904, 211–24.

Gairdner, J., ed. *The Historical Collections of A Citizen of London.* London, 1876.

Giesey, Ralph E. *The Royal Funeral Ceremony in Renaissance France.* Geneva, 1960.

Gilbert, A. P. M. *Description historique de l'église metropolitaine de Notre-Dame de Rouen.* Rouen, 1816.

Godefroy, Frédéric. *Dictionnaire de l'ancienne langue française et de tous ses dialectes du IXe au XVe siècles,* 12 vols. Paris, 1880.

Gouellain, Gustave. "Eglise de Saint-Maclou de Rouen, Dégradations." *Bulletin de la Commission des Antiquités du département de la Seine-Inférieure* 8 (1889–90), 227.

Guenée, Bernard, and Françaíse Lehoux. *Les Entrées royales françaises de 1328 à 1515.* Paris, 1968.

Guitard, M. L. "La draperie à Rouen." *Bulletin de la Commission des Antiquités du département de la Seine-Inférieure* 8 (1889–90), 88–112.

———. "La draperie à Rouen, des origines aux réformes de Colbert." Thèse, Ecole des Chartes, 1933.

Hahn, H. *Die frühe Kirchenbaukunst der Zisterzienser.* Berlin, 1957.

Hahnloser, H., ed. *Villard de Honnecourt: Kritische Gesamtausgabe des Bauhuttenbuchs ms. fr. 19093 der Pariser Nationalbibliothek,* 2d. ed. Graz, 1972.

Hall, Edwin. *The Arnolfini Betrothal: Medieval Marriage and the Enigma of Van Eyck's Double Portrait.* Berkeley and Los Angeles, 1994.

Harbison, Craig. *Jan van Eyck: The Play of Realism.* London, 1991.

———. *The Mirror of the Artist: Northern Renaissance Art and Its Historical Context.* New York, 1995.

Harvey, John. *The Perpendicular Style, 1330–1485.* London, 1978.

Heliot, P. "Triforiums et coursières dans les églises gothiques de Bretagne et de Normandie," *Annales de Normandie* 19 (1969), 115–54.

Héron, Alexander, ed. *Deux chroniques de Rouen.* Rouen, 1900.

Herval, René. *Histoire de Rouen.* 2 vols. Rouen, 1947.

———. *Saint-Maclou de Rouen.* Rouen, 1933.

Horn, Walter, and Ernst Born. *The Plan of St. Gall,* 2 vols. Berkeley and Los Angeles, 1979.

Huard, George. *L'art en Normandie.* Paris, 1928.

Huizinga, J. *The Waning of the Middle Ages: A Study of the Forms of Life, Thought, and Art in France and Netherlands in the Fourteenth and Fifteenth Centuries.* New York, 1989 (first published 1924).

James, John. *The Template Makers of the Paris Basin.* Leura, 1989.

Johnes, Thomas, Esq., trans. *The Chronicles of Enguerrand de Monstrelet,* 2 vols. London, 1853.

Jolimont, T. de. *Les principaux édifices de la ville de Rouen en 1525.* Rouen, 1845.

Jouen, Alfred Léon. *La cathédrale de Rouen.* Rouen, 1932.

———. "Eglise de Saint-Maclou." *Congrès archéologique de France* (Rouen, 1926), 127–41.

Julien, Henri. "Clé de voûte de la chapelle de la Vierge à Caudebec-en-Caux." *Monuments historiques de la France* 1 (July-September 1955), 116–20.

Kaye, Joel. "The Impact of Money on the Development of Fourteenth-Century Scientific Thought." *Journal of Medieval History* 14, no. 3 (September 1988), 251–270.

Kimpel, Dieter. "Le développement de la taille en série dans l'architecture mediévale et son rôle dans l'histoire économique." *Bulletin Monumental* 135, no. 3 (1977), 195–222.

———. "Les méthodes de production des cathédrals," trans. Anseime Schimpf. In *Les Bâtisseurs des cathédrals gothiques,* ed. Roland Recht, Strasbourg, 1989, 103–9.

Kleinbauer, W. Eugene, ed. *The Art of Byzantium and the*

Medieval West: Selected Studies by Ernst Kitzinger. Bloomington, Ind., 1976.

Kletzl, O. "Ein Werkriss des Frauenhauses von Strassburg." *Marburger für Kunstwissenschaft* 11 (1938–39), 1–56.

Koepf, Hans. *Die gotischen Planrisse der Wiener Sammlungen Wien.* Cologne, 1969.

Koerner, Joseph Leo. *The Moment of Self-Portraiture in German Renaissance Art.* Chicago, 1993.

Laborde, Léon de. *Etude sur la bibliothèque de la cathédrale de Rouen: le portail des libraires.* Paris, 1919.

Lafond, Jean. *La cathédrale de Rouen.* Paris, 1936.

———. "La prétendue maquette de l'église Saint-Maclou de Rouen." *Gazette des Beaux Arts* 83 (1974), 65–74.

Lance, Adolphe. *Dictionnaire des architectes français.* 2 vols. Paris, 1872.

Lanfry, Georges. *La cathédrale après la conquête de la Normandie et jusqu'à l'occupation anglaise.* Rouen, 1960.

———. *La cathédrale dans la cité romaine et la Normandie ducale.* Rouen, 1956.

———. *La cathédrale de Rouen.* Rouen, 1957.

———. *La façade occidentale de la cathédrale de Rouen.* Rouen, 1957.

Langlois, E.-H. *Stalles de la cathédrale de Rouen.* Rouen, 1838.

Langlois, Abbé P. *Les jubés de la cathédrale de Rouen.* Rouen, n.d.

———. *Nouvelles recherches sur les bibliothèques des archevêques et du chapître de Rouen.* Rouen, 1854.

Lasteyrie, Robert Charles de. *L'architecture religieuse en France à l'époque gothique,* 2 vols. Paris, 1926.

Lavallée, Daniel. "Notes sur l'église Saint-Vivien de Rouen." *Revue Sociétés Savantes de Haute-Normandie—Préhistoire—Archéologie* 26 (1962), 53–65.

La Quérière, A. "L'Aître Saint-Maclou." *Bulletin de la Société des Amis des Monuments rouennais* (1907), 99–105.

La Quérière, Eustache de. *Notice sur le clocher de l'église de Saint-Maclou.* Rouen, n.d.

———. *Saint-Laurent, ancienne église paroissiale de Rouen.* Rouen, 1866.

Lebeuf, Abbé. *Histoire de la ville et de tout le diocèse de Paris,* I, 1754.

Lebeurier, P. F. *Etat des anoblis en Normandie de 1545 à 1661 avec un supplément de 1398 à 1687.* Evreux, 1866.

Le Cacheux, Paul. *Actes de la Chancellerie d'Henri VI concernant la Normandie sous la domination anglaise, 1422–1435,* I. Rouen, 1907.

———. *Correspondance de la famille d'Estouteville, 1460–1535.* Rouen, 1935.

———. "Le modèle de l'église Saint-Maclou de Rouen." *La Normandie* (December 1906), 249–54.

———. *Rouen au temps de Jeanne d'Arc et pendant l'occupation anglaise, 1419–1449.* Paris, 1931.

Lefèvre-Pontalis, Germain. "La guerre des partisans dans la Haute Normandie, 1424–1429: Les Rouennais." *Bibliothèque de l'Ecole des Chartes* 57 (1896), 5–54.

Legendre. L. *Vie du Cardinal d'Amboise, premier ministre de Louis XI.* Rouen, 1724.

Le Goff, Jacques. "Labor Time in the "Crisis" of the Fourteenth Century: From Medieval Time to Modern Time." In *Time, Work, and Culture in the Middle Ages,* trans. A. Goldhammer, Chicago, 1980, 43–52.

———. "Merchant's Time and Churches' Times in the Middle Ages." In *Time, Work, and Culture in the Middle Ages,* trans. A. Goldhammer, Chicago, 1980, 29–40.

Le Lieur, Jacques. *Livre des fontaines de Rouen.* Bibliothèque municipale de Rouen, 742 MS g.3, 1525.

Le Reboulet, Christiane. "Recherches sur les confréries des métiers à Rouen XIII au XVe siècle." Thèse, Ecole des Chartes, 1960.

Leroi, André. "Rouen au temps de Jeanne d'Arc." *Connaître Rouen* (1970), 16–24.

Le Trésor de la Cathédrale de Rouen. Musée des Antiquités de la Seine-Maritime. Rouen, 1993.

Lettres de Charles VI du mois de novembre 1441 octroyant divers privilèges et exemptions aux artillieurs, charpentiers et tailleurs de pierres à bombardes. Bibliothèque municipale de Rouen, Collection Lebers, 3187 (5702).

Le Verdier, Pierre. *Entrée du roi Louis XII et de la reine à Rouen 1508.* Rouen, 1900.

Lewis, P. S. *The Recovery of France in the Fifteenth Century.* London, 1971.

———. "War Propaganda and Historiography in Fifteenth-Century France and England." *Transactions of the Royal Historical Society,* 1965, 1–21.

Loisel, Armand. *La cathédrale de Rouen.* Paris, n.d.

Loriquet, Henri. *Le Beffroi de Rouen avant la sédition de la Harelle.* Rouen, 1906.

Loth, Julien. *L'Aître de Saint-Maclou.* Rouen, 1910.

———. *La cathédrale de Rouen.* Rouen, 1879.

———. "Rouen, Eglise de Saint-Maclou, états des dégradations." *Bulletin de la Commission des Antiquités du département de la Seine-Inférieure* 12 (1900), 5–69.

———. *Saint-Maclou de Rouen: L'église—la paroisse.* Rouen, 1913.

———. *Une visite à l'église Saint-Maclou.* Rouen, 1892.

Mâle, Emile. *Religious Art in France: The Late Middle Ages, A Study of Late Medieval Iconography and Its Sources,* ed. Harry Bober, trans. Marthiel Mathews, Bollingen Series 90:3. Princeton, N.J. 1986.

Martin, Abbé. *Répertoire des anciennes confréries et charités du diocèse de Rouen approuvées de 1434 à 1610.* Fécamp, 1936.

Masson, André. *L'Abbaye de Saint-Ouen de Rouen.* Rouen, 1930.

———. "Le bouchement des piliers de la croisée à Saint-Ouen de Rouen en 1441." *Bulletin monumental* 85 (1926), 307–16.

———. "Eglise Saint-Ouen." *Congrès archéologique de France* (Rouen, 1926), 102–26.

———. *Etudes sur l'abbaye de Saint-Ouen: Les Pierres tombales du XIIIe siècle à la fin du XVIe siècle.* Rouen, 1926.

———. "Saint-Ouen de Rouen." Positions des Thèses de l'Ecole des Chartes, 1922.

Mayr, Otto. "The Rise of the Clock Metaphor." In *Authority, Liberty and Automatic Machinery in Early Modern Europe.* Baltimore, 1986, 28–54.

Meckseper, Cord. "Über die Fünfeckkonstruktion bei Villard de Honnecourt und im späteren Mittelalter." *Architectura* 1, no. 13 (1983), 31–40.

Menut, A. D. "The French Version of Aristotle's *Economics* in Rouen, Bibl. Municipale, MS 927." *Romance Philology* 4 (1950–51), 55–62.

Michel, André. *Histoire de l'art depuis les premiers temps chrétiens jusqu'à nos jours.* Paris, 1907.

Michel, T. "L'Eglise de Notre-Dame de Vernon." In *La Normandie monumentale et pittoresque,* Le Havre, 1896, I, 122.

Miller, David B. "Monumental Building as an Indicator of Economic Trends in Northern Rus' in the Late Kievan and Mongols Periods, 1138–1462." *American Historical Review* 94 (1989), 360–90.

Millin, Aubin-Louis. *Antiquités nationales: ou. Recueil des monumens, pour servir a l'histoire générale et particulière de l'empire françois, tels que tombeaux, inscriptions, statues, vitraux, fresques, etc.: tirés des abbayes, monastères, châteaux, et autre liuex devenus domaines nationaux,* 5 vols. Paris, 1799.

Mirot, Albert, and Bernard Mahieu. "Cérémonies officielles à Notre-Dame au XVe siècle." *Huitième centenaire de Notre-Dame de Paris,* Congrès 1964, Paris (1967), 223–90.

Mirot, Léon. "Paiements et quittances de travaux exécutés sous le règne de Charles VI (1380–1422)." *Bibliothèque de l'Ecole des Chartes* 81 (1920), 183–304.

Mojon, Luc. *St. Johannsen. Saint-Jean de Cerlier: Betrage zum Bauwesen des Mittelalters, aus den Bauforschungen in der ehemaligen Benediktinerabtei 1961–1984.* Bern, 1986.

Mollat, Michel. *Le commerce maritime normand à la fin du moyen âge.* Paris, 1952.

———. *Histoire de Rouen.* Toulouse, 1979.

Monographie sur l'église Saint-Maclou de Rouen avec plan des abords de l'église 1938–1941. Bibliothèque municipale de Rouen, Fonds Coutan, 3F5.

Montelos, Jean Marie Pérouse de. *Principes d'analyse scientifique en architecture, Méthode et Vocabulaire,* 2 vols. Paris, 1972.

Montreuil, Guillaume de. *Chronique de Cousinol, Chronique de la Pucelle, La Chronique de Normandie de Pierre Cochon.* 1859

Morris, Richard. "The Development of Late Gothic Mouldings in England, c. 1250–1400, part I and part II." *Architectural History: Journal of the Society of Architectural Historians of Great Britain* 21 (1978), 18–57; 22 (1979), 1–48.

Mortet, V. "La maîtrise d'oeuvre dans les constructions du XIIIe siècle et la profession d'appareilleur." *Bulletin Monumental* 70 (1906), 263–70.

Mortet, V., and Paul Deschamps. *Recueil des textes relatifs à l'histoire de l'architecture et à la condition des architectes en France au moyen âge,* 2 vols. Paris, 1929.

Murray, Stephen. *Building Troyes Cathedral: The Late Gothic Campaigns.* Bloomington, Ind., 1987.

———. "The Choir of the Church of Saint-Pierre, Cathedral of Beauvais." *Art Bulletin* 63 (1980), 533–51.

———. "Master Jehançon Garnache and the Construction of the Vaults and Flyers of the Nave of Troyes Cathedral." *Gesta* 19 (1981), 37–49.

Murray, Stephen, and J. Addis. "Plan and Space at Amiens Cathedral: With a New Plan Drawn by James Addis." *Journal of the Society of Architectural Historians* 49, no. 1 (March 1990), 44–65.

Naillon, Edgar. *Les églises de Rouen.* Rouen, 1941.

———. *Rouen, ville d'art et d'histoire, églises, chapelles et cimetières à travers les âges,* 2 vols. Rouen, 1937.

Neagley, Linda E. "Elegant Simplicity: The Late Gothic Plan Design of St.-Maclou in Rouen," *Art Bulletin* 74, no. 3 (September 1992), 395–422.

———. "The Flamboyant Architecture of Saint-Maclou, Rouen, and the Development of a Style." *JSAH,* 47, no. 4 (December 1988), 374–96.

———. "The Parish Church of Saint-Maclou and Late Gothic Architecture in Rouen." Ph.D. dissertation, Indiana University, 1983.

Neumeyer, A. "The Meaning of the Balcony Scene at the Church of Muehlhausen in Thuringia: A Contribution to the History of Fourteenth-Century Illusionism." *Gazette des Beaus-Arts* (1957), 305–10.

Neuwirth, Joseph. *Die Wochenrechnungen und der Betrieb des Prager Dombaues.* Prague, 1890.

Newhall, R. A. *The English Conquest of Normandy.* New Haven, 1926.

———. "Henry V's Policy of Conciliation in Normandy, 1417–22." *Anniversary Essays in Medieval History by Students of Charles Hommer Haskins.* Boston, 1929.

Ouin-Lacroix, Charles. *Histoire de l'église et de la paroisse de Saint-Maclou de Rouen.* Rouen, 1846.

———. *Histoire des anciennes corporations d'arts et métiers et des confréries religieuses de la capitale de la Normandie.* Rouen, 1850.

Panofsky, Erwin. *Early Netherlandish Painting: Its Origins and Character.* Cambridge, 1964.

———. *Gothic Architecture and Scholasticism.* New York, 1951.

Pause, Peter. *Gotische Architekturzeichnungen in Deutschland.* Bonn, 1973.

Periaux, Nicétas. *Dictionnaire indicateur et historique des rues et places de Rouen*. Rouen, 1870.

———. *Histoire sommaire et chronologique de la ville de Rouen*. Rouen, 1874.

Perrot, F. "Le Vitrail à Rouen." *Connaître Rouen* (1972), 27.

Perroy, Edouard. *The Hundred Years' War*, trans. W. B. Wells. London, 1951.

———. "Social Mobility among the French Nobles in the Later Middle Ages." *Past and Present* (1962), 25–38.

Picard, M. *Répertoire des rues de Rouen avec l'indication des paroisses auxquelles elles appartenaient avant 1789*. Rouen, 1950.

Pigoreau, B. *L'Eglise de Caudebec-en-Caux*. Evreux, 1976.

Pillet, M. *L'Aître Saint-Maclou ancien cimetière paroissial de Rouen*. Paris, 1924.

Pillion, L. *Les portails latéraux de la cathédrale de Rouen*. Paris, 1907.

Pinel, Robinet. *Entrée de Charles VIII à Rouen en 1485*. Paris, 1902.

Pommeraye, François. *Histoire de l'abbaye royale de Saint-Ouen de Rouen*. Rouen, 1686.

———. *Histoire de la cathédrale de Rouen*. Rouen, 1686.

———. *Histoire des archêveques de Rouen*. Rouen, 1667.

———. *Sanctae Rotomagensis ecclesiae concilia ac synodalie decreta*. Rouen, 1677.

Pottier, André. "Portrait d'Alexandre de Berneval, architecte de Saint-Ouen de Rouen." *Revue de Rouen* (1849), 675–76.

Prak, N. "Measurement at Amiens Cathedral." *Journal of the Society of Architectural Historians* 25 (1966), 209–12.

Prevost, Chanoine L. *Histoire de la paroisse et des curés de Saint-Maclou depuis la fondation jusqu'à nos jours*. Rouen, 1970.

Prieur, Lucien. "L'Eglise Saint-Germain d'Argentan." *Congrès archéologique de France* (Orne 1953), 91–105.

Quenedey, Raymond. *Les anciens faubourgs de Rouen*. Rouen, 1936.

———. *Anciens termes normands de charpente*. Rouen, n.d.

———. "Les anciennes mesures de longueur de Rouen." *Bulletin philologique et historique de Comité des Travaux historiques et scientifiques* (1920), 301–9.

———. "Un devis de charpenterie de 1393 à Rouen, les etablis de Fécamp." *Bulletin Archéologique du Comité des Travaux historiques et scientifiques* (1913), 66–92.

———. *L'Habitation rouennaise: étude d'histoire, de géographie et d'archéologie urbaines*. Brionne, 1926.

———. *Métrologie rouennaise. Instruments et mesures de longueur*." *Bulletin philllogique et historique du Comité des Tavaux historiques et scientifiques* (1920), 301–9.

———. "Le prix des matériaux et de la main d'oeuvre à Rouen de XIVe au XVIIIe siècle." *Bulletin de la Société Libre d'émulation du commerce et de l'industrie de la Seine-Inférieure* (1925), 331–56.

Quicherat, Jules. "Documents inédits sur la construction de Saint-Ouen de Rouen." *Bibliothèque de l'Ecole des Chartes* 3 (1852), 464–76.

Rabb, Theodore K., and Jerrold E. Seigle, eds. *Action and Conviction in Early Modern Europe: Essays in Memory of E. H. Garbison*. Princeton, N.J., 1969.

Rapport sur les travaux de réédification de la flèche de l'église Saint-Maclou. Bibliothèque municipale de Rouen, F173. Rouen, 1873.

Recht, R., ed. *Les Bâtisseurs des Cathédrales Gothiques*, exh. cat. Strasbourg, 1989.

Recht, R., and A. Chatelet. *Automne et Renouveau, 1380–1500*. (Le Monde du Gothique), 1988.

Régnier, Louis. "Document du XIVe siècle relatif à l'achèvement de l'église Notre-Dame d'Andely." *Bulletin philologique et historique du comité des travaux historiques et scientifiques* (1917), 118–26.

Reinhardt, Hans. *La Cathédrale de Reims*. Paris, 1963.

Renaud, Abbé Edmond. *Eglise Saint-Vincent*. Rouen, 1885.

Richard, Charles. *Rouen, fortifications, porte Martainville*. Rouen, 1844.

Richard-Rivoire, J. "La reconstruction de Notre-Dame des Andely à l'époque flamboyante." *Actes du 81ième congrès national des Sociétés savantes* (Rouen-Caen, 1956), 81–87.

Rigoldus, Odo. *The Registers of Eudes of Rouen*, trans. Sydney M. Brown. New York, 1964.

Rivoire, Monique. "L'Architecture religieuse flamboyante dans les anciens archidiocèses du vexin normand." Thèse, Ecole des Chartres, 1943.

Robinée, André. "Origine et histoire des rues de Rouen." *Connaître Rouen* (1972), 27–34.

Rowe, B. J. H. "The Estates of Normandy under the Duke of Bedford, 1422–1435." *English Historical Review* 46 (1931), 533.

———. "Henry VI's Claim to France in Picture and Poem." *The Library*, 13th ser., 4 (1932–33), 77–78.

Ruskin, John. *Seven Lamps of Architecture*. Boston, 1880; reprint, New York, 1989.

———. *The Stones of Venice*, ed. Jan Morris. Boston, 1981.

Saint Paul, Anathyme de. "L'Architecture française et la guerre de cent ans." *Bulletin Monumental* (1908), 5–40, 209–302; (1909), 387–436.

———. "Les origines du gothique flamboyant en France." *Bulletin Monumental* (1906), 483–510.

Sanabria, Sergio. "A Late Gothic Drawing of San Juan de los Reyes in Toledo at the Prado Museum in Madrid." *JSAH* 51, no. 2 (June 1992), 161–73.

Sanfaçon, Roland. *L'Architecture flamboyante en France*. Québec, 1971.

———. "La rôle des techniques dans les principales mutations de l'architecture gothique." *Cahiers d'études mediévales* 7 (1982), 93–129.

Sanson, Victor. *Le livre enchaîné ou Livre des fontaines de Rouen par Jacques Le Lieur*. Rouen, 1911.

Sarrazin, Albert. *Jeanne d'Arc et la Normandie au quinzième siècle*. Rouen, 1896.

Sauvage, Abbé. "Note sur un dessin original du XVe siècle appartenant au chapître de Rouen." *Revue de l'art chrétien* 7 (January 1889).

Savoie, Anne. "Saint Vincent de Rouen, paroisse de marchants au XVe siècle." Thesis, D.E.S., Faculté des lettres de Caen, 1965.

Seidel, Linda. *Jan van Eyck's Arnolfini Portrait: Stories of an Icon*. Cambridge, 1993.

Snyder, James. *Medieval Art*. Englewood Cliffs, N.J., 1985.

Stein, Henri. *Les architects des cathédrales gothiques*. Paris, 1909.

Steinke, William. "The Flamboyant Gothic Church of Caudebec-en-Caux: A Neglected Masterpiece of French Medieval Architecture." Ph.D. dissertation, New York University, 1982.

Stevenson, Joseph. *Letters and Papers Illustrative of the Wars of the English in France*, 3 vols. London, 1861–64.

Strayer, Joseph Reese. *The Administration of Normandy Under Saint Louis*. Cambridge, 1932.

Taillepied. *Recueil des antiquitez et singularitez de la ville de Rouen*. Rouen, 1587.

Taralon, Jean. "L'Eglise de Saint-Maclou, caractères." *Les Monuments historiques de la France* 4 (1958), 151–62.

———. "Le Mobilier et le Trésor." *Les Monuments historiques de France* (1956), 119–20.

Taveau, Isabelle. "L'Architecture civile et religieuse à Paris sous la règne de Charles VI." Thèse de 3e cycle, University of Paris, Sorbonne, 1987.

Thorel, O. "Le 'Bort d'illand' à la cathédrale d'Amiens." *Bulletin Trimestriel de la Société des Antiquaires de Picardie* (1915), 53–79.

de Tolnay, Charles. *Le Maître de Flémalle et les frères Van Eyck*. Brussels, 1939.

Tractenberg, Marvin. "Gothic/'Italian' Gothic: Toward a Redefinition." *Journal of the Society of Architectural Historians* 50, no. 1 (March 1991), 22–37.

Tuetey, A, ed. *Journal d'un Bourgeois de Paris, 1405–1449*. Paris, 1881.

Vale, R. *Charles VII*. Berkeley and Los Angeles, 1974.

Vallery-Radot, J. "Remarques sur le style des église des Andelys." *Bulletin monumental* 83 (1924), 293–303.

van Moé, Emile. "Les éthiques politiques et économiques d'Aristote traduits par Nicole Oresme." *Les trésors des Bibliothèques de France* 3 (1930), 3–15.

van Puyvelde, L. *L'agneau mystique*. Paris, 1946.

Vesley, Léon de. "Inventaires du mobilier d'art des édifices religieux églises Saint-Maclou et Saint-Ouen de Rouen." *Bulletin de la Société des Amis des Monuments rouennais* (1909), 139–54.

Viollet-le-Duc, E. *Dictionnaire raisonné de l'architecture française du XIe au XVIe siècle*, 10 vols. Paris, 1870–73.

Walsh, David. "Measurement and Proportion at Bordesley Abbey." *Gesta* 19, no. 2 (1980), 109–13.

White, Lynn. *Medieval Technology and Social Change*. Oxford, 1962.

———. "Natural Science and Naturalistic Art in the Middle Ages." *American Historical Review* 52 (1947), 421–35.

Wilson, Christopher. *The Gothic Cathedral: The Architecture of the Great Church, 1130–1530*. London, 1990.

Zephirin, Yolande. "Saint-Yves et sa chapelle parisienne de la rue St. Jacques." *Société historique et archéologique des 9e, 13e, 14e arrondissements* (November 1954), 2–7.

Index

Illustrations

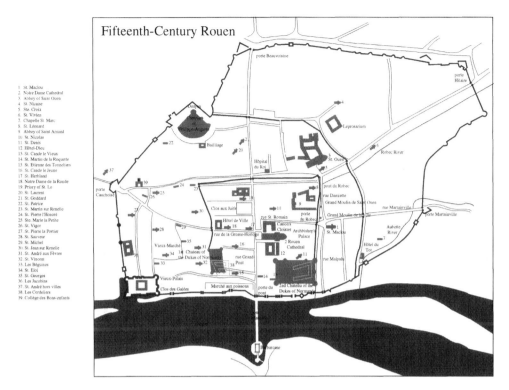

Fig. 1. Map of Rouen in the Late Middle Ages.

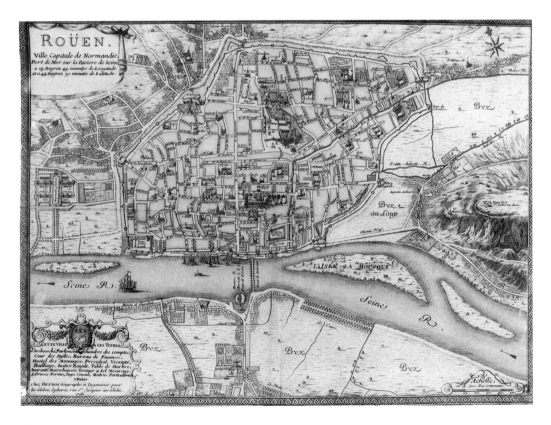

Fig. 2. Map of Rouen in 1766.

Fig. 3. Parish of Saint-Maclou in 1525, Rouen, detail from *Livre des Fontaines*, made by Jacques Le Lieur for the Counsellors of Rouen to commemorate the construction of new fountains in the city.

Fig. 4. Detail of Saint-Maclou (in 1532?), from stained-glass windows of Saint Vincent, Rouen, now in church of Sainte-Jeanne d'Arc, Rouen.

Fig. 5a. Model of Saint-Maclou, Musée des Beaux-Arts.

Fig. 5b. Model of Saint-Maclou, Musée des Beaux-Arts.

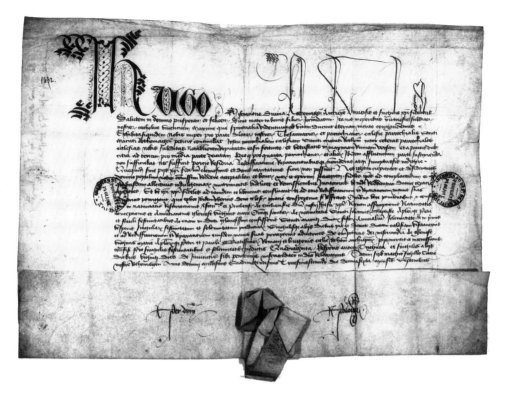

Fig. 6. Letter of indulgence from the archbishop of Rouen, Hugues d'Orgues, to the parishoners of Saint-Maclou. Dated 16 September 1432 and conferred by Robin Le Vigneron, notary, 3 September 1436.

Fig. 7. Rouen, Saint-Maclou, inscription, choir, Chapel of the Virgin (NEIAII).

Fig. 8. Rouen, Saint-Maclou, inscription, nave, Chapel of Saint Anthony of Padua (SIIWII), formerly Chapel of the Annunciation.

Fig. 9. Rouen, Saint-Maclou, Construction Sequence I, 1436–37. Master masons Pierre Robin, Oudin de Mantes, and Simon Le Noir.

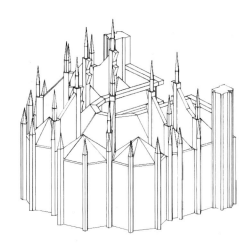

Fig. 10. Rouen, Saint-Maclou, Construction Sequence II, 1437–50. Master mason Simon Le Noir.

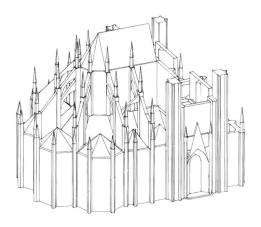

Fig. 11. Rouen, Saint-Maclou, Construction Sequence III, 1450–60. Master mason Jehan Chauvin.

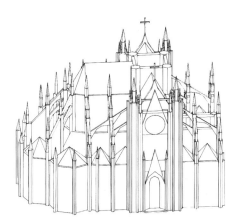

Fig. 12. Rouen, Saint-Maclou, Construction Sequence IV, 1460–90. Master mason Ambroise Harel.

Fig. 13. Rouen, Saint-Maclou, Construction Sequence V, 1490–1521. Master masons Jacques Le Roux, Jean Le Boucher, and Pierre Grégoire.

Fig. 14. Rouen, Saint-Maclou, general view of interior.

Fig. 15. Rouen, Saint-Maclou, general view of interior.

Fig. 16. Rouen, Saint-Maclou, south nave aisle, before 1944.

Fig. 17. Rouen, Saint-Maclou, ambulatory, before 1944.

Fig. 18. Rouen, Saint-Maclou, west facade.

Fig. 19. Rouen, Saint-Maclou, general view of exterior from southeast, before 1944.

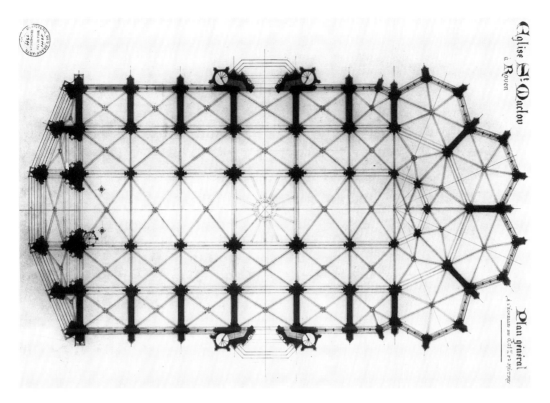

Fig. 20. Rouen, Saint-Maclou, ground plan, by Vincent, 1899.

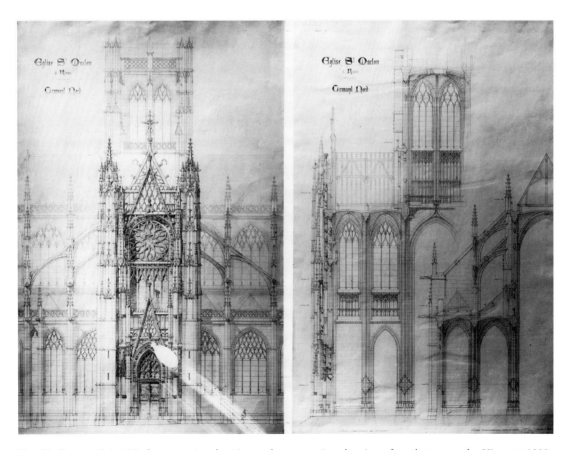

Fig. 21. Rouen, Saint-Maclou, exterior elevation and cross-section drawing of north transept, by Vincent, 1899.

Fig. 22. Rouen, Saint-Maclou, nave triforium/clerestory.

Fig. 23. Rouen, Saint-Maclou, choir elevation.

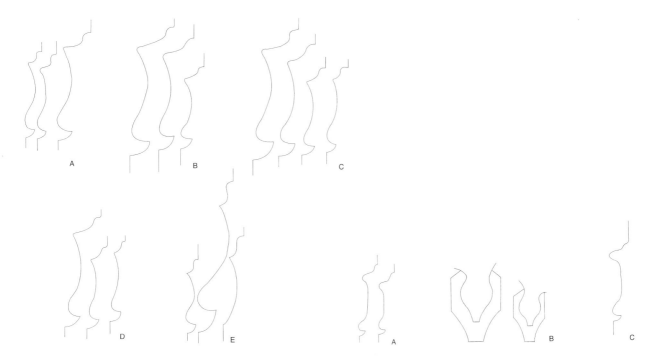

Fig. 24a. Rouen, Saint-Maclou, the fillet base, lower-levels of interior: A. nave pier nw1; B. chapel opening pier n1wl; C. transept crossing pier nw; D. choir chapel n1e1; E. core moldings.

Fig. 24b. Rouen, Saint-Maclou, the fillet base, west facade and upper levels of interior: A. west facade, embrasure molding base profiles; B. west facade, embrasure molding base sections; C. nave triforium.

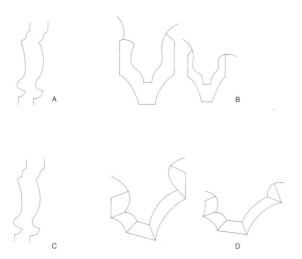

Fig. 24c. Rouen, Saint-Maclou, the fillet base, transept exterior: A. north transept, embrasure molding base profiles; B. north transept, embrasure molding base sections; C. south transept, embrasure molding base profiles; D. south transept, embrasure molding base sections.

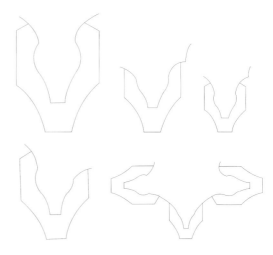

Fig. 25. Rouen, Saint-Maclou, graded sizes of fillet plinth and base sections.

Fig. 26. Rouen, Saint-Maclou, nave pier nw1.

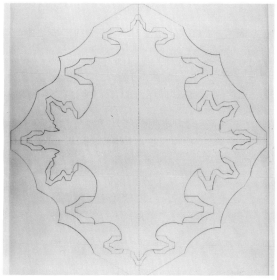

Fig. 27. Rouen, Saint-Maclou, cross-section drawing of nave pier nwl.

Fig. 28. Rouen, Saint-Maclou, chapel opening pier n1w1.

Fig. 29. Rouen, Saint-Maclou, transept crossing pier nw.

Fig. 30. Rouen, Saint-Maclou, attached pier and wall molding nw3.

Fig. 31. Rouen, Saint-Maclou, continuous and disappearing moldings, nave chapel SIIWI.

Fig. 32. Rouen, Saint-Maclou, west facade, central portal, embrasures sw3.

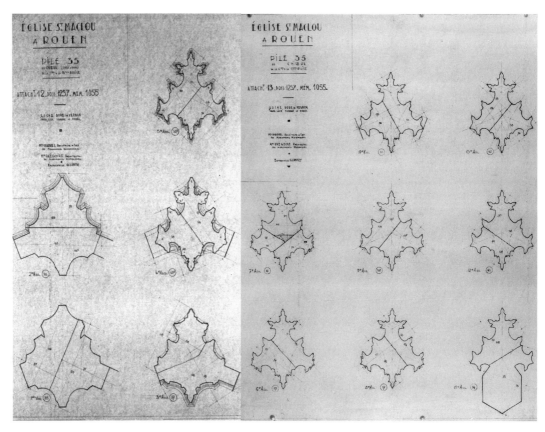

Fig. 33. Rouen, Saint-Maclou, restoration drawing for axial pier of choir hemicycle. (a)

Fig. 34. Rouen, Saint-Maclou, axial pier. (a)

Fig. 35. Rouen, Saint-Maclou, axial pier. (a)

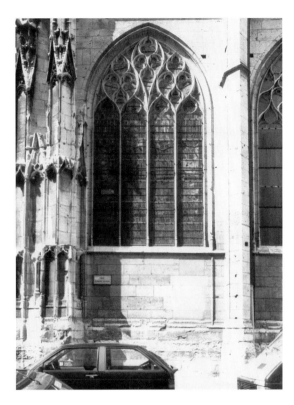

Fig. 36. Rouen, Saint-Maclou, nave chapel window tracery SIIWIII.

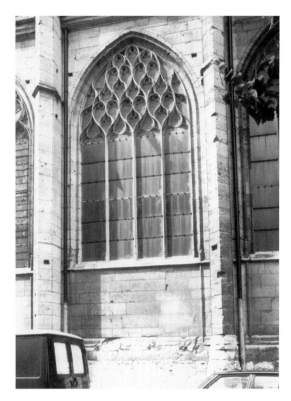

Fig. 37. Rouen, Saint-Maclou, nave chapel window tracery SIIWII.

Fig. 38. Rouen, Saint-Maclou, interior nave chapel NIIWI.

Fig. 39. Rouen, Saint-Maclou, interior choir chapel NEIAII.

Fig. 40. Rouen, Saint-Maclou, interior triforium sculpture.

Fig. 41. Rouen, Saint-Maclou, west facade portal detail.

Fig. 42. Rouen, Saint-Maclou, west facade portal detail.

Fig. 43. Rouen, Saint-Maclou, nave aisle and central vessel vaults.

Fig. 44. Rouen, Saint-Maclou, keystone NIWI, Baptism of Christ.

Fig. 45. Rouen, Saint-Maclou, keystone NIWIII, Amyot Coat-of-Arms.

Fig. 46. Rouen, Saint-Maclou, keystone.

Fig. 47. Rouen, Saint-Maclou, keystone.

Fig. 48. Rouen, Saint-Maclou, keystone.

Fig. 49. Rouen, Saint-Maclou, keystone.

Fig. 50. Rouen, Saint-Maclou, south transept vaults.

Fig. 51. Rouen, Saint-Maclou, south transept vault pendant keystone.

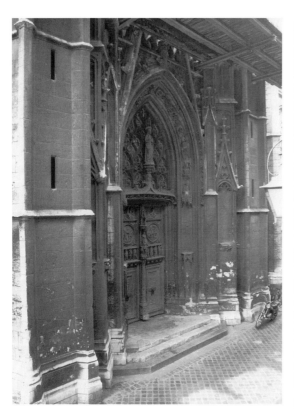

Fig. 52. Rouen, Saint-Maclou, north transept portal.

Fig. 53. Rouen, Saint-Maclou, upper portion of north transept.

Fig. 54. Rouen, Saint-Maclou, south transept.

Fig. 55. Rouen, Saint-Maclou, west facade.

Fig. 56. Rouen, Saint-Maclou, west facade porch platform (above portals).

Fig. 57. Rouen, Saint-Maclou, post-1944 damage to choir.

Fig. 58. Rouen, Saint-Maclou, flying buttresses below aisle roof, south nave aisle.

Fig. 59. Rouen, Saint-Maclou, relieving arches below triforium passage.

Fig. 60. Rouen, Saint-Maclou, *tas-de-charge*, high vaults north transept.

Fig. 61. Rouen, Saint-Maclou, lantern tower before 1944.

Fig. 62. Rouen, Saint-Maclou, choir flying buttresses.

Fig. 63. Rouen, Saint-Maclou, transept flying buttresses.

Fig. 64. Rouen, Saint-Maclou, exterior clerestory passage between transept and nave.

Fig. 65. Rouen, Saint-Maclou, spur buttresses of chapels NIIEI and NIIEII.

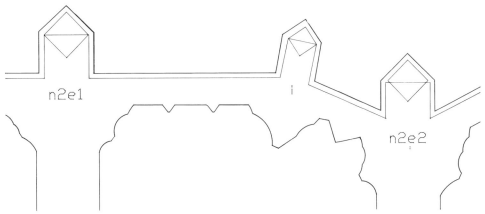

Fig. 66. Rouen, Saint-Maclou, cross-section of spur buttresses of chapels NIIEI and NIIEII.

Fig. 67. Rouen, Saint-Maclou, spur buttress of nave.

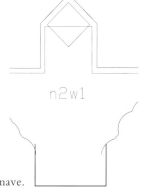

Fig. 68. Rouen, Saint-Maclou, cross-section of spur buttress of nave.

Fig. 69. Rouen, Saint-Maclou, buttress salient, radiating chapel.

Fig. 70. Rouen, Saint-Maclou, buttress salient, choir straight bay chapel.

Fig. 71. Rouen, Saint-Maclou, buttress salient, nave, south side.

Fig. 72. Rouen, Saint-Maclou, buttress salient, nave, north side.

 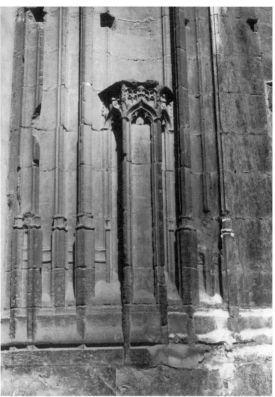

Fig. 73. Rouen, Saint-Maclou, west facade, south portal.

Fig. 74. Rouen, Saint-Maclou, south transept portal embrasure.

Fig. 75. Rouen, Saint-Maclou, south transept triforium block.

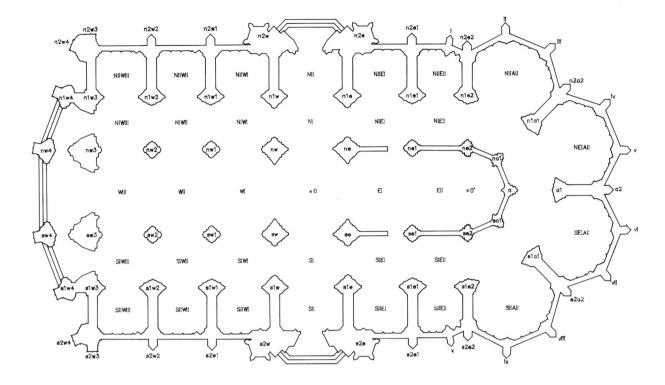

Fig. 76. Rouen, Saint-Maclou, plan, nomenclature.

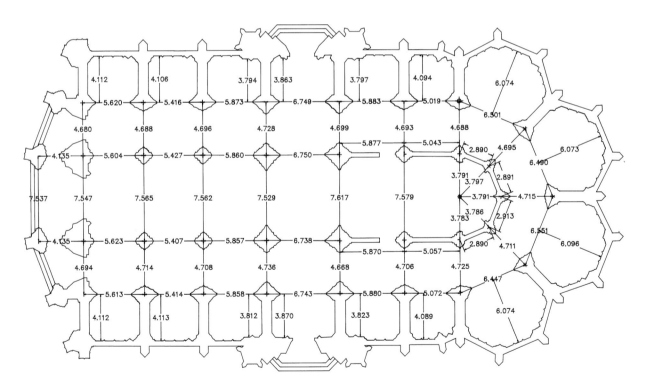

Fig. 77. Rouen, Saint-Maclou, plan, grid dimensions.

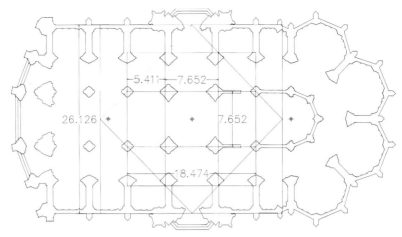

Fig. 78a. Rouen, Saint-Maclou, design scheme, transept macro module.

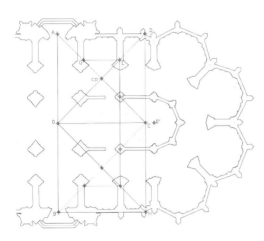

Fig. 78b. Rouen, Saint-Maclou, setting-out procedure of transept and straight bays of choir using constructive geometry.

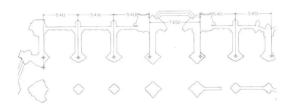

Fig. 79. Rouen, Saint-Maclou, dimensions of straight bays, north side.

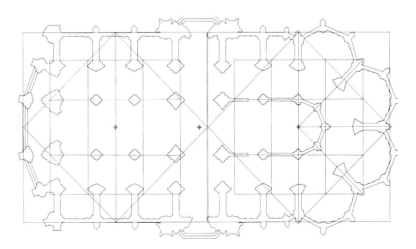

Fig. 80. Rouen, Saint-Maclou, overall design scheme, based on transept macro module.

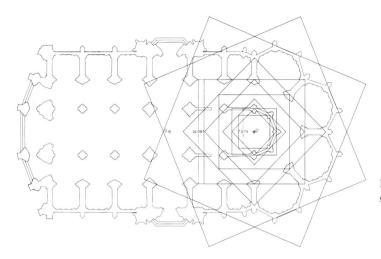

Fig. 81a. Rouen, Saint-Maclou, design scheme, east end.

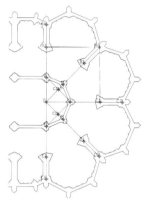

Fig. 81b. Rouen, Saint-Maclou, setting-out procedure of turning bays using constructive geometry.

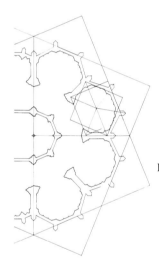

Fig. 82a. Rouen, Saint-Maclou, design scheme, radiating chapel.

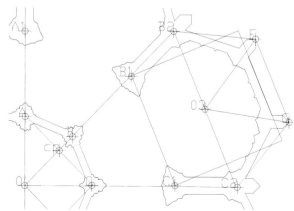

Fig. 82b. Rouen, Saint-Maclou, setting-out procedure of radiating chapels using constructive geometry.

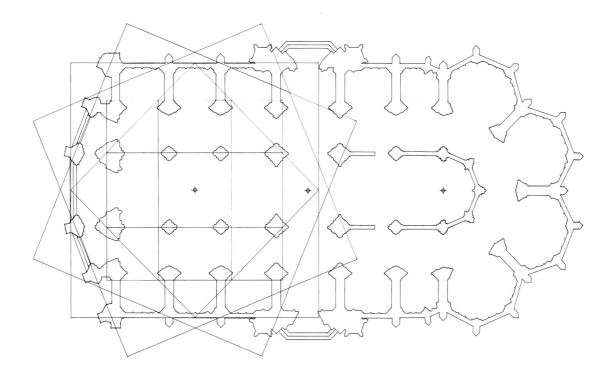

Fig. 83a. Rouen, Saint-Maclou, design scheme, western porch.

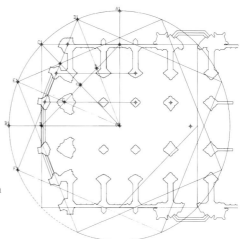

Fig. 83b. Rouen, Saint-Maclou, setting-out procedure of western porch using constructive geometry.

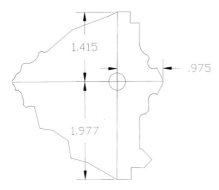

Fig. 84a. Rouen, Saint-Maclou, cross-section of western porch buttress with multiples of .325m "foot".

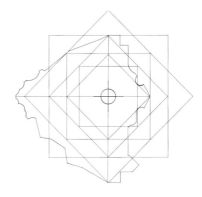

Fig. 84b. Rouen, Saint-Maclou, design scheme of western porch buttress.

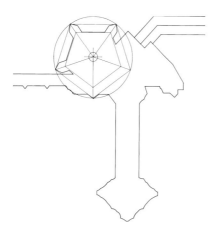

Fig. 85a. Rouen, Saint-Maclou, design scheme of staircase turret nw2.

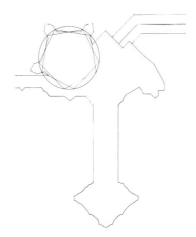

Fig. 85b. Rouen, Saint-Maclou, staircase turret nw2, defines width of spur buttress. Rotation of pentagon 18 degrees according to master 2 from Villard de Honnecourt's portfolio.

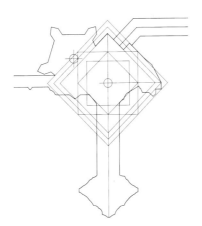

Fig. 86. Rouen, Saint-Maclou, design scheme, north portal embrasure.

Fig. 87. Dufour family presented to Virgin by its patron saint, Saint-Maclou, from *Grand Chartrier* (Rouen, Archives Seine-Maritime, G6873).

Fig. 88. Detail of Figure 87.

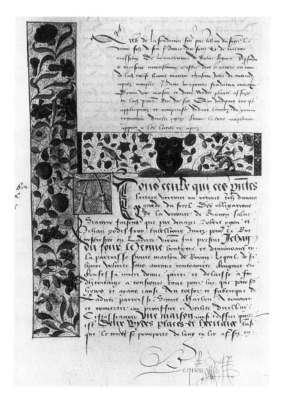

Fig. 89. Coat-of-arms, Dufour family, *Grand Chartrier* (Rouen, Archives Seine-Maritime, G6873).

Fig. 90. Coat-of-arms, Amyot family, *Grand Chartrier* (Rouen, Archives Seine-Maritime, G6873).

Fig. 91. Life of Saint-Maclou with cityscape of Rouen, from *Grand Chartrier* (Rouen, Archives Seine-Maritime, G6873).

Fig. 92. Detail of Figure 91.

Fig. 93. *Livre des Fontaines de Rouen*, made by Jacques Le Lieur for the Counsellors of Rouen in 1525 to commemorate the construction of new fountains in the city. General view of Rouen from the left bank of the Seine (Rouen, Bibliothèque municipale, no. 3833).

Fig. 94. Paris, Saint-Yves, engraving from Du Chemin de Carpentier, 1751.

Fig. 95. Rouen, Priory of Saint-Lo, south portal, 1441.

Fig. 96. Paris, Saint-Yves, engraving, 1702.

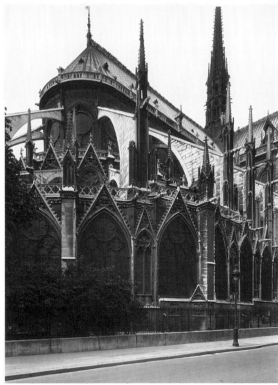

Fig. 97. Paris, Notre-Dame, exterior choir.

Fig. 98. Vernon, Notre-Dame, nave arcade pier base.

Fig. 99. Vernon, Notre Dame, nave arcade pier capital.

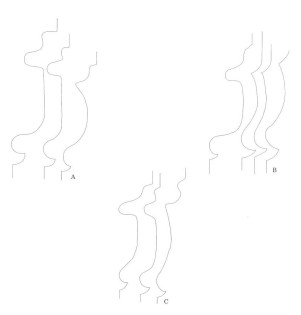

Fig. 100. Vernon, Notre-Dame and Le Grand Andely, Notre-Dame, base profiles: A. Vernon, Notre-Dame, nave pier; B. Vernon, Notre-Dame, Chapel Sainte Geneviève pier; C. Le Grand Andely, Notre-Dame, south transept pier.

Fig. 101. Vernon, Notre-Dame, Chapel Sainte Geneviève, pier capital.

Fig. 103. Vernon, Notre-Dame, nave triforium.

Fig. 102. Vernon, Notre-Dame, Chapel Sainte Marguerite, pier continuous moldings.

Fig. 104. Le Grand Andely, Notre-Dame, south transept pier base.

Fig. 105. Le Grand Andely, Notre-Dame, south transept triforium and clerestory.

Fig. 106. Rouen Cathedral, interior nave elevation.

Fig. 107. Rouen Cathedral, north transept.

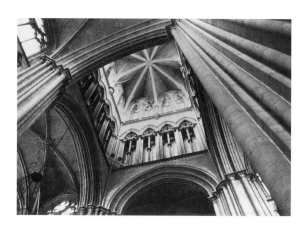

Fig. 108. Rouen Cathedral, lantern tower.

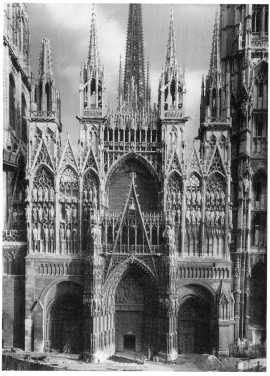

Fig. 109. Rouen Cathedral, west facade.

Fig. 110. Rouen Cathedral, west facade, right portal, attached shaft of Perier's Porch.

Fig. 111. Rouen Cathedral, choir clerestory.

Fig. 112. Rouen Cathedral, *Avant Portail* by Guillaume Pontis.

Fig. 113. Rouen Cathedral, library staircase by Guillaume Pontis, north transept.

Fig. 114. Rouen Cathedral, choir chapel *clôture* by Guillaume Pontis.

Fig. 115. Rouen Cathedral, Tour Saint Romain.

Fig. 116. Rouen Cathedral, *Tour de Beurre* by Guillaume Pontis and Jacques Le Roux.

Fig. 117. Fécamp, La Trinité, tabernacle of the *Pas de l'Ange*.

Fig. 118. Fécamp, La Trinité, tabernacle of the *Pas de l'Ange*. (detail)

Fig. 119. Rouen, Saint-Ouen, south transept, Porch of the Marmosets.

Fig. 120. Rouen, Saint-Ouen, south transept, Porch of the Marmosets, interior.

Fig. 121. Rouen, Saint-Ouen, north transept, inner wall.

Fig. 122. Rouen, Saint-Ouen, south transept, inner wall.

Fig. 123. Rouen, Saint-Ouen, south transept chapel, window.

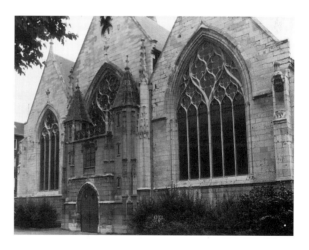

Fig. 124. Rouen, Saint-Vivien, west facade.

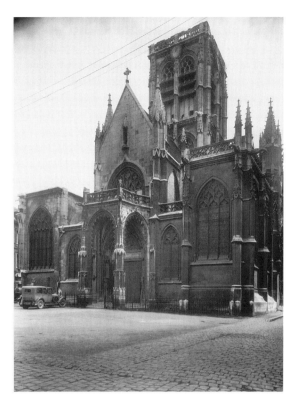

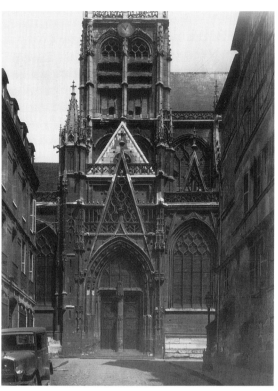

Fig. 125. Rouen, Saint-Vincent, west façade porch by Ambroise Harel, before 1944.

Fig. 126. Rouen, Saint-Vincent, south transept façade, before 1944.

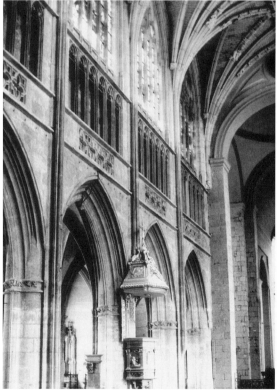

Fig. 127. Argentan, Saint-Germain, nave elevation.

Fig. 128. Alençon, Notre-Dame, nave elevation.

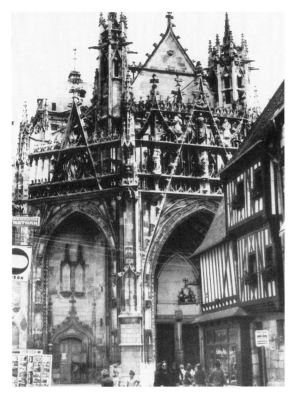

Fig. 129. Alençon, Notre-Dame, facade.

Fig. 130. Caen, Saint-Pierre, interior.

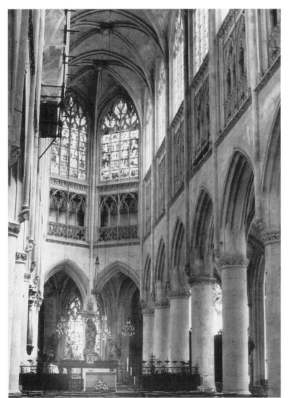

Fig. 131. Caudebec-en-Caux, Notre-Dame, interior.

Fig. 132. Le Neuborg, Saint Paul, interior.

Fig. 133. Paris, Saint-Séverin, ambulatory.

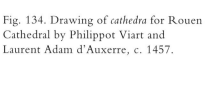

Fig. 134. Drawing of *cathedra* for Rouen Cathedral by Philippot Viart and Laurent Adam d'Auxerre, c. 1457.

Fig. 135. Drawing of late gothic portal, anonymous, 1470–1500.

Fig. 136. Tomb from Saint-Ouen, c. 1340–50, anonymous architect of choir.

Fig. 137. Tomb from Saint-Ouen, 1441– , Alexander and Colin de Berneval.

Fig. 138. Funerary plaque for Guillaume Le Tellier, master mason of Notre Dame, Caudebec-en-Caux, 1484.

Fig. 139. Saint Barbara by Jan van Eyck, 1437.

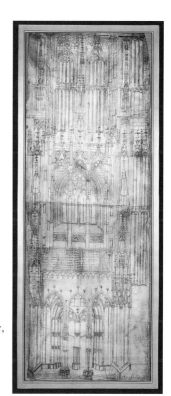

Fig. 140. Ulm Cathedral, drawing of western tower attributed to Moritz Ensinger, c. 1476.

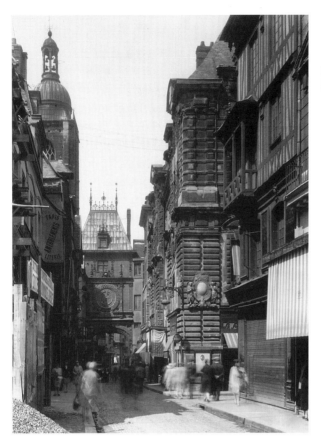

Fig. 141. *Gros horloge* or communal clock, on rue Saint Romain, begun 1389.

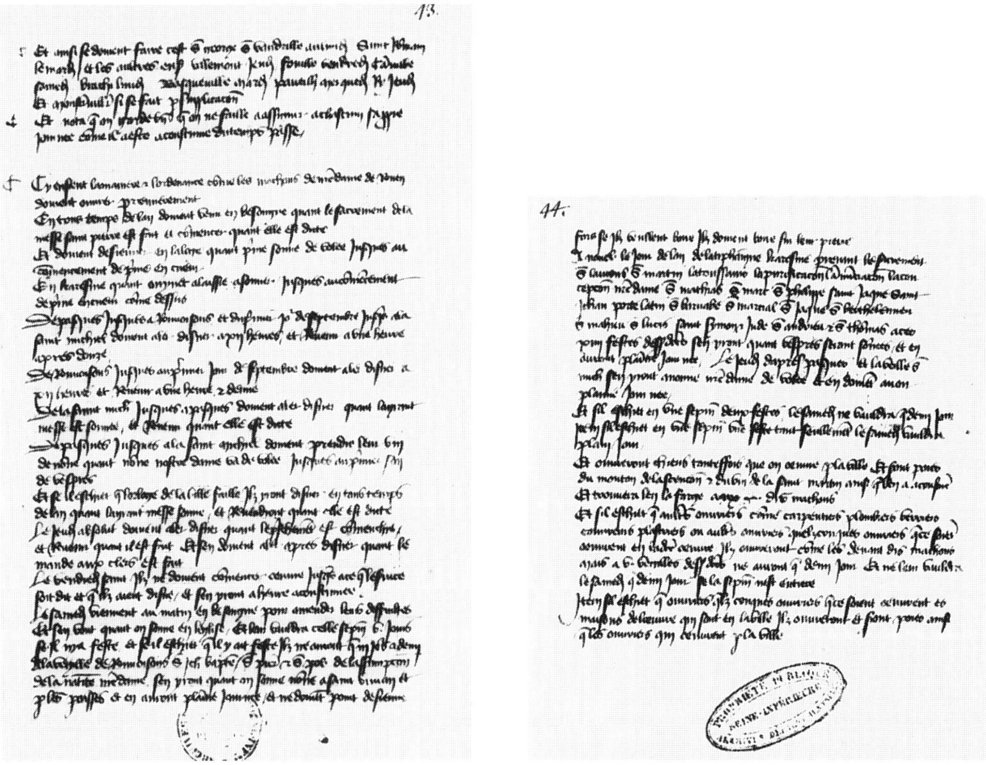

Fig. 142. Contract between masons and cathedral chapter, c. 1450 (Rouen, Archives Seine-Maritime, chapter deliberations, G2094).

Fig. 143. Temperance Among the Cardinal and Theological Virtues, MSS.

Fig. 144. Rouen Cathedral, Temperance, stained glass, south transept.

Fig. 145. Rouen, Saint-Maclou, exterior wall of nave chapel NIIWII.

Fig. 146. Rouen, Saint-Maclou, interior wall of nave chapel NIIWII.

Fig. 147. Rouen, Saint-Maclou, staircase for *jubé* by Pierre Gregoire.

Fig. 148. Detail of Figure 147.